SCIENCE AND INTERNATIONAL ENVIRONMENTAL POLICY

SCIENCE AND INTERNATIONAL ENVIRONMENTAL POLICY

Regimes and Nonregimes in Global Governance

Radoslav S. Dimitrov

ROWMAN & LITTLEFIELD PUBLISHERS, INC.

Lanham • Boulder • New York • Toronto • Oxford

ROWMAN & LITTLEFIELD PUBLISHERS, INC.

Published in the United States of America
by Rowman & Littlefield Publishers, Inc.
A wholly owned subsidiary of The Rowman & Littlefield Publishing Group, Inc.
4501 Forbes Boulevard, Suite 200, Lanham, Maryland 20706
www.rowmanlittlefield.com

P.O. Box 317, Oxford OX2 9RU, UK

British Library Cataloguing in Publication Information Available

Library of Congress Cataloging-in-Publication Data

Dimitrov, Radoslav S., 1971–
  Science and international environmental policy : regimes and nonregimes in global
governance / Radoslav S. Dimitrov.
    p. cm.
  Includes bibliographical references and index.
  ISBN 0-7425-3904-0 (cloth : alk. paper) — ISBN 0-7425-3905-9 (pbk. : alk. paper)
  1. Environmental policy—International cooperation. 2. Environmental law—
International cooperation. I. Title.
  GE170.D56 2006
  363.7—dc22
                                                                    2005019290

Printed in the United States of America

♾™ The paper used in this publication meets the minimum requirements of American
National Standard for Information Sciences—Permanence of Paper for Printed Library
Materials, ANSI/NISO Z39.48-1992.

To Zlatka Ivanova

Contents

Acknowledgments

AN ANCIENT MASAI PROVERB BRINGS us the sunny, earthy wisdom of Africa once again: "It takes a village to raise a child." Similarly, it takes an intellectual community to produce a book. Work on this project has benefited enormously from the ideas and moral support of a number of people. My gratitude goes first to Martin Sampson who has the grace and patience to nurture scholars from promising and unpromising students. His timeless kindness, unwavering commitment to people, rich intellect, and steadfast support truly made all the difference. I am also thankful to Richard Price for teaching me to escape academic dogmatism and to let moral concerns guide academic inquiry. His scholarship has provided me with a paragon of research that really matters to the world outside and inside the ivory tower. I thank Bob Holt for relentlessly pushing me to do my science homework and for showing me that intellectual sophistication and elegance derive from a simple logic of analysis; Bud Duvall for his encouragement and dedicated support; and Jeff Broadbent for his professionalism and kindness. Above all, work on the book benefited from the constant help and meticulous attention to detail of my wife Nanda whose ubiquitous warm presence, gentle love, patience, and tenacious support keep me in quiet awe.

Oran Young, Peter Haas, Robert O. Keohane, Jørgen Wettestäd, Frank Alcock, Elizabeth DeSombre and anonymous reviewers for Rowman and Littlefield, *International Studies Quarterly*, and *International Organization* provided valuable comments on various aspects of the research. I also wish to thank the numerous negotiators and policy makers from around the world,

United Nations officials, and scientists who spent valuable time on my interviews. The information they provided greatly enriched this study.

Work on the project was funded by the following institutions whose sup-
port I gratefully acknowledge: the Institute for the Study of World Politics in
Washington, D.C., the MacArthur Foundation's Interdisciplinary Program on
Global Change, Sustainability and Justice, and the University of Minnesota's
Graduate School and Consortium on Law and Values in Health, Environment
and the Life Sciences.

Abbreviations

CBD	Convention on Biological Diversity
CCD	Convention to Combat Desertification
CCOL	Coordinating Committee on the Ozone Layer
CFCs	chlorofluorocarbons
EC	European Community
EMEP	Cooperative Programme for the Monitoring and Evaluation of the Long-Range Transmission of Air Pollutants in Europe
EPA	U.S. Environmental Protection Agency
FAO	Food and Agriculture Organization
FRA	Forest Resource Assessment
GCRMN	Global Coral Reef Monitoring Network
GDP	gross domestic product
ICRAN	International Coral Reef Action Network
ICRI	International Coral Reef Initiative
IFF	Intergovernmental Forum on Forests
IPF	Intergovernmental Panel on Forests
ITTA	International Tropical Timber Agreement
ITTO	International Tropical Timber Organization
IUCN	International Union for the Conservation of Nature
LRTAP	Convention on Long-Range Transboundary Air Pollution
MSAs	multilateral scientific assessments
NASA	U.S. National Aeronautics and Space Administration
NGO	nongovernmental organization
NOAA	National Oceanic and Atmospheric Administration

NOZE	National Ozone Expedition
NRC	U.S. National Research Council
ODS	ozone-depleting substance
OECD	Organization for Economic Cooperation and Development
POPs	persistent organic pollutants
RAINS	Regional Acidification Information and Simulation
UNCED	United Nations Conference on the Environment and Development
UNDP	United Nations Development Programme
UNECE	United Nations Economic Commission for Europe
UNEP	United Nations Environment Programme
UNFCCC	United Nations Framework Convention on Climate Change
UNFF	United Nations Forum on Forests
UV	ultraviolet radiation
VOCs	volatile organic compounds
WCMC	World Conservation Monitoring Center
WHO	World Health Organization
WMO	World Meteorological Organization

1

Success and Failure in Environmental Regime Formation

WHEN THE SUN ROSE over the New York headquarters of the United Nations at six o'clock in the morning on February 11, 2000, a photographer for the *Earth Negotiation Bulletin* pulled the heavy curtains of conference room 4. The sunrays of dawn entered a room crowded with fatigued diplomats who wore crumpled clothes and weary faces. They had spent the night and the previous two weeks attempting to reach a compromise on international policy to combat deforestation. Negotiations had now reached the end of a five-year-long process of international deliberations regarding forestry issues. Countries advocating the creation of a global forest treaty had met enduring and concerted opposition from the United States, Brazil, and most developing countries. After futile attempts to bridge irreconcilable differences, delegates decided to forgo negotiations on a legally binding treaty and to instead create yet another institutional platform for nonbinding discussions, the United Nations Forum on Forests (UNFF). This would be the fourth in a series of institutionalized initiatives to devise international forest policy.

Why do some environmental negotiations succeed while others fail to produce policy agreements? A distinct historical development in modern international relations has been the phenomenal proliferation of global environmental institutions (Meyer et al. 1997). In recent decades, states have constructed more than three hundred multilateral policy agreements addressing ecological issues, making the environmental arena the fastest growing sector of international law. The multitude of accords and the steady progression of conferences might lead us to conclude that environmental multilateralism has a secure place in world politics. It is equally important to recognize, however, that this area of international relations is rife with intractable conflict. States do not engage in joint environmental management on all ecological issues, and there are sharp contrasts in negotiation outcomes. When twenty-four states signed the Montreal Protocol on Substances that Deplete the Ozone Layer in 1987, the event was hailed as a remarkable success in global politics and a clear confirmation that chronic discord among nations can yield to cooperation. In contrast, there has been little progress in discussions on other prominent ecological issues such as deforestation, where decade-long talks have not resulted in international policy instruments. Such variance in political outcomes deserves close attention and provides an excellent opportunity to explore the conditions under which intergovernmental cooperation occurs.

Analytical Directions

The creation of multilateral institutions is influenced by a large host of political, economic, social, and cultural factors. This book focuses on the role of scientific information in the formation of policy agreements. The central question that guides the inquiry is whether shared knowledge derived from scientific research can help explain collective action in environmental policy. The task is to investigate how government decisions regarding cooperation are affected by research-derived information about particular aspects of the ecological problems at hand. The broader goal is to explore the interplay between knowledge, interests, and power in world politics, and illuminate how perceived characteristics of shared problems affect policy responses.

The investigation deploys an innovative analytical framework designed to gain greater leverage over how shared knowledge affects collective action. Two central characteristics distinguish the project from previous works on regime formation and the influence of expert knowledge. First, the concept of knowledge is disaggregated in order to distinguish between different types of information and analyze their uneven roles in international decision-making. I draw a distinction between three "sectors of knowledge" about an ecological problem that comprise information about its (1) extent or magnitude, (2) causes, and (3) consequences. Instead of asking whether "science matters," the study explores which kind of expert information about a problem matters most and what other types are less influential.

The book also introduces nonregimes into the regime literature and compares cases of successful regime formation with cases where international deliberations have not produced environmental policy agreements. It is a structured and focused comparison of intergovernmental initiatives regarding four environmental problems: ozone depletion, acid rain, deforestation, and coral reef degradation. In the first two cases, states constructed a series of legally binding international treaties. The Montreal Protocol to the Vienna Convention on the Protection of the Ozone Layer and its subsequent amendments constitute a strong international regime to regulate substances that deplete the ozone layer. Similarly, the problem of acid rain is subject to international regulations under the Convention on Long-Range Transboundary Air Pollution (LRTAP) and its protocols. By contrast, deliberations on deforestation and coral reef degradation have not led to policy agreements. States concluded the last meeting of the Intergovernmental Forum on Forests (IFF) in February 2000 without agreeing on the need for a global treaty on forest policy. And despite wide recognition of the problem of coral reef degradation, governments have only endorsed a nonbinding International Initiative on Coral Reefs that has no policymaking mandate.

Scientific Mysteries

The perspective offered here differs markedly from previous knowledge-based approaches to the study of international institutions. A long list of publications explore the interface between science and politics and examine international environmental policymaking in conjunction with shared scientific knowledge (Andresen and Østreng 1989; Jasanoff 1990; Haas 1992a; Litfin 1994; Andresen et al. 2000; Miller and Edwards 2001a; SLG 2001; Lidskog and Sundqvist 2002; Parson 2003; Harrison and Bryner 2004a). These works have made major advances in illuminating the interplay between science and politics and the conditions under which information influences policy processes. Yet, the literature has created more theoretical puzzles than it has solved. Namely, intuitive expectations that information is a requirement for policy action are repeatedly contradicted by empirical findings that states create policy regimes in spite of significant gaps of information and scientific uncertainty.

As a result, international relations (IR) scholarship on the link between shared scientific knowledge and collective action in environmental policy is in a state of profound malaise. This literature has been unable to extricate itself from the conflict between theoretical expectations and empirical findings: many scholars embrace the theoretical premise that knowledge affects action but discover that international policy is most often launched in the absence of key information about issues at hand. Again and again, studies show that at the time when states decided to address a problem collectively and made legally binding international commitments, significant scientific uncertainties and gaps of knowledge about the problem at hand remained (Haas 1992b;

Litfin 1994; Andresen et al. 2000; Lidskog and Sundqvist 2002; Harrison and Bryner 2004a). Logically, their authors conclude that the formation of cooperative policy regimes cannot be explained by the existence of scientific knowledge. Such claims contradict not only expectations but also results of other investigations that report that, over the long term, international policy clearly corresponds with scientific research (SLG 2001). These contradictions have caused considerable confusion, which helps explain why recent works on the topic have forsaken ambitions to make causal inferences or to formulate even tentative hypotheses and are explicitly and emphatically atheoretical (SLG 2001; Harrison and Bryner 2004a).

This apparent puzzle creates problems for people with rationalist and constructivist intellectual orientations alike. If reliable knowledge were not necessary for collective action, rational choice theory would lose one of its fundamental premises, namely, that actors make decisions on the basis of information. For constructivists, on the other hand, who see politics as a process of social learning and who focus on the construction and diffusion of ideas, the implications of the puzzle are equally considerable. If shared information is not required for institutional development, why should we care who constructs, frames, and diffuses knowledge in the social world and how it happens? In other words, if shared knowledge is not an important independent variable, why study it as a dependent variable? Thus, the puzzle I address here presents a challenge to theorists of various persuasions that they cannot afford to ignore.

The origin of the theoretical predicament can be found in faulty concepts and assumptions that hamper the analysis and can explain why previous knowledge-based approaches have failed to deliver consistent and persuasive accounts of the impact of shared scientific knowledge. The reason we have no clear answers is that we have not asked the right questions. By asking "Does knowledge matter?" scholars implicitly treat knowledge in the singular, both grammatically and conceptually. Previous studies on the role of science share the problematic analytical assumption that scientific knowledge is a single variable: "knowledge about the problem." They have not given sufficient scrutiny to differences between *types* of information and how distinct kinds of knowledge affect collective action.

In the case of ozone depletion, for instance, when the key Montreal Protocol was created, there was indeed no conclusive evidence of the *extent* of ozone depletion. There was also some uncertainty about the *causes* of the depletion. However, there was reliable information and complete scientific consensus about the negative *consequences* of ozone depletion (e.g., skin cancer and eye cataracts). The mechanisms through which increased ultraviolet radiation damages human health, terrestrial plants, and aquatic life were well understood and never disputed by either scientists or negotiators. This widely accepted knowledge existed from the very beginning of global discussions and provided an important zone of agreement that facilitated treaty negotiations. We can see this only if we make the distinction between types of information. Scholars who lump "scientific knowledge about the problem" together make themselves vulnerable to blind spots in their fields of vision. They discover the uncertainties about the extent of depletion and prematurely conclude that science was not there, overlooking the existing scientific consensus on consequences of ozone depletion and thus throwing the baby out with the bathwater.

Instead of asking whether knowledge matters, it is more productive to inquire what *type* of knowledge matters. What kinds of things are important to know in order to engage in collective action? Conversely, what type of uncertainty hampers decision-making and reduces actors' willingness to cooperate in environmental management? Pursuing such questions brings us to findings that are more consistent with theoretical expectations. Investigating the roles of different types of information leads to the discovery that some matter critically and others do not. The key distinction here is between three aspects of a problem: (1) its extent, (2) its causes, and (3) its transboundary consequences. In addition to these three, we could identify other types of relevant knowledge such as information about possible solutions to the ecological problem, technological options, and their costs, feasibility, and effectiveness. Examining the impact of other kinds of data is a worthwhile exercise but remains outside the scope of this book. Four stories of global environmental politics advance the argument for a differentiated concept of knowledge. Each case study investigates the state of scientific knowledge about extent, causes, and consequences of a problem and observes how each type of input affects the international policymaking process. A refined notion of knowledge allows us to observe that different types of research-derived information play uneven roles in international policymaking.

Regimes and Nonregimes

The phenomena of interest are international regime formation and, conversely, collective decisions to abstain from policy coordination. Regime is defined here as a formal intergovernmental policy agreement that involves specific commitments to policy targets and timetables and has entered into force according to the terms of the legal text.[1] This is one way to operationalize

Stephen Krasner's classical definition of regimes as "implicit or explicit principles, norms, rules, and decision-making procedures around which actors' expectations converge in a given area" (Krasner 1983, 2).[2] Success in regime formation is the conclusion of a legally binding international accord that involves clearly defined goals and policy commitments and enters into force. This formal definition centers on intergovernmental policy coordination and poses a lighter analytical burden than broader conceptions of governance through social norms and nongovernmental activity.

Why study legally binding agreements? Clearly, international treaties are not the only sources of global governance (Young 1997). Students of constructivism have cogently argued that behavioral patterns and regularized activities in international relations are upheld not only by formal rules but also by shared norms, collectively held beliefs, and reciprocal expectations (Keohane 1988). Such ideational convergence allows us to speak of regimes. In addition to such cognitivist notions, regimes can be conceptualized as collections of behavioral practices that may occur even in the absence of formal accords. And aside from government initiatives, nonstate actors can create and maintain effective mechanisms of governance such as certification schemes that rely on market forces to promote sustainable forest management (Bernstein and Cashore 2004; Cashore et al. 2004).[3]

In the case of coral reefs (chapter 6), numerous nongovernmental organizations (NGOs) worldwide help communities develop capacity for sustainable coral reef management; states such as Australia and the United States have established extensive marine protected areas; others have entered bilateral partnerships to promote solutions to reef decline. Thus, the absence of a coral reefs treaty does not equate absence of governance. Some even question whether cooperation among governments is desirable, on the premise that it is states themselves that destroy the environment.

At the same time, there is a post-realist consensus in the study of world politics that intergovernmental institutions matter, and that policy agreements affect state behavior. This notion is supported by empirical studies on the implementation of regimes and their impact on national policies for environmental management (Sand 1992; Victor et al. 1998; Young 1999; Miles et al. 2002). International treaties may not be the only levers for regulating behavior, but as long as we attribute any significance to them, the study of their formation remains an important realm of research, with practical as well as theoretical ramifications. The choice to focus on interstate legal regimes is not motivated by a conviction that treaties occupy the top of the hierarchical order of governance institutions; rather, it is made for analytical expediency: formal institutions are sites of interaction between science and politics, between ideas and behavior.

Why Study Nonregimes

The literature on the creation of international cooperative arrangements is conspicuously short on comparative studies that offer generalizable conclusions. Much previous work consists of single case studies, such as Edward Parson's (2003) book on the ozone regime, Matthew Paterson's (1996) work on climate change, or Peter Haas's (1990) study on Mediterranean cooperation to combat marine pollution. These and other works provide thorough treatment of individual cases and have generated important ideas as well as useful data. We have little inkling, however, of how their conclusions may or may not apply to other cases.

The development of systematic knowledge about the human world requires comparative work that seeks to reveal patterns and make generalizations. An attempt to make even tentative conclusions about the forces that shape world politics needs to rest on a broad empirical base that is built through structured analysis of multiple and various cases. The few existing comparative projects on international environmental policy move in that direction but cover only successful cases of regime formation (Andresen and Østreng 1989; Haas 1992a; Young and Osherenko 1993; Andresen et al. 2000).[4] These works have greatly advanced our understanding of the conditions under which international policy is made, but their claims have not been examined against negative cases of policy creation.

A comprehensive attempt to understand the emergence of global governance institutions should cover cases of failure to create policy regimes as well as cases of success. After all, what better way to study the obstacles to regime creation? Such impediments can best be analyzed in cases of nonregimes where their impact has shaped not only the process but also the outcome. The absence of policy regimes in an issue area is an outcome of theoretical interest, just like regime formation. It is a result of collective political decisions. Such decisions could be explicit (when international deliberations fail to produce a regime) or implicit (absent formal negotiations).

Students of global environmental politics have so far focused their attention exclusively on cases where legal regimes were formed, and have ignored issues that states have not addressed through international policy agreements. In seeking to understand when cooperation emerges, it is indeed reasonable to explore instances where states engage in coordinated collective action. Yet, cases where states choose *not* to cooperate are at least equally useful in theorizing about collective action. Absence of policy coordination is also a result of a collective decision that is either explicit or implicit (absent formal negotiations). Negative cases of noncooperation can help us evaluate the strengths of theoretical propositions regarding cooperation.[5]

Properly formulated, the important question is not why states cooperate but why they cooperate on some issues and refuse to cooperate on other issues. Why do some negotiations produce an agreement and others do not? Why do some environmental problems trigger coordinated policy response and others do not? To give a thorough treatment to these questions, it is indispensable that we study nonregimes as well. The absence of research on negative cases of nonregimes is a major gap in the regime literature that hampers the development of knowledge. This problem is recognized in several respected literature reviews (Hasenclever et al. 1997, 79; Zürn 1998; Sprinz 1999).[6] This book responds to the challenge to study nonregimes and throws light not only on why institutions for collective action form but also why, when, and how they do not come into being.

Defining Nonregimes

How would we know a nonregime if we saw one? Defining a nonregime is not a straightforward exercise, because it hinges on ontological notions that are shaped by the particular intellectual interests of the observer. It is common-sensical to conceptualize nonregimes by inverting the definition of a regime. The mere absence of a regime is thus a central ontological element of the phenomenon: a nonregime is a case where a regime for policy coordination does not exist.[7]

A more complicated question pertains to whether political efforts to create a regime are a condition for classifying a case as a nonregime. What level of activity toward creating a regime should be detected before we can regard a case as a nonregime? Two principal views merit attention here. According to one of them, there must be a clearly identifiable political movement toward creating an institutional arrangement for policy coordination, manifested in negotiations (that fail) or political calls by governments to establish a mechanism for international governance.[8] Examples of such failed efforts range from the case of small arms control, where UN meetings were ruptured by disagreements and failed to produce a treaty, to failed negotiations on a forest convention, to the failure of the secret Security Council meetings four weeks after September 11 to produce a multilateral agreement on combating terrorism. Each of these cases can be regarded as a nonregime.

According to another view, any absence of a regime is a nonregime even if states have not attempted to create one. The problems of Arctic haze, coral reef degradation, and international tax evasion, for instance, have not triggered negotiations on how to coordinate policy regarding these issues. Conceivably, these cases are nonregimes because the absence of political efforts does not alter the factual absence of a regime. The premise underlying this view is that the problem is absence of collective action—not merely failure of negotiations. The absence of initiatives toward regime creation could make cases all the more interesting. If we frame the collective action problematic in terms of preferences and ask when and why actors *want* to cooperate, then cases where no actor desires cooperation are theoretically informative. Such cases reflect social consensus among actors who agree that there is no perceived need to coordinate policy or that the prospects for success are so minimal that states are unwilling to attempt coordination. What makes coral reef degradation remarkable is not simply that there is no international treaty on coral reef management, but that no state has even raised the issue of a treaty. Although popular journals shape a public perception that reef decline is a global issue, countries do not consider policy coordination necessary.

The choice between these alternative definitions depends on the exact theoretical question that guides the inquiry. If the conundrum is formulated as "when and why do negotiations fail?" we automatically make negotiations an integral part of the nonregime phenomenon. Clearly, then, we need to have negotiations that fail so that we can study them. The existence of high levels of regime-making activities becomes a requirement for a case to qualify as a nonregime. Alternatively, the intellectual interest that drives research may be formulated as "when do social actors seek collective action?" If the question is formulated in this way, the existence of state efforts to create a regime is no longer a prerequisite. We could then consider zero-activity cases when social actors do not seek collective action. This would allow us to look at issues in world politics that have not been the subject of formal negotiations and that have not motivated governments to seek a policy agreement.

This book favors the latter view and adopts a broad definition of a nonregime as a public policy arena characterized by *the absence of an interstate policy agreement where states have either tried and failed to create one, or when governments have not even initiated negotiations.* A "public policy area" is a space for potential public policy activity that is actually occupied by institutionalized policy in at least three countries. In the absence of such activity at the national level, we should not expect a multilateral regime. In the presence of such national policies, the absence of an international regime is a nonregime even if states never attempted to create one. The attention given to regime formation in IR scholarship was motivated by a broader intellectual interest in collective action—and not in negotiations per se. The growth of this academic literature was driven by curiosity about the conditions that facilitate collective action. Today, proponents of various schools of thought continue to disagree on a number of points but would agree that preferences shape political behavior. Institutionalists focus on configurations of preferences, while constructivists want to know how these preferences are formed; both groups agree on their quintessential role in social behavior. If the problematic of collective action can be framed in terms of preferences, then absence of collective action can be framed in terms of absence of preferences (or at least of sufficiently strong ones). Cases where governments deem regimes unnecessary can inform us when and why actors seek collective action and when they do not.

The Cases

The problem of ozone depletion was first theorized in scientific research in the 1970s. Ozone occurs naturally at higher altitudes of the Earth's stratosphere and absorbs ultraviolet radiation of the sun that is detrimental to living organisms. In 1974, two academic publications theorized that certain human-made industrial chemicals rise in the atmosphere and reduce concentrations of stratospheric ozone, causing thinning of the protective shield. Because the effects of increased solar radiation were known to be detrimental, ozone depletion was believed to have negative consequences on human health and the immune systems of plants and marine species. In the late 1970s, the United States adopted national policies to restrict the domestic use of ozone-depleting substances. The international political movement to address the problem emerged at the turn of the decade and met opposition from companies that produced or used these substances. Initially, the United States was the lone advocate of policy action and European governments were unresponsive. In 1985, after years of deliberations, governments signed a general framework agreement, the Vienna Convention for the Protection of the Ozone Layer. Subsequent negotiations began immediately after and resulted in the 1987 Montreal Protocol on Substances that Deplete the Ozone Layer. This treaty stipulated 50-percent reductions in the production of several ozone-depleting substances. A series of amendments made in 1990, 1992, and 1997 required complete elimination of these and additional chemicals. Today, virtually all countries are parties to the ozone regime.

Similarly, governments addressed the problem of transboundary air pollution, commonly referred to as acid rain, through a series of binding policy agreements among European and North American countries. Common industrial emissions associated with energy production and transportation form acidic chemical compounds that come down with rain, snow, and fog or are directly deposited on surfaces. This has a number of negative impacts on terrestrial and aquatic ecosystems, including soils, plants, freshwater species, and human health. In the 1960s, scientific research in Scandinavian countries revealed that this acidification can be caused by pollutants originating in distant countries, and that the transboundary transport of emissions occurs on a large scale. Sweden and Norway issued a call for international regulations of acidifying pollutants, and the political movement slowly gained momentum, with more and more governments seeking a treaty. The economic as well the social costs of proposed policies were significant because controls would affect major industries. Despite business concerns, by the mid-1980s governments signed the first binding agreement to reduce sulfur emissions, and over the following years built a strong international policy regime consisting of numerous agreements to control emissions of sulfur and nitrous oxides, volatile organic compounds, and persistent organic pollutants.

In contrast, no policy agreement to address deforestation has come into being. The forest cover of the planet is known to be dwindling due to human activities such as commercial logging and clearing of agricultural land and pastures. Deforestation and forest degradation are well-known problems that figure prominently in public discourse. Forests are popularly known as the lungs of the planet and have become emblematic of the natural environment. Their destruction has long been a matter of concern to a variety of actors. Despite popular support for halting deforestation and despite consensus among governments regarding the unsustainable rates of forest degradation, negotiations at a number of international forums have consistently failed to produce a binding policy agreement. While there are elements of soft law such as Chapter 11 of Agenda 21 as well as tools for private forest governance operated by nonstate actors, a forest policy regime based on hard international law is absent.

The 1990s saw an impressive array of global and regional state initiatives to introduce international policies for sustainable forest management. In preparing for the 1992 United Nations Conference on Environment and Development (UNCED) in Rio de Janeiro, industrialized states attempted to launch negotiations on a global forest convention but failed due to concerted opposition by developing countries. In 1995, states embarked on a two-year process under the Intergovernmental Panel on Forests (IPF) to discuss policy priorities and options regarding forest management. Major disagreements and an apparent lack of progress prompted governments to continue discussions under a new institutional body, the Intergovernmental Forum on Forests (IFF). After eight rounds of negotiations, states did not reach agreement on the need for a global forest convention and decided to create instead a nonbinding UNFF that does not have a mandate for policymaking.

Similarly, a treaty on coral reef management does not exist and is not even on the global political agenda. Coral reefs are ecosystems that are particularly rich in biodiversity and are believed to provide habitats to one-fourth of all marine species. They are being degraded by a host of natural and human-related factors, including marine pollution, destructive fishing practices, and climate change. Scientific communities and environmental activists portray the worldwide degradation of coral reefs as a global issue that requires a policy response. Yet, an international legal regime on coral reefs is not on the global agenda. The only policy development at the global level is the International Coral Reef Initiative (ICRI) launched in 1994. ICRI is an informal network of governments, international development banks, NGOs, scientists, and corporate actors who meet annually for nonbinding discussions. It neither develops, funds, nor implements policy; its purpose is to merely identify policy needs at local and national levels. The case is thus characterized by the absence of a legal regime and by an apparent absence of attempts to create one.

Several considerations inform this particular selection of episodes in global environmental politics. First, the set of cases displays sharp differences in negotiation outcomes and thus variance on the dependent variable: efforts to form legal regimes have succeeded in the first two cases and have failed in the latter two. For reasons elaborated above, it is useful and necessary to compare successes with failures at international cooperation. Selecting cases on the dependent variable can be problematic: it biases results by creating overrepresentation of positive cases (King et al. 1994). The solution to this problem is to include both negative and positive cases (Mahoney and Goertz 2004), a tactic used here. By exploring a set of cases that includes two successes and two failures, this book combines Mill's method of difference with the method of agreement (Skocpol 1984). The method of difference comes into play in the juxtaposition of cases with different outcomes (ozone and acid rain versus forests and reefs). The method of agreement is used in comparing the two successes with each other (ozone and acid rain) as well as in comparing the two failures with each other (forests and reefs).

Second, international forest management and global coral reef politics are seriously understudied, and even the mere compilation of information about them provides a useful contribution to a number of academic disciplines. Just as deforestation and coral reefs are left outside the realm of international law, the two cases have been left out of the literature on global environmental politics. Hardly anyone in the study of IR has examined the global politics of coral reef management or recent negotiations on global forest policy.[9] Published work on these prominent environmental issues is ostensibly missing from the burgeoning literature on international cooperation in environmental policy. Although the chief purpose of this book is theory development, it also seeks to make important contributions to data collection.

Choosing these particular cases also allows us to hold constant several factors that could otherwise explain differences in political outcomes. This complies with the "most-similar research design" established in comparative politics whose central principle is that cases should be as similar to each other as possible, except for their value on the dependent variable (Skocpol 1984, 378). According to Przeworski and Teune (1970), cases "as similar as possible with respect to as many features as possible constitute the optimal samples for comparative inquiry" (p. 32). All cases examined here deal with issues with global dimensions that involve many countries. Thus, the number of actors involved in negotiations and cultural differences among them—both of which are variables that could affect the chances of collective action—can be taken out of the equation. In regional or bilateral efforts at negotiation, a common culture and/or the relatively small number of actors may affect the dynamics of negotiations and the chances of success in establishing policy coordination. By selecting only broadly international issues, these two independent variables are held roughly constant.

Finally, the selection of cases controls for the international normative context that otherwise could explain disparate outcomes by selecting issues that arose on the international agenda at approximately the same time, in the 1980s. The environmental problematic emerged on the international scene recently, in the late 1960s and the 1970s, and eventually concerns about ecology gained a prominent place in global politics. One could argue that environmental protection was more likely in the 1990s than in the early 1970s, when environmental health was a novel concept that was not accorded much priority. All of the cases examined here, however, evolved in the 1980s, when the level of environmental awareness and the strength of environmental norms were roughly the same. In short, choosing these particular cases eliminates the possibility that norms or the number of actors involved, or cultural differences among them, can explain differences in outcomes. Control for such background features helps achieve greater leverage for causal analysis.

Defining Science and Its Sources: Data Collection

The political outcomes of these cases can be interpreted in light of common perceptions of ecological problems that derive from scientific knowledge. This conclusion is reached based on research using three modes of data collection: analysis of multilateral scientific assessments, interviews with experts and policy makers, and participant observation in negotiations. Each case study takes stock of the existing scientific knowledge about three aspects of the problem (its extent, causes, and consequences), evaluates the level of reliability and scientific consensus around it, and examines how the state of knowledge on each aspect relates to the dynamics of international policymaking and its outcomes.

The main goal is to observe how the existence or absence of reliable information in each "sector of knowledge" affects the international policy process and whether it correlates with the general outcomes of regime-making efforts. Does scientific consensus on the extent of a problem correspond with a collective decision to cooperate in addressing it? Conversely, what is the political outcome when such knowledge is missing or is subject to considerable controversy? Similarly, does the absence of reliable information on the consequences of a problem correspond with collective refusal by states to cooperate?

The central explanatory factor (the independent variable) under examination here is shared scientific knowledge: a stock of information that is scientifically derived and shared by policy makers cross-nationally. Attempts to evaluate existing knowledge are inevitably highly subjective exercises since knowledge is a mental entity that is difficult to measure. One imperative is to ascertain that policy makers indeed possess certain knowledge. Scientific data may exist in print, but decision makers are not necessarily aware of it. If that is the case, "available" information may not affect their perceptions of the problem and therefore not exercise influence on decision-making. Therefore, it is important that we distinguish between information and knowledge. Information becomes "knowledge" only when actors are aware of it and accept it as valid. The implication for research is that we need to verify that scientifically derived information is indeed available and actually used by decision makers.

The natural scientific literature on each ecological problem is vast. It consists not only of academic publications but also includes reports from research institutions in various countries, government agencies, and international organizations. Multiple sources produce sometimes conflicting scientific reports and give rise to competing expert opinions. Scientific controversy is perhaps even more likely when science is politicized and actors seek in it justifications for preferred political positions. The dissonance among experts places additional burdens on researchers who seek to evaluate the state of knowledge regarding an ecological issue and identify areas of scientific consensus.

To cope with these challenges, I operationalize "shared scientific knowledge" in terms of information contained in multilateral scientific assessments and use interviews to supplement the analysis of assessment reports. The attention here is primarily on multilateral scientific assessments (MSAs) coordinated by international institutions. Those include: the joint studies on ozone depletion by the World Meteorological Organization (WMO) and the National Aeronautics and Space Administration (NASA) of the United States; research on acid rain conducted in the international research network that provides input to the Convention on Long-Range Transboundary Air Pollution (LRTAP); the regular assessments of global forest resources commissioned by the United Nations Food and Agriculture Organization (FAO); and the reports of the Global Coral Reef Monitoring Network (GCRMN) comprising a large number of researchers around the world. Each of them is a broadly multilateral research program. Even the ozone assessments, considered American-dominated, in fact involved 150 scientists from eleven countries. They were sponsored by the WMO, the United Nations Environment Programme (UNEP), NASA, the National Oceanic and Atmospheric Administration (NOAA), the European Community Commission, and the German Ministry of Science and Technology.

There are at least five good reasons to focus on multilateral assessments.

First, multilateral research programs monitor ecological problems at a global scale. Country-based research on environmental problems usually pertains to local and national ecological scales, whereas information on their global dimensions is typically provided through multilateral scientific endeavors.[10]

Second, MSAs include comprehensive reviews of existing scientific knowledge and offer useful summaries of otherwise vast literatures. Consulting them is an efficient way to review the state of knowledge on a problem that is accumulated through hundreds or thousands of publications over decades.

Third, MSAs are written to bridge the science and policy worlds. They are intended to assist decision-making, and reports from them always include executive summaries for policy makers that are comprehensible to broad audiences. This is not necessarily the case with other sources of information such as academic journal articles whose language is highly idiosyncratic and forbidding to people other than scientists in the particular discipline.

Fourth, unlike local and national sources of data, reports from MSAs are made widely available to political actors in all countries. While decision makers in a particular country may be oblivious to publications and studies in another country, they are more likely to be familiar with multilateral reports coming from international organizations. Thus, multilateral assessments are sources of truly shared information.

Finally, of all sources of scientific data, MSAs tend to represent the highest degree of scientific consensus. National sources of information may produce data and conclusions that contradict those coming from elsewhere, partly because state interests and preferences on an issue may affect research funding, the composition of advisory bodies, and consequently the conclusions of research. The most skeptical scientific voices on climate change have come from the United States, arguably because the American government opposes international cooperation on the problem and favors skeptics who stress scientific uncertainty. Studies sponsored by industries tend to serve corporate interests and often contradict information compiled by environmental groups. Therefore, it would be highly problematic to rely on such information and treat it as shared knowledge. In comparison, multilateral assessments are conducted by multinational teams of experts, and this parity reduces the potential biases associated with pressure from governments. When scientists on these multinational teams disagree, the tug-of-war could eventually lower the least common denominator in the reported results, but, at the same time, it increases the degree of consensus around the conclusions. The emerging reports from these assessments are less likely to be disputed by scientific experts, and that increases our confidence that the state of knowledge contained in these reports is indeed accepted and agreed upon.

What constitutes reliable knowledge or scientific uncertainty? When assessments speak in general terms about the transboundary consequences of deforestation but offer neither concrete evidence nor specific measurements, this signals lack of reliable information and a weak knowledge base. Scientific assessments on coral reefs, for instance, do not contain any information whatsoever on the consequences of coral reef degradation. Moreover, they explicitly state that knowledge on this aspect is at a very primitive level and that gaps of information will not be filled in the foreseeable future. When this is the case, one needs no sophisticated techniques to conclude that the state of knowledge is poor. On the other hand, knowledge is strong when abundant information, detailed measurements, and concrete numbers regarding a particular aspect of a problem are provided and when assessments explicitly conclude that there is high confidence in the data.[11]

The conclusions also draw on interviews with a wide variety of individual actors: natural scientists, members of governmental delegations, officials and policy makers in pertinent national ministries, representatives of NGOs and international organizations, and staff members of international convention secretariats. Interviews ascertain what these actors know about each aspect of the problem and whether their perceptions are consistent with scientific assessments or considerably deviate from them. The questions in these interviews pertain to their personal knowledge on the ecological problem, their views on how reliable the available scientific information is, and their perception of relevant characteristics of the ecological problems. In addition, they respond to questions about the extent to which scientific views and information figured in political discussions, the types of information adduced most frequently in the talks, and the rationale behind the negotiating positions of different countries. The accounts of people with first-hand experience take us closer to the actual process of regime formation and help protect the study from reaching "library" conclusions that run counter to what actually took place.

The investigation is further strengthened by participatory observation of international negotiations, including several rounds of international deliberations at the UNFF and the IFF. Observing meetings provides a closer perspective on negotiating processes and offers an opportunity to follow the dynamics of formal discussions as well as informal interaction between political actors behind the curtains. This brings to the reader aspects of the story that would otherwise remain hidden from the outside world: negotiating positions of individual countries as expressed in their official statements and debate "interventions," the arguments that they offered in support of these positions, and the extent to which delegates discussed scientific research and the perceived character of the problem. Are there any disagreements and uncertainties about any particular aspect of the problem? Do actors who oppose policy try to dispute the reliability of existing information? How do negotiators use existing knowledge about the problem during bargaining? What aspect of the problem do they emphasize?

Exploration of these matters reveals how shared knowledge on each aspect of the problem correlates with the policy process and outcome. Eventually, we can see patterns between variance in the state of knowledge on a particular aspect, on the one hand, and variance in the dynamics and outcomes of negotiations, on the other. In cases of dramatic new additions of information, I follow whether and how changes in the stock of knowledge correlate with major turning points in the course of negotiations.

The Arguments

The successful creation of agreements to address ozone depletion and acid rain contrasts with the repeated failure to introduce a treaty on deforestation and with the unwillingness of states to coordinate policies on coral reef management. The difference between the outcomes of these stories can be interpreted in terms of a particular type of existing scientific knowledge about these ecological problems. On the basis of extensive and detailed empirical evidence, I make the following arguments:

1. *Different types of information matter differently and play uneven roles in collective decision-making.* The sectors of knowledge on various aspects of a problem vary independently of each other and should be treated as distinct variables. Is good scientific information crucial for environmental policy coordination among governments? Some types are and other types are not. As long as we treat scientific knowledge as a single variable, we may not be in a good position to adequately assess its role in decision-making or to fully understand the connection between science and politics. The book demonstrates that accurate

identification of the role of science in international policymaking requires that we distinguish between different types of scientific information.

2. *Reliable scientific knowledge about negative transboundary consequences of a problem is essential for creating international policy agreements* to address the problem. There is a clear correspondence between the state of knowledge on the transboundary impact of a problem and the overall dynamics of regime making processes. This type of information exerts influence on the formation of interests along three main pathways: by making utility calculations possible, by portraying the degree of interdependence involved in the issue, and by offering fuel for rhetorical arguments.

As the empirical evidence from the four cases shows, the availability of reliable information about the negative cross-border effects of ecological developments corresponds to collective decisions as to whether to address a "problem" in a coordinated manner through binding multilateral policy agreements. When there is consensual shared knowledge about detrimental transboundary consequences, states seek to cooperate under treaties (ozone and acid rain). In contrast, when reliable information about cross-border effects is missing, states either fail to create cooperative arrangements or do not even attempt to do so. Therefore, reliable information about the cross-border effects of a problem appears to be an important requirement in the process of policy deliberations, and increases the likelihood for international environmental agreements.

Arguing that there is a single reason for creating regimes is not my intention. Not all actors who support international environmental agreements are motivated primarily by a desire to escape the impacts of an ecological problem. States create institutions and engage in policy coordination for a variety of reasons, and some of these reasons are unrelated to ecological impacts. Concerns about economic competitiveness and desires to secure level playing fields, obtain information about other countries' policies, or strengthen political alliances often provide the rationale for seeking international institutions. Hence, it is possible to identify existing regimes in cases where science about transboundary ecological impacts is incomplete. Rather, I argue that when states are concerned about an ecological problem, the state of knowledge on its cross-border impacts is of primary importance for the emergence of a policy regime. This is the scope of the theoretical argument (Walker and Cohen 1985).[12]

Expert information does not exercise its influence in policymaking in a deterministic way. Scientific input cannot dictate the particular choice of policy and therefore cannot explain the particular design of a regime. Reliable scientific evidence of negative consequences does not guarantee policy action but it is an important enabling condition because it allows meaningful discussion of the problem and calculation of interests. Knowledge about transboundary effects of a problem does not determine the outcomes of decision-making and negotiations. Rather, it facilitates utility calculations regarding the need for international cooperation and helps establish the parameters of political discussion as well as the range of policy options under consideration.

3. Before we hasten to declare triumph for rationalism, however, it is important to emphasize that other types of information that are seemingly highly relevant in fact do not appear to affect international policy processes significantly. In particular, *conclusive information about the precise extent of a problem is not a critical requirement for international policy coordination.* Having reliable data on the extent of a problem is not sufficient for regime formation, as the forestry and coral reef cases demonstrate. Moreover, it is not even necessary for collective action. The ozone regime was created despite considerable uncertainty about the extent of ozone depletion in the stratosphere. Decision makers tolerate high degrees of uncertainty regarding the exact magnitude of a problem and can take costly policy action, even in the absence of such knowledge.

4. The influence of information about the causes of a problem is nuanced. On the one hand, *principal knowledge about human-related causes needs to be established before policy action can be undertaken.* Such knowledge affects the design of the regime by informing actors what socioeconomic activities cause the problem and may need to be regulated. At the same time, however, *complete information about the causes of a problem does not appear to be required for regime formation.* States do occasionally take action without having precise estimates about the relative contributions of different causal factors. Various natural processes as well as anthropogenic (i.e., human) substances, for instance, cause ozone depletion. At the time when states committed themselves to collective action towards eliminating human-made ozone depleting substances, scientists could not determine the relative contribution of these substances vis-à-vis natural causes.

5. *Existing knowledge about ecological problems is not a function of sociopolitical power.* According to an intellectual tradition in social sciences, powerful social actors manipulate the production as well as the use of information in decision-making, and the state of existing expert knowledge comes to match their interests and preferences. The evidence from the four cases considered here largely refutes this claim. If knowledge was a puppet in the hands of powerful actors, one would logically expect such actors to "produce" information that suits their interests and, conversely, to contest information that undermines their negotiating positions. This did not happen in any of the four histories examined here. Contrary to expectations generated by the above theory, available scientific information on various important aspects of the problems did not suit the preferences of major states. Too often, powerful players such

as the U.S. government were not able to present conclusive evidence that would support their negotiating positions. Furthermore, governments are rarely successful in disputing data that are unfavorable to their desired political outcomes. Most important, they sometimes do not even attempt to refute information that runs counter to their preferences. Some actors have strong scientific research capabilities and the political interests to manipulate data, but apparently these do not translate into a capacity for unbridled production of knowledge.

The distinction between scientific process and output is highly salient. In his work, Robert Merton (1973) taught us that governments have a good measure of control over interest groups and scientific projects because they control the funds on which such groups depend. More recently, Weale and Williams (1998) point out that the very production of knowledge presupposes institutional structures that only political authority can provide. In the cases examined here, such characteristics of the scientific *process* did not affect critically the scientific *output*. Governments often try to bend research but—as in the case of acid rain—even the results of government-commissioned research spin out of control and go against the preferences of the patrons.

On Causal Inference

The political processes that lead to the creation of multilateral treaties are intricate and take place in multiple arenas at national and international levels. Their dynamics are affected by many political, economic, and cultural factors, and it is often difficult to disengage science and politics in this complicated picture. The present analysis deliberately simplifies and abstracts reality in order to reveal patterns between shared knowledge and policy outcomes. I consider such simplification not a flaw but a helpful tool in illuminating complex conditions for the establishment of international institutions. The goal is not to produce exhaustive accounts but to use the specific cases to flesh out empirical patterns. The book ascertains a strong connection between global policy coordination and a particular type of shared knowledge. Establishing a plausible link between information and collective action comprises four analytical stages: (1) identifying scientific information in research reports; (2) verifying that this information was used by decision makers; (3) identifying collective decisions and observing how they relate to available scientific knowledge; and (4) refuting alternative explanations of the apparent correspondence between information and behavior.

The analysis suggests that a specific type of research-derived knowledge helps explain why some global ecological problems are addressed in a coordinated manner while others may be a subject of discussion but do not lead to international treaties. Some may question whether I am proposing a causal explanation. The notion of causality is the subject of major disagreements in the social sciences. As Peter Railton (1989) points out in his brilliant essay, much of the difference among particular views on causation lies in fundamental metaphysical disagreements that have no definitive resolution. Because such controversies are intractable, they should not preclude analyses that follow reasonable and well-established epistemological lines. My personal view on explanation follows closely Philip Kitcher's "unification" approach whose essence is captured in the following statement: "The growth of science is driven in part by the desire for explanation, and to explain is to fit the phenomena into a unified picture in so far as we can. . . . Proponents of the unification approach are committed to viewing factors as *explanatorily relevant* if they figure in a unified treatment of the phenomena (Kitcher 1989:495, 500; emphasis added).

Accordingly, we cannot ascribe strict causality to the impact of science. The cases do indeed display variance on research-derived information that could be treated as a causal factor; but they also vary along a number of other axes, including the distribution of power across negotiating coalitions, the policy impact on economic sectors, and the distribution of costs and benefits among domestic actors. Furthermore, the two regimes tackle atmospheric pollution problems, while the two nonregimes involve natural resource use, and such typology of issues may hold additional explanatory power. These important factors offer ground for various alternative explanations of the outcome of any of the four cases, and the account offered here is not intended to refute those. Rather, it illuminates the impact of certain types of information that, in conjunction with other factors, have made regime formation easier in some cases and more difficult in others.

Significance and Limitations of the Study

Exploring the connection between scientific knowledge and international environmental policy is important for several reasons. Theoretically, it pertains to several topics that are central to the study of international relations: the conditions under which actors cooperate with each other; the relationship between knowledge and action; the impact of information on decision-making; the rationality of human action; and the role of ideas in the evolution of institutions. These themes reflect fundamental intellectual interests pursued through much of the history of human thought. They are significant not only for international relations theory but for social science scholarship in general.

The book introduces the concept of nonregimes into the literature on global governance and demonstrates the value of exploring negative cases. By broadening the scope of comparative work to include cases where cooperation does not occur, the book produces conclusions that are more reliable and more widely generalizable. The analysis advances the knowledge-action research agenda by extricating it from the tangles and contradictions in the existing knowledge-based literature on environmental cooperation. It does so by disaggregating the concept of knowledge, drawing distinction between types of information and studying their differential roles in decision-making. The added value of this analytical approach is considerable: it enables us to produce internally consistent findings that disperse the tensions and contradictions of previous studies. This innovative analytical framework reveals clearer patterns and consistent trends in multilateral environmental policymaking. Observing global environmental politics through this new lens increases our confidence in the proposition that reliable information is an essential ingredient in international policy formation.

Apart from its intellectual import, the analysis has practical implications for environmental management. Ecological issues are increasingly recognized as posing serious threats to human well-being, and their gravity has prompted some academics and policy makers to discuss them as matters of human security. Since many ecological developments do not recognize national borders, international cooperation is sometimes indispensable for addressing them effectively. Achieving such cooperation is an arduous process that can be helped by analyzing what facilitates cooperation and what hampers it and applying the lessons learned from the past in future initiatives on ecological issues. The analysis here produces recommendations that can guide global cooperation on other common problems. The findings can also be useful to natural scientists who seek to assist policymaking and are often frustrated when policy makers disregard their input or when the policy output does not correspond with scientific advice.

It may be useful to specify at the outset what this book is *not* about. First, it does not seek to explain the particular timing of policy formation. A longitudinal study may discover connections between the time when certain information emerged and the creation of a regime, but this connection is not likely to be strict because additional factors can delay the adoption of policy until long after consensual scientific knowledge emerges. The book also does not seek to explain the particular design of international agreements. There is a splendid variety of policy regimes in terms of scope of regulation, ambition in targets and timetables, range of participation, decision-making procedures, levels of funding for implementation, and the particular mechanisms for verifying compliance. This project does not profess to explain why the Montreal

Protocol involved 50-percent rather than 10- or 85-percent cuts in ozone depleting substances, or why it was created fourteen and not five or twenty-five years after the first scientific publication on ozone depletion.

Nor is the goal here to discuss success and failure in policy *implementation*. By joining a treaty, states agree to cooperate. There are few guarantees that they will keep their promises and will indeed comply with the agreement. Furthermore, compliance itself does not guarantee that the ecological problem will be ameliorated. The quality of the environment depends on many natural biophysical processes that are beyond the sociopolitical realm. The creation of legal treaties is an important step but only one political element in the long tale of environmental protection. The timing of regime formation, its particular design, the level of compliance with it, and its effectiveness are all important topics that are given deserved attention elsewhere (Wettestäd and Andresen 1991; Haas et al. 1993; Victor et al. 1998; Young 1999; Miles et al. 2002). This book focuses on the general phenomenon of policy cooperation and explores collective decisions to create or forgo legally binding policy agreements.

Finally, this is not primarily an exploration of social constructivist processes of knowledge production and legitimation. Many works focus on the political, cultural, and institutional forces that shape the production and validation of scientific claims (see chapter 2). This important topic is not given priority here. The primary focus is on knowledge as an independent— not a dependent—variable. Once knowledge is produced, legitimized, and accepted, how does it affect decision-making and what is its impact on state negotiations and international policymaking? The possibility that political actors control and manipulate the generation of information is investigated only as a possible explanation of the observed patterns—and refuted by the discovery that the scientific claims that were accepted did not match the preferences of powerful actors. Finally, the micro-dynamic process of interaction between scientists and policy makers as political actors is deliberately left aside. Others have given thorough treatment to this (Haas 1990, 1992a; Sabatier and Jenkins-Smith 1993; SLG 2001).

A number of caveats warrant caution in drawing conclusions about the role of science.

First, neither type of expert information is likely to be sufficient for undertaking collective action because various other obstacles can thwart efforts at cooperation. Even if science brings governments to a consensus about an ecological problem, collective action problems may still prevent cooperation. How these problems are solved remains a major question about which knowledge-based explanations may have little to say.

Second, certain knowledge does not directly or necessarily lead to particular decisions because the ultimate choice of what goals to pursue depends also on values. "Neither science nor logic can tell us where we ought to head" (E. Haas 1982, 239). All incoming information is interpreted through filters that are partly defined by values that help shape the preferences regarding a perceived problem.

Third, the ideas advanced here may not be capable of explaining differences in national policies or negotiating positions (Skolnikoff 1997). The transition from science to policy is structured by social relations between scientific and policy communities that vary across countries. Organizational and cultural differences between political systems may affect the selection of information that is used in policy (Brickman et al. 1985; Jasanoff 1986). Even when policy makers are given the same information, the preferences of different delegations at the negotiating table continue to diverge. This is where studies of domestic politics, values, norms, and social discourse may hold particular promise.

Finally, the conclusions presented here likely pertain better to environmental management and may not hold equally well in other issue areas of international politics such as arms proliferation, human rights, or international trade. Ecological scientific research produces highly specialized knowledge that does not have exact equivalents in other realms such as human rights protection. In areas such as security and arms control, expert information is more relevant but may be less objective than natural scientific data or exert less significant influence on policy processes. Exploring the role of information in those realms may offer useful insights about the differences among issue areas.

Organization of the Book

The remainder of the book is organized as follows. Chapter 2 offers a critical review of the relevant literature on shared knowledge and collective action in environmental politics, to reveal why previous works produce contradictions and have fallen short of persuasive accounts of internal logical consistency. It then introduces an alternative analytical framework for investigating the role of information in the formation of environmental regimes. This framework is then applied in a structured comparison of four cases: ozone depletion (chapter 3), transboundary air pollution (chapter 4), deforestation (chapter 5), and coral reef degradation (chapter 6). The case studies are divided uniformly into several sections. After a description of the ecological problem at hand, each chapter delves into the history of international policy deliberations of the issue. It then discusses scientific research activities and explores in detail the state of knowledge that existed during the political efforts at regime formation. The last section analyzes how scientific information and the degree of its reliability affected the political processes. Each individual case study ends with brief conclusions. Chapter 7 summarizes the findings of the overall project and the patterns that they reveal, provides a theoretical explanation of these patterns, discusses alternative explanations, and draws conclusions about the interplay between knowledge, power, and interests in global environmental politics. The chapter elaborates on the implications of the study for international relations theory, international law, and environmental policymaking and offers recommendations for policy makers and scientists that can strengthen efforts to introduce responsible environmental policy at the international level.

Notes

1. Such definition is consistent with Robert Keohane's conception of regimes as "institutions with explicit rules, agreed upon by governments, that pertain to particular sets of issues in international relations" (1989, 4).

2. For an illuminating review of alternative definitions, consult Hasenclever et al. 1997, chapter 2.

3. For another discussion of forest-related nonstate governance, see Lipschutz 2001.

4. To take one instance, a project funded by the Ford Foundation seeks to identify the "determinants of success" through a comparison of five empirical cases of successful regime formation (Young and Osherenko 1993). All of the cases under its consideration pertain to natural resource management in the Arctic region. This thematic as well as regional focus may further limit the generalizability of the conclusions.

5. It is important to note that if X is a necessary but not sufficient condition, all regimes would be characterized by A, yet not all nonregimes may be characterized by –X. Cooperation may not materialize even in the presence of A; failure may be due to other factors.

6. "The discipline still lacks a good study which explores under which circumstances international regimes do *not* come into being" (Sprinz 1999).

7. From this perspective, ineffective regimes do not qualify as nonregimes because the basic requirement for absence of regime is not met. One could argue that regimes exist only by virtue of actual behavior, and if there is no policy under ineffective regimes, there is no regime. However, since our definition of a regime is premised not on behavior but on institutional rules, it is reasonable to regard ineffective regimes as regimes nonetheless.

8. The premise underlying this view is that the main problem is *failure* in regime formation—and failure presupposes attempt.

9. One exception is work by Humphreys (2003, 2004). The early history of forest negotiations is analyzed by David Humphreys (1996) and Deborah Davenport (2005).

10. Occasionally, data used in multilateral assessments come primarily from a single country whose scientific authorities have virtual monopoly in a particular realm of research. Examples here are NASA's studies of stratospheric ozone, the results of which

were widely used in many countries that did not have the technological and scientific capacity to conduct similarly comprehensive studies of their own.

11. Data are interpreted and analyzed qualitatively. The attention is on several indicators related to the quantity and quality of information: the availability of concrete evidence, the level of detail, and explicit conclusions in the reports regarding the state of knowledge on each aspect of the problem. Particular attention was paid to the gaps of information that the reports identify and the explicit evaluations of the reliability of existing data that such assessments always provide.

12. Scope conditions pertain to the parameters within which a given theory is expected to be valid (Walker and Cohen 1985).

2

Shared Knowledge and Collective Action in Global Environmental Politics

SCHOLARLY WORK ON INTERNATIONAL COOPERATION has a long and prolific tradition. Theories of regime formation can be grouped in three categories that focus on the role of power, interests, and knowledge, respectively.[1] Debates among these contending approaches have not reached clear denouements, and many scholars regard as dim the prospects for reaching generalizable conclusions about the forces that shape regime formation. Most rigorous analyses conclude that all three types of factors affect international processes and that it is difficult to discern the relative importance of each. One prominent study, funded by the Ford Foundation, tests various theoretical schools of thought against five empirical cases and concludes that none of the contending explanatory hypotheses could fully account for the outcomes, and therefore all of them have to be viewed as complementary (Young and Osherenko 1993). The only agreement appears to be on a "fundamentally messy, contingent, and ambiguous intermingling of knowledge, power, interests, and chance in the workings of the world" (Parson and Clark 1995, 457). Eventually, we join Plato in knowing that we do not know.[2]

Science and Politics

The role of science in international policymaking falls within the purview of knowledge-based explanations of international cooperation. A growing number of studies explore the interface between science and politics on the international arena (Andresen and Østreng 1989; Jasanoff 1990; Haas 1992a; Litfin

1994; Andresen et al. 2000; SLG 2001; Parson 2003).[3] These works have improved understanding of the relationship between knowledge and action and the conditions under which information influences policy processes. At the same time, they have led to conflicting findings and confusion. While some studies support the intuitive claim that information matters, many other investigations conclude that scientific knowledge does not have a critical role in the formation of international regimes. Intuitive expectations that knowledge should be a prerequisite for policy action are repeatedly contradicted by empirical findings that states form policy regimes despite significant gaps of information and scientific uncertainty.

Thus, IR scholarship on the link between shared scienctific knowledge and collective action in environmental policy is in a state of profound malaise. It has been unable to extricate itself from the contradiction between theoretical expectations that knowledge affects action and the empirical findings that international policy is often launched in the absence of key information. This contradiction has hampered the research agenda and has contributed to skepticism about the idea that scientific knowledge could help explain international cooperation in environmental policymaking. At the very least, it has left knowledge-based approaches at a pre-theoretic stage[4] and has precluded them from moving beyond the recognition that the relationship between science and policy is complex, precarious, and poorly understood (Andresen et al. 2000; SLG 2001; Parson 2003; Harrison and Bryner 2004b). Recently, a major review of diverse bodies of knowledge-policy literature[5] concluded that "Neither tradition has been particularly successful in showing how or under what conditions . . . ideas affect issue development" (SLG 2001, vol. 1, 12).

Knowledge-Based Regime Theory: Facts Get in the Way

Knowledge-based explanations of international regimes and cooperation, in particular, suffer from three interrelated problems. The main, unresolved, problem derives from a contradiction between theoretical expectations and empirical findings. While some maintain that scientific input is a critical component of policymaking (Clark et al. 2002; Parson 2003), several comparative projects have concluded that scientific information does not have a decisive influence and therefore cannot explain international policy.[6] A recent collaborative study found that reliable information is not a requirement for collective action because decision makers took regulatory action on two ecological problems in the absence of conclusive evidence (Andresen et al. 2000).

Contradictions between and within scholarly investigations are remarkable. Looking at the role of science in the formation of the ozone regime, for instance, there is a considerable dissonance among observers about the degree of scientific certainty and the role that it played in influencing negotiations. Some maintain that scientific knowledge about the problem helps explain the emergence of the policy regime (DeSombre and Kauffman 1996; Benedick 1998; Miller and Edwards 2001b; Parson 2003). "Clearly, . . . expert knowledge was a sine qua non of the Montreal Protocol on ozone-depleting substances and its successors" (Miller and Edwards 2001b, 3). Others insist that considerable scientific uncertainty persisted throughout the negotiations and conclude that science cannot explain regime formation (Haas 1992b; McInnis 1992; Litfin 1994; Harrison and Bryner 2004b). "What we know about the ozone layer pales in comparison to what we do *not* know. . . . The voluminous research failed to produce certainty about the actual amount of ozone depletion caused by CFCs" (McInnis 1992, 132–134).

Even Peter Haas, whose name is associated with knowledge-based explanations in international relations (IR), emphasizes scientific uncertainty about ozone depletion and argues that science does not easily explain the successful formation of the regime: "Analytically, the ozone case is revealing because international cooperation on a highly technical issue was reached before complete scientific consensus emerged" (Haas 1993, 152). Karen Litfin also claims that "a detailed process tracing of the process shows that the treaty was not fundamentally rooted in consensual knowledge" (1994, 79). Thus, knowledge-based works are, in fact, rather skeptical of the proposition that scientific data inform decision-making in environmental politics.

Interestingly, the skeptics receive indirect vindication from the pro-science camp, when even publications asserting the important role of science display internal contradictions and tensions between claims and evidence. A recent collaborative project on science and politics in international environmental regimes examines what governs the transformation of scientific input into premises for political decisions (Andresen et al. 2000). Its major starting point is the assumption that scientific information matters critically: "We assume that . . . adequate knowledge about the problem itself and available response options is a *necessary*—although by no means sufficient—condition for designing and operating effective international regimes" (Andresen et al. 2000, 3). Contrary to its premise, the study explicitly concludes that "conclusive evidence is *not* a necessary condition for collective action" (p. 184), since in two out of five cases under consideration, decision makers took regulatory action in the absence of conclusive evidence about the problem.[7] Another book argues that scientific assessments had a critical impact in the formation of the ozone regime. On closer reading, however, it explains this outcome with negotiaton dynamics where "the crucial factor was aggressive leadership by the group of U.S. officials who became the driving force for strong controls" (Parson 2003, 143). The reason why scientific research results take backstage in this account is the author's discovery of the uncertainties and "unverified claims of global depletion" at the time.

Thus, existing scholarship on the science-policy interface tends to refute the notion that environmental policy is based on science. This counterintuitive conclusion is particularly bewildering in relation to environmental politics. What distinguishes this issue from international policy realms such as security maintenance or human rights protection is that it involves phenomena taking place in the biophysical world. Consequently, natural scientific research is indispensable in obtaining information about these issues. "Environmental management necessarily has a high scientific and technical component at its core; indeed, policy makers would often not be aware that certain scientific problems existed unless those problems had first been identified by scientific research" (Weale and Williams 1998, 84). Because such research is the main outlet of information about the natural environment, one would logically expect scientific input to play an important role in environmental politics and international policymaking. Indeed, knowledge-based analyses of international environmental policy have gained considerable currency in IR theory, partly because the natural element to environmental problems shifts attention to the role of expert information (Haas 1992a; Litfin 1994; Andresen et al. 2000). In this context, the claim that knowledge does not have significant influence is highly problematic.

What Knowledge-Based Theory?

The second problem with knowledge-based accounts of international environmental policy is that, strictly speaking, there are none. All cognitivist explanations focus on factors other than the available information per se: actors, institutions, or processes. For instance, the literature on epistemic communities that has gained prominence in the study of IR in the last decade focuses on the role of transnational networks of scientists with an authoritative claim to policy-relevant knowledge, who share beliefs and values, and who are politically empowered by their governments. They seep into the decision-making apparatus and can bring their governments to agreements that lead to the successful adoption of institutional frameworks for relevant policies (Haas 1990, 1992a).[8]

Supposedly knowledge based, the entire epistemic communities literature in fact advances an interest-group explanation of outcomes. It explains international cooperation not with information per se but with the political activism of groups who have been described as "coalitions of believers" or as "knowledge brokers" (Sebenius 1992, 364; Litfin 1994). Scholars in this tradition are concerned less with the content of information and more with the mechanisms for transmitting it. This suggests that what accounts for the outcome is not knowledge but the carriers of knowledge whose political power derives from their status as experts. They explain outcomes not with science, then, but with scientists. The latter distinction is of considerable importance: it implies that scientists can critically influence the process and outcomes, even if the existing knowledge derived through scientific research is not reliable and does not fully justify corrective action. This facile replacement of knowledge with "knowers" is clearly captured in the following summary of knowledge-based explanations:

> Knowledge is the key to understanding the decision making process. Those who are perceived to have a monopoly of knowledge, or at least privileged access to it are highly valued in times of policy uncertainty. . . . Therefore, to explain instances of international co-operation, one should look to those who control knowledge (be they individuals or groups) and the ways in which they interact with those in decision making circles. (Rowlands 1995, p. 25)

A transition is made between knowledge to those who handle knowledge. Eventually, we are treated not to a cognitivist explanation of outcomes but to one that focuses on an interest group that joins the political jumble of regime formation. And "scientists, once organized into institutions giving policy advice, are no more 'trustworthy' than most other respectable pressure groups" (Boehmer-Christiansen 1989, 150).

Epistemic communities may affect the policy process, but so do all other groups of actors involved, and the relative impact of experts remains unspecified. These analyses have not shown linkage between scientific activities and actual impact on policy process. "Little more than ad hoc generalizations are offered on the precise conditions under which the influence of epistemic coalitions will show up in outcomes" (Sebenius 1992, 326). Some even question the existence of epistemic communities, pointing at the lack of evidence of actual coordination between scientists toward a political goal (Harrison and Bryner 2004b).

Other analyses shift the emphasis not to actors but to institutions, practices, and processes. A Harvard project addressing the connection between knowledge and action seeks to explain variation in the influence of scientific assessments and focuses on the role of institutions in mediating the impact of scientific assessments (Clark et al. 2002). The scrutiny thus shifts from information as an independent variable to institutions as intervening variables. Another recent study, while affirming the importance of scientific input in policymaking, shifts the explanatory weight away from scientific results themselves and onto processes of conducting scientific assessments (Parson 2003, 7). The analytical attention goes to the procedural mechanisms through which expert activities make an impact, and not to the actual content of research results. Constructivists, on the other hand, speak of broad discursive practices. When Karen Litfin finds significant gaps in the existing stock of knowledge on ozone depletion, she gives a reflectivist account of the story of the ozone regime and argues that the regime was a product of discursive practices; that is, "linguistic practices embedded in networks of social relations and tied to narratives about the construction of the world" (Litfin 1995, 252–253). Interests were not objective but were shaped in discourse. According to her, imperfect knowledge about ozone depletion was framed in terms of the precautionary principle and discourse was shaped to obscure scientific data. Once again, this twist is driven by the finding that science was not reliable and therefore could not explain the outcome.

By shifting the focus from science onto scientists as political agents or onto social practices, previous investigations take us away from the original proposition that *information* matters. The implication of Haas's proposition is that epistemic communities could successfully push for environmental action even without bringing reliable information or when the available information does not warrant policy action. Indeed, we cannot separate completely scientific results from the activities and actors who produce them. Science is indeed closely related to scientists: ideas cannot exist without heads. However, the two cannot be conflated either and should not be used interchangeably. Actors do not have unlimited ability and freedom to shape ideas and present them in any way they want. Natural scientists, in particular, have methods and instruments, and if results are consistent they cannot be distorted infinitely, at the whim of political interests. In any case, there are limits to how much a piece of evidence can be interpreted and manipulated. The precise extent to which facts and events can be (mis)represented, the range of possible interpretation, the limits of malleability, and the boundaries of social construction are all important topics on which good studies are still waiting to be written.

Lumping "Science" Together

The third and cardinal flaw in existing explorations of the role of science in politics is in the prevailing analytical assumption that scientific knowledge is a single unitary entity. Most, although not all, of those who consider the role of science typically treat scientific input as a single, dichotomous variable: knowledge about the problem. There is a lump "science" that can be either certain or uncertain. The question that the existing literature has addressed is "Does knowledge matter?" and/or "How much does knowledge matter?"

In two prominent compendiums of studies on the role of science in environmental politics (Andresen and Østreng 1989; Andresen et al. 2000), "knowl-

edge" is in the singular, both grammatically and conceptually. "The general assumption is that other things being equal, the less conclusive the evidence, the
less likely that it will be utilized as a basis for joint policy decisions" (Andresen
et al. 2000, 15). No attempt is made to specify: evidence *about what*? In another
study on cooperation on local and international levels, a team of scholars examine asymmetries in information as an explanatory variable but also treats
information as unitary and do not distinguish between various objects of information (Keohane and Ostrom 1995).[9]

In important recent work, some scholars are mindful of different attributes
of scientific input and are attentive to questions of what kind of knowledge
matters to whom and for what reasons (GEA 1997; SLG 2001). In a major
comprehensive study, the Social Learning Group considers distinct aspects of
a problem in the context of issue framing and explores how ideas about a
problem's causes, effects, and policy solutions figure in elite public discourse.
Yet, the group does not study the state of scientific knowledge on each of these
aspects, nor does it attempt to establish patterns between policy responses and
levels of scientific certainty on particular aspects of a problem.[10]

As long as we treat knowledge as a single variable, we may not be in a good
position to adequately assess its role in decision-making or to understand
the connection between science and politics. Suppose that we investigate the
role of science in the successful formation of an international policy regime
on an environmental problem. If we implicitly treat "knowledge about the
problem" as a single variable, as soon as we find scientific uncertainty about
any given aspect of the problem, we would be logically led to conclude that
information could not explain the outcome. In the meantime, we may overlook other areas of knowledge where information was reliable! Indeed, previous analysts of the ozone regime are preoccupied with the uncertainty
about the *extent* of depletion but fail to see that there was reliable information and scientific consensus on the shared *consequences* of the problem.
This is how problematic analytical assumptions preclude proper understanding of the role that scientific knowledge plays in the formation of environmental regimes.

The Alternative Approach: Sectors of Knowledge

Clearly, we need to calibrate our analytical tools more finely and consider the
possibility that different types of shared knowledge play uneven roles in influencing collective decisions. What kinds of things are important to know in
order to introduce an international legal regime? Conversely, what types of
uncertainty hamper cooperative action to protect the environment? Is one

type of information more important than other types? Knowledge about which aspect of a problem is most influential in decision-making?

There are a number of possible ways to categorize information. Here I break up scientific knowledge into three basic sectors: (1) knowledge about the extent of the problem; (2) knowledge about the causes of the problem; and (3) knowledge about its consequences for human societies. The first sector comprises data relevant to the identification of an ecological development and the appraisal of its extent: whether ozone concentrations are declining and how much ozone is depleted or whether forested lands are shrinking and what area of forests is being degraded. The second sector contains information about what causes such changes and the relative contributions of different human activities and/or natural factors. Finally, the third sector is a pool of information about the socioeconomic consequences of the trends.[11]

The three sectors of knowledge are related and sometimes difficult to distinguish. Calculations regarding causes are related to those regarding extent: how could one discuss the causal role of chlorofluorocarbons (CFCs) in ozone depletion if there is no knowledge of ozone depletion? Also, information about the extent and consequences are interlinked: the impact of a problem is a function of its magnitude as well as its principal consequences. While separating them is a somewhat artificial exercise, the distinction is nonetheless useful for analytical purposes. This new analytical premise not only allows us to observe a more nuanced relationship between science and politics but also significantly alters the results of empirical investigation into the role of information.

The central idea of disaggregating "expert knowledge" can be extended further in a number of directions. Other types of relevant information are not examined here, such as knowledge about policy options and the ecological changes that they are likely to induce. The ability of scientists to inform policy makers regarding the feasibility of policy options, the ecological problem-solving effectiveness of solutions, or the socioeconomic impacts of policies is likely to be an important factor in policy formulation. Examining the role of this and other types of knowledge would be a useful continuation of the research agenda.

Why should we differentiate between different types of information? The primary value of disaggregating knowledge is in helping us solve puzzles that previous approaches have not been able to address effectively. The new analytical premise leads us to findings that are more consistent with theoretical expectations and increases confidence in the proposition that reliable information is a requirement for policy regime formation. Eventually, the innovative approach helps us to extricate ourselves from the apparent contradictions encountered by other approaches.

This alone would justify the approach taken here. In addition, there are conceptual, methodological, and theoretical reasons for distinguishing between types of information. Ecological research in the natural sciences is an enormously complex, multi-component endeavor that involves many separate academic disciplines: chemistry, physics, biology, meteorology, geology, medicine, atmospheric chemistry, etc. Conceptually, therefore, it is not realistic to assume a singularity of science. Moreover, the state of knowledge in different areas does not progress evenly or simultaneously. Variance in the state of knowledge on the extent of a development is not necessarily reciprocated by variance in the state of knowledge on its causes or consequences. There is no reason to assume, for instance, that advances in atmospheric chemistry on measurements of ozone concentrations would also trigger a breakthrough in medical research on the health effects of ozone depletion. The two are separate realms of research that do not go hand in hand but make progress independently from each other.

This has significant methodological implications for social scientific research on the impact of information on policy. If bodies of information on different aspects of a problem vary independently from each other, they constitute distinct variables. By treating "knowledge about the problem" as a lump entity, we would be grouping several variables together and become unable to isolate the independent role of each in the political process.

Indeed, the four cases in this book could not be adequately explained by existing knowledge-based approaches with their assumption of knowledge as a single variable. In the many studies of the ozone case, scholars see the enormous gaps of information on the extent of depletion but overlook the complete scientific consensus on the consequences of depletion; hence, their conclusion that science could not explain the story is hasty. The scholarly tradition of the epistemic communities would be amiss in interpreting the forest and coral reefs cases, too. On a regular basis, various scientific assessments turn up solid data about the extent and causes of deforestation. And forest research, in particular, is institutionalized as forest experts are firmly embedded in policymaking government agencies as well as international organizations. In view of these factors, previous knowledge-based approaches could not explain the persistent failure of states to form a regime on forest management and their utter lack of interest in creating a coral reefs treaty.

Disaggregating knowledge allows us to observe a more nuanced relationship between science and politics, and to reveal clear patterns. Most importantly, it significantly alters the results of empirical investigation into the role of information in regime formation. Analysis of the four empirical cases suggests that reliable information about the shared consequences of a problem is essential for the formation of international environmental regimes, while complete knowledge about the precise extent or causes of a problem is neither necessary nor sufficient for regime formation.

At the time when countries made international commitments to protect the ozone layer, there was indeed little certainty about how much ozone was actually depleted. Nor was there clear understanding of the relative roles of the many possible causes of depletion. There was, however, reliable and consensual knowledge about *the effects* of ozone depletion (if it occurred). Combined with the probability of depletion, solid information about the shared consequences provided a zone of agreement and facilitated the calculations of interests. Similarly, scientific research on acid rain provided ample evidence about the negative cross-border consequences. In the two failed cases of forests and coral reefs, on the other hand, the picture is reversed. Multilateral assessments of forest resources and coral reefs health provide reliable information about the extent of their decline and the causes for it, but there is remarkably little information about the shared consequences of the two problems and much of it is unreliable. This gap hampers utility calculations and helps explain the failure of regime-making efforts.

The Skeptics

Social scientists are defensive about the idea that natural scientific information affects social dynamics and outcomes. With our long tradition of dwelling on the subjectivity of human thought, the complexity of human behavior, and the mystery of history, we are conditioned to be skeptical about the idea that scientific input shapes social output. Most IR scholars are inclined to regard knowledge as a dependent variable shaped by the exercise of power, and projects in this realm of research are preoccupied with the extent to which political actors control processes of generating, ordering, and using information.

Rational models of policymaking posit that science drives policy by diagnosing a problem and identifying alternative solutions from which decision makers choose (Brewer and DeLeon 1983). An ideal model of the science-policy process would be as follows: impartial scientists who use objective criteria produce "objective" and definitive information that enjoys their full consensus. This information then enters the decision-making apparatus undistorted, and policy makers make rational calculations and devise policies that reflect the scientific input. This rational model of policymaking has come under various radical criticisms, and linear models of information-based decision-making have been rejected. In the real world, scientists are not impartial; they rarely share consensus; the information is never definitive but constantly evolving; research data can be intentionally or unintentionally distorted; calculations are not rational in the technical sense; and, finally, policy decisions do not fully match the scientific information.

Reservations about the idea that scientific information can shape policy are based on two principal objections. One of them stems from the recognition that scientific information is not an objective reflection of physical reality but a product of subjective cognitive processes. A number of important works have examined the production of knowledge as a sociological phenomenon, and the unifying theme among them is the claim that knowledge is socially constructed (Kuhn 1970; Mulkay 1978; Latour and Woolgar 1979; Miller and Edwards 2001a; Lidskog and Sundqvist 2002). The second grand caveat is that science cannot dictate policy because politics gets in the way, and values, power, and institutions shape the transition between information and interest formation (E. Haas 1975; Douglas and Wildavsky 1982; Jasanoff 1990; Litfin 1994; Munton 2001; SLG 2001).

Together, these two stipulations have strongly inclined scholars in the social sciences to doubt that scientifically derived information could determine social processes or outcomes. Although all agree that the science and policy realms affect each other in a dialectic relationship, many scholars choose to focus on knowledge as shaped by political, social, and cultural factors. The majority of projects in this line of research study the conditions under which knowledge is influenced by and influences policy, how it is affected by the way the science-policy dialogue is organized, and the social processes through which experts persuade other actors (Jasanoff 1986, 1990; GEA 1997; Haas 1997; Andresen et al. 2000; Miller and Edwards 2001a; Munton 2001; SLG 2001).

Previous work has put forward several claims that every exploration of the role of knowledge must acknowledge. First, knowledge is not objective but socially constructed. Scientific information is not an objective output of mechanistic inquiry but a product of social processes among scientists and other social actors. The producers of knowledge are not insulated from politics or impartial participants in it: their political orientation, personal values, agendas, and financial interests in research funds affect their work and its products. At the very least, scientific research relies on funding whose allocation is highly political, and because sponsors have political biases, the impartiality of research cannot be guaranteed. Some even argue that facts cannot be separated from values and that science and politics mingle inextricably in advisory processes (Jasanoff 1990; Lidskog and Sundqvist 2002).[12] Mandated science for policy is supposedly a different type of science that is not an exclusive domain of scientists. The need for policy-relevant information sets research goals and influences the methods (Shackley and Wynne 1995).

Second, knowledge is rarely consensual. There are conflicting claims and competing scientific views (Collingridge and Reeve 1986, ix–x; Jasanoff 1990; Andresen et al. 2000). Because consensus among experts is rarely complete, information is often controversial. This is especially pertinent to ecological studies because they constitute a new realm of science. "In fact, environmental policies will almost always be made on the basis of imperfect information about important aspects of the problem" (Andresen et al. 2000, 4). Knowledge is always evolving, and what we know to be true is constantly being reconsidered in light of new information and/or new beliefs. "[Knowledge] is not so much like a building, eventually to be finished, but more like an airport, always under construction" (Douglas and Wildavsky 1982, 194). Such perpetual contestation does not signal inferior data—rather, it is inherent in the production of knowledge. The process of developing consensus is also open to sociological analysis. Its social nature makes it not only possible but also necessary to study the role of power.

Furthermore, transmitting knowledge from the scientific to the political realm is also a social process in which information does not arrive intact. How information is framed and interpreted by decision makers is yet another separate issue. Any given information could be interpreted in a number of ways, shaped by existing interests and values. Mary Douglas and Aaron Wildavsky (1982) argue that risk assessment depends on the values of the assessors, that societies address dangers selectively, and that the selection of risks is a political process guided not by facts but by values and beliefs. Policy is not and cannot be directly and automatically derived from information; more important is how the information is interpreted, and interpretation is inextricable from values and beliefs. The mere presence of scientific information on an issue does not guarantee that this issue will be chosen as a problem to be addressed through policy. Even if it is elected onto political agendas, it may be framed through discourse in various ways, using the same scientific information. Both the selection and the framing of an issue are products of social discourses that are influenced by many actor considerations and exogenous factors. In the end, even consensual information cannot resolve political conflicts over values and interests (E. Haas 1975). Deciding whether to accept a certain level of risk and what level of risk is acceptable involves values and sociopolitical judgment and is not delegated to experts alone (Lowrance 1976; Jasanoff 1986). Because of this, different countries may respond differently to the same discoveries (Lundqvist 1980; Brickman et al. 1985; Vogel 1986; Boehmer-Christiansen and Skea 1991).

Many scholars elaborate on these matters, arguing that policy outcomes cannot be easily explained with information. "However useful, *knowledge can be neither the master of, nor a substitute for politics*" (Andresen et al. 2000, 5;

original emphasis). Therefore, scientific information cannot be a sufficient condition for policymaking. John Kingdon (1984), for instance, argues that policy often occurs almost accidentally at the convergence of problems, policies, and politics, whereby decision makers may use problems to advance their own political agendas and promote solutions that serve their political interests. In other words, policy may be less a rational response to a problem identified by science and more a function of interests unrelated to the problem.

So What?

The above caveats are to be taken seriously, but their practical implications are less than clear. It does not *necessarily* follow from these objections that science-based knowledge does not affect decision-making and collective action in important ways. It has not been shown, for instance, whether social processes of knowledge production and utilization affect the *content* of scientific output. Regardless of scientific debates and disagreements, at the end of the day, certain knowledge is generally accepted as valid and is being used by decision makers. Whether science is objective or not, we all agree on the chemical composition of water and on myriads of other truths about the natural world. Furthermore, we all do use information to make decisions. Before we go on a trip for the weekend, most of us consult the weather forecast, regardless of our theoretical views about meteorology and the nature of knowledge. As Ernst Haas (1975, 874) points out, "we must admit that too much is already 'objectively' known to enable us to write off science as a willing handmaid, to be used or ignored as our moral commitments dictate." Indeed, a recent comparative study found that the influence of scientific input in decision-making is not affected by either the malignancy of political conflicts or by the way the science-policy dialogue is organized (Andresen et al. 2000).

As long as certain knowledge is commonly accepted and identifiable, and as long as people use it to make decisions, we can study the independent influence of scientific information in international policymaking. If knowledge is not an important independent variable, why care about it as a dependent variable? If information does not exercise influence over behavior, why care who produces information? In this regard, it is indicative that even scholars who emphasize the constructivist aspects of social reality cannot help referring to its objective aspects. While arguing that risk assessment is a matter of subjective judgment, Douglas and Wildavsky write: "Pollution dangers are not imaginary dangers. The more real and grave, the better they qualify [for policy response]" (1982, 40).

The relationship between science and politics, between knowledge and action, is indeed a complex one, and there is no straightforward way of deriving policy from knowledge. Yet, "Even the most cynical observer would have to admit that international environmental regimes tend to rely heavily . . . on inputs that originated in science" (Andresen et al. 2000, 6). It is unfortunate that general caveats have unnecessarily led scholars to shun the notion of science as an independent variable and have inclined them to regard knowledge as a dependent variable. And studies that do examine the impact of information in policy making are constrained by the analytical assumptions that they rely upon.

To summarize: the role of scientific information has not received the adequate examination it deserves. Most study it as a dependent variable shaped in social discourse by power and values. Those who examine it as an independent variable have run against seemingly conflicting findings and have failed to solve an apparent contradiction between theoretical premises and empirical results. A reason for this confusion is the failure to distinguish between types of information and the failure to examine their roles separately. Those who seek to explain policy action with scientific knowledge treat the latter as a lump entity, while those who notice differences between types of knowledge are not interested in information as an independent variable. Absent from the literature is a systematic analysis of how different types of information affect the likelihood of collective policy responses. This is what subsequent chapters set out to accomplish.

Notes

1. An extensive inventory of regime theories is provided in Hasenclever et al. 1997. See also Rittberger and Meyer 1993 and Haggard and Simmons 1987.

2. Janice Stein believes that "Our evidence does not permit us to draw more than tentative conclusions about when and why parties get to the table" (1989, 261). Oran Young is cautious, too: "I conclude . . . that there are no necessary conditions for change in international regimes and that any of a variety of factors may be sufficient to precipitate major changes in prevailing social institutions in real-world situations" (1989, 206). Ten years later, he acknowledged that "We are nowhere near a definitive resolution of this debate" (Young 1998, 12).

3. With the exception of Jasanoff (1990) and Litfin (1994), each of these publications is a compendium of case studies on the topic.

4. "None of [the literature] suggests that learning theories are yet ready to generate tight theories or crisp predictions of social change" (SLG 2001, vol. 1, 13).

5. Relevant to this topic is scholarship on issue framing (Nelson 1984; Schon and Rein 1994; Hajer 1995), problem definition (Rochefort and Cobb 1994), agenda set-

ting (Kingdon 1984), issue dynamics (Baumgartner and Jones 1993), stages of policy development (Jones 1984; DeLeon 1999), and on risk assessment as a social process (Beck 1992; Wynne 1995; NRC 1996). At the international level, in particular, there is IR literature on the role of shared beliefs in stabilizing coalitions of actors (Hall 1989; Haas 1990; Goldstein and Keohane 1993; and Blyth 1997).

6. The first of these is a string of studies edited by Andresen and Østreng 1989.

7. The authors themselves acknowledge this contradiction in a footnote (p. 200) and make a less than convincing attempt to explain it by stating that science may precipitate action but not determine the content of policy.

8. See also other contributions to Haas 1992a as well as work on advocacy coalitions (Sabatier and Jenkins-Smith 1993), and on advocacy networks (Keck and Sikkink 1998).

9. Other variables that the project considers are the number of actors and differences in their capability and preferences.

10. The study is conceptually sophisticated and explicitly atheoretical, and it refrains from making causal inferences. It is described by the authors as a "preliminary historical reconnaissance" to document patterns of potentially important variables. See chapter 1 of volume 1, pp. 1–19, and the concluding chapter 22 in volume 2, pp. 181–197.

11. There are other types of relevant information as well, such as knowledge about policy options and the ecological changes that they are likely to induce. Whether scientists can tell policy makers what a particular policy measure would lead to in ecological and socioeconomic terms is likely to be an important factor in policy formulation. Examining the role of this and other types of knowledge would be a useful continuation of the research agenda.

12. There is a small debate regarding the desirability of insulating science from politics. Some argue that attempts at strict separation may hurt advisory processes (Jasanoff 1990), while others observe that separation is beneficial at early stages of knowledge production and engagement between scientists and policymakers is better for later stages of policy formulation (Andresen et al. 2000).

3

Out of Thin Air:
The Regime on Stratospheric
Ozone Depletion

The Montreal Protocol constitutes an outstanding model of international
cooperation, particularly between developed and developing countries.

—UNEP Executive Director Klaus Töpfer[1]

THE FORMATION OF THE POLICY REGIME for the protection of the ozone layer
has been hailed as a spectacular success in international environmental
politics, and a shining example of overcoming obstacles to policy coordination. The regime consists of several legal instruments: the Vienna Convention
for the Protection of the Ozone Layer (1985), the Montreal Protocol on Substances that Deplete the Ozone Layer (1987), the London Amendments to the
Protocol (1990), the Copenhagen Amendments (1992), the Montreal Amendments (1997), and the Beijing Amendments (1999). Each of them is legally
binding, and, except for the Convention, involves concrete commitments to
meet specific targets and timetables in reducing emissions of substances that
deplete the ozone layer. Virtually all countries have joined most or all of the
agreements.

The case is by no means idiosyncratic in its political dimensions, as it dis-
played all the usual obstacles to cooperation in environmental politics. It involved a conflict between environmental concerns and economic interests.
Large industrial establishments either produced or used the chemical products
that were allegedly causing the ecological problem. Worldwide, $385 billion in
equipment were dependent on chlorofluorocarbons (CFCs) and regulations
would affect thousands of jobs (Benedick 1998, 134). There were sharp disagreements among nations about the need for action and later about alternative

policy options, and the North-South divide was as wide as ever. Despite these hurdles, the denouement of negotiations favored environmental protection over economic concerns. The story is made particularly astonishing by the fact that the largest producer of CFCs (the United States) became one of the leaders in the movement to phase them out, despite initial opposition from its own corporate sectors. Similarly, Germany was the largest producer within the European Community (EC) and yet became one of the first European countries to support international regulations. Nations made commitments before they had empirical proof of the ecological problem, and the treaty set up deadlines for specified reductions in emissions before alternative technologies were widely available (Benedick 1998). Such features of the case make it puzzling for many of the theoretical approaches used in the study of international cooperation, and thus particularly interesting to examine.

What was the role of scientific information in the formation of the regime? Ozone depletion is an ecological problem discovered purely through scientific research. Unlike deforestation or water pollution that can be observed directly by unaided eyes, the occurrence of ozone depletion in the stratosphere is not apparent to the public, and the layperson cannot observe either its extent or its consequences. Political deliberations on this issue proceeded in parallel with intense scientific research at national and international levels. Could expert information explain the adoption of policies to address the problem? Was "science" reliable in the first place? A straightforward answer to this latter question is impossible because the quality of information varied from one aspect of the problem to another. This makes it imperative to examine various types of scientific knowledge and analyze their roles separately. Instead of searching for a "blanket" answer, we need to formulate a series of more precise propositions regarding the differential and uneven roles of several types of information. One factor that made the regime possible was the reliable scientific information about detrimental and globally shared consequences of ozone depletion.

The Problem of Ozone Depletion

The Earth's stratosphere is the stratum of the atmosphere that lies between 10 and 50 kilometers in altitude. It contains a relatively small quantity of ozone molecules that are widely dispersed and, if compressed, would form a layer that is only several millimeters thick. They play an important role in shielding the planet from ultraviolet (UV) radiation and protect living organisms from its harmful effects. Solar radiation is absorbed in a process that converts ozone into oxygen. The reverse reaction also takes place, and the dynamic balance between the two processes in a normal state of affairs keeps the ozone levels stable. In 1974, Sherwood Rowland and Mario Molina of the University of California at Irvine advanced a theory that certain human-made chemicals speed up the destruction of stratospheric ozone and tip the balance. Stable compounds containing chlorine were theorized to rise to the stratosphere where solar energy breaks them apart, and the released chlorine atoms serve as catalysts for the reaction in which UV radiation converts ozone into oxygen (Rowland 1986; Stolarski 1988).

The list of man-made substances that deplete stratospheric ozone includes CFCs, halons, methyl chloroform, hydrochlorofluorocarbons, nitrous oxides, and carbon tetrachloride. CFCs, in particular, were invented in the 1930s and since then have been used as refrigerants, propellants in aerosols, fire-fighting agents, solvents for cleaning computer microchips, and in air conditioning (Benedick 1998, Table 2.1). CFCs were the "miracle chemicals": stable, non-toxic, noncorrosive, nonflammable, and inexpensive. These qualities made them convenient, economical, and widely applicable. The Rowland-Molina hypothesis alerted societies to the possibility that these compounds were corroding the ozone shield of the Earth, with grave consequences. Every percent of ozone loss was estimated to cause a 2-percent increase in surface UV-B that, in turn, leads to a 2-percent increase in skin cancers.[2] Beyond a certain threshold, increased UV radiation also causes eye disorders, suppresses the human immune system, stunts plant growth, affects agricultural productivity, and hurts marine life (Titus 1986).

Creating the Ozone Policy Regime

The formation of the international legal regime on protection of the ozone layer has been well documented (Roan 1989; Cagin and Dray 1993; Litfin 1994; Benedick 1998; Tolba and Rummel-Bulska 1998). Recently, we received a particularly thorough account of the entire evolution of the policy regime and the development of scientific knowledge base (Parson 2003). A brief sketch of the political developments should suffice here.

Beginning in the mid-1970s, the purely scientific theory of ozone depletion generated academic conferences, further research, and eventually public debate. Despite business opposition, several countries, including the United States, introduced domestic legislation to limit or ban uses of CFCs. The first international round of deliberations on the ozone problem was a meeting sponsored by the United Nations Environment Programme (UNEP) that took place in Washington, D.C., in March 1977. The meeting was heavily research oriented. Representatives from thirty-three nations gathered to hear a set of presentations on scientific studies and adopted a Plan of Action for international cooperation in research on atmospheric chemistry, ozone trends, emissions trends, and the health and ecological effects of ozone depletion. Those at the meeting also recommended the creation of a Coordinating Committee on the Ozone Layer (CCOL), consisting of government as well as nongovernment organization (NGO) experts. UNEP adopted the Plan of Action and formed the CCOL two months later.

In 1982, at the formal request of Scandinavian countries, UNEP convened the first meeting of a negotiating committee to prepare an international agreement on ozone depletion. During the following three years, national preferences contrasted sharply. Western European countries as well as Japan and the Soviet Union were strongly opposed to control measures while Canada, Finland, Norway, Sweden, and the United States (the so-called Toronto Group) supported regulation.[3] Developing countries did not participate at this early stage of the international policy process. Disagreements could not be resolved, and negotiations produced only a general agreement to cooperate on further research and data exchange. The 1985 Vienna Convention for the Protection of the Ozone Layer did not impose any specific obligations to reduce the production or the use of ozone-depleting substance (ODS), and the text did not even identify the ODSs that the agreement covers.

The only concession that the Toronto Group gained in exchange for the absence of any control measures was a clause in the text requiring negotiations on a subsequent protocol to the Convention. Talks were organized in four rounds that took place in December 1986 and in February, April, and September 1987. The Toronto Group advocated a freeze followed by a 95-percent multistage reduction in production output over ten to fourteen years. As late as April 1987, the EC would not agree on more than a freeze in production *capacity*. Some European countries began breaking ranks, and by 1986, Belgium, Denmark, Germany, and the Netherlands were increasingly supportive of stricter regulations. Except for Germany, these states were not producers of CFCs and they met the opposition of France, Italy, and the United Kingdom, which were producers (Benedick 1998).

A compromise was reached, and twenty-four countries signed the Montreal Protocol in September 1987. It stipulated 50-percent reductions of ODSs by the year 1990, using the 1986 levels as a baseline. In many ways, the Protocol was impotent: it did not include financial arrangements or provisions for monitoring and enforcing compliance. Nevertheless, it is widely considered as a political success in overcoming traditional obstacles to international cooperation. It was a binding treaty between industrialized countries that made specific commitments to a detailed action plan to address a global environmental problem that was caused by industrial practices.

An important element of the agreement pertained to scientific input. The goal of 50-percent reductions and the list of chemicals to be controlled were left open to change by the provision that measures should be reconsidered in light of new scientific evidence. The Protocol provided for periodical scientific assessments and allowed for revising the controls accordingly. Article 6 required that: "Beginning in 1990, and at least every four years thereafter, the Parties shall assess the control measures provided for in Article 2 on the basis of available scientific, environmental, technological and economic information."[4] This provision gave the treaty a distinct flexibility and facilitated subsequent evolution of the regime (Benedick 1998).[5]

The Role of U.S. Leadership

The decision of the United States to combat ozone depletion is interesting, given that American companies were the largest producers of CFCs. The government did not protect corporate interests but introduced domestic regulations and pushed for international ones. This makes it tempting to give a realistic interpretation of the case: the United States wanted a treaty and it got one. However, there are several reasons why the case cannot be completely understood from this perspective. First, the will of the powerful did not have an effect on the decisions of the weak. Regardless of Western preferences and despite the stick-and-carrot approach that was used, not a single developing country signed onto the Montreal Protocol (see below). Second, the position of the United States was not consistent until very late; it vacillated between support and skepticism, between interest and nonchalance.

The United States was not the driving force behind negotiations, the Scandinavian countries were. Since the late 1970s, the Nordic countries repeatedly asked for initiating formal negotiations on an international agreement to address the problem. In 1981, UNEP's Governing Council approved a Swedish motion to create a negotiating working group. When the group convened for its first meeting in Stockholm, in January 1982, the Scandinavian proposal met little support: no other country wanted controls. The American delegation in particular came unprepared and, like Japan and European countries, were unwilling to engage in substantive discussion (Parson 1993, 37).

The United States was undecided about signing the Vienna Convention. As the meeting proceeded, their delegation was receiving mixed messages due to a conflict within the State Department as to whether to sign onto the agreement or not. Undersecretary of State for Economic Affairs Allen Wallis recommended that the delegation not sign the convention "precisely because he saw it as a forerunner of international regulation" (Benedick 1998, 46). The real possibility that the United States would make a last-minute decision to renege was the reason for a series of frantic midnight phone calls between Vienna and Washington. Even two years later, the U.S. preference regarding the Montreal Protocol was a matter of bitter disputes, and a high-level interagency process was established with the express purpose to reconsider the national interest regarding ozone depletion (Benedick 1998, 58–65). The American position was not finalized until June 18, 1987, when president Ronald Reagan reaffirmed the initial stance of support (Parson 1993, 43–44). Thus, the ozone regime cannot be interpreted as a function of U.S. leadership, since its position was far from consistent or stable.

What made "good knowledge" possible? The pro-environment stance that the United States took on the international scene was the end result of a chain reaction at home. Regulation first came through state legislation. New York and Oregon adopted anti-aerosol laws, and by 1976, two dozen states were considering similar legislation (McInnis 1992, 137). This put industries in regulated states at a competitive disadvantage and led them to seek national regulation that would level the national playing field.[6] Equilibrium was restored in 1976 when Congress passed the Toxic Substance Control Act that led to the ban of CFCs as aerosol agents nationwide; in 1978, their use as propellants was prohibited as well.

The United States was the only country to regulate even essential uses of CFCs in the 1970s (Stoel 1983, 69). These domestic regulations placed American producers of CFCs at a competitive disadvantage on the world markets. Between 1974 and 1985, their market share declined from 46 to 28 percent, while the market share of European producers increased from 38 to 45 percent (McInnis 1992, 137–140). American producers were faced with a choice between this undesirable state of affairs and international regulation that would impose similar burdens on their European competitors. DuPont launched programs to develop substitutes, and, when it succeeded, it joined the U.S. government in advocating international regulations. The decision of American companies to move toward substitutes and to support an international agreement helped stabilize the official position of the U.S. government, and, at the same time, undermined the opposition of EC countries, which were arguing that a transition away from ODSs was not economically prudent. The support of American industries automatically invalidated opposing claims by their European counterparts.[7]

Corporate Influences

Industries exerted efforts to influence the policymaking process, but their opposition did not prevent policy, and their subsequent support does not explain the formation of the regime. Corporate representatives were members of

European and Japanese delegations at negotiation meetings, particularly at the early stages of the process. Moreover, at particular times, U.S. companies embraced regulations as useful mechanisms for marketing industrial substitutes for ODSs. To interpret the international ozone regime as a function of corporate interests, however, would ignore the early stages of regime formation. Capital did not have an interest in government regulations of ODSs. Quite the opposite; companies contested science and bitterly opposed regulations at both national and international levels for a long time. Industries in all negotiating countries lobbied against regulations, yet some governments favored an agreement and others opposed one. National regulations in the United States were adopted in the 1970s and 1980s against consistent opposition from business. When the U.S. Environmental Protection Agency (EPA) issued a proposal for comprehensive CFC controls in 1980, industries formed a new lobby group, the Alliance for Responsible CFC Policy, a coalition of more than 500 businesses that included both producer and consumer companies and that waged a campaign against controls (Parson 1993, 35–36). As late as the summer of 1986, just prior to the adoption of the Montreal Protocol, no segment of industry supported the official position of the United States regarding international regulations (Litfin 1995, 262). This changed only in late 1986, when the Alliance announced its support for international controls on the *rate* of CFCs growth (Parson 1993, 41).

The reversal of the U.S. corporate position was not proactive but reactive: when companies saw that they were losing the battle, they rolled with the punches. Some observers suggest that these companies supported international controls because they had developed substitutes for CFCs and regulations would create new market for them. However, the development of substitutes occurred in reaction to national regulations and the political movement toward an international agreement. DuPont and others began research programs to develop substitutes because they faced domestic regulations. As the political climate shifted with the advent of the Reagan administration, the programs were abandoned in early 1980s, only to resume again in late 1986 when the negotiation process to devise a protocol to the Vienna Convention was established. DuPont's most promising substitutes (hydrochlorofluorocarbons and hydrofluorocarbons) were two to five times more expensive than CFCs (Parson 2003, 53–54) and therefore not economically preferable as far as business was concerned. In short, the formation of regulatory regimes was against corporate interests and took place despite business opposition.

Consequently, the Montreal Protocol added incentives for the further development of substitutes. Between 1988 and 1989, international limitations on production pushed prices of CFC-11 and CFC-12 up 30–60 percent in the

United States and 15 percent in Europe (Hunter 1989). For producers, this meant higher profits. The EPA estimated that implementation of the provisions of the Montreal Protocol together with domestic regulations would produce windfall profit for U.S. producers of $1.8 to $7.2 billion by the end of the century (McInnis 1992, 147). For the industrial *users* of CFCs, on the other hand, regulation meant that they would have to pay more for CFCs. Higher CFC prices made the development of substitutes financially viable because it reduced their relative cost. After the creation of the Protocol, in March 1988 DuPont announced that it would stop producing CFCs by the end of the century, and, before any government suggested it, proposed a complete international phase-out of ODSs (Benedick 1998, 111–112).

Bringing in Developing Countries

Bringing developing countries into the treaty was important. Per capita consumption rates in these countries were negligible when compared to those of advanced industrialized countries, but the *growth* rates of consumption were higher (Benedick 1998, 49–50). Thus, their nonparticipation could eventually offset the positive ecological effects of regulation in the North. Negotiators used a stick-and-carrot approach that produced limited results. Article 4 of the Montreal Protocol contained a provision for trade sanctions against nonparties to the treaty and introduced restrictions on trade with ODSs, with products that contained ODSs, and finally, with products made with ODSs (DeSombre and Kauffman 1996). At the same time, the treaty allowed developing countries to postpone implementation for ten years. During this time, they could increase their consumption up to 0.3 kilograms per capita. These negative and positive incentives proved insufficient to attract more parties to the treaty. Only one developing country, Mexico, signed the protocol, and key players, including Brazil, China, and India stayed out.

This situation changed only after financial arrangements were offered. In 1990, parties to the regime established the Montreal Protocol Multilateral Fund to assist developing countries with the costs of phasing out ODSs. Initially, the fund was $130 million and was later increased to $240 million. China accepted the provisions of the agreement immediately after the establishment of the Fund, and Brazil and India joined in 1992. By 1994, most developing countries had joined the treaty. Despite world economic recession, the Fund was expanded to $510 million annually for 1994–1996 and further to $540 million for 1997–1999 (DeSombre and Kauffman 1996; Benedick 1998, 252–255).

Political and financial accommodation had symbolic significance for developing countries. The largest contributors to the Fund were those countries that had created the ecological problem in the first place: the EC with 34.6

percent, the United States with 25 percent, and Japan with 13.3 percent of contributions. Moreover, developed and developing countries were given equal representation on the executive committee responsible for the administration of the Fund (DeSombre and Kauffman 1996, 99–100). Donor countries, on the other hand, could view the money they put into the fund as investment in future markets for the substitutes they were developing. Eventually, the creation of the Fund contributed to the formation of the regime by eliminating two major impediments. It helped assuage the suspicions that the regime was an attempt to hamper the economic development of poor countries by denying them the industrial benefits of available and cheap chemicals. Second, it made financially possible the shift to substitutes of ODSs that would have been difficult for countries with limited resources. So, financial arrangements not only facilitated the implementation of the regime but were also an important factor in its creation.

· The Montreal Protocol entered into force on January 1, 1989, with ratification from twenty-nine countries that accounted for 83 percent of global consumption of CFCs and halons. The initiative was soon accelerated, and the regime was strengthened significantly. At a London conference in early spring of 1989, more than one hundred nations agreed in principle on complete elimination of ODSs, and the idea of phase-outs before the end of the century was officially endorsed at the first meeting of the parties to the Montreal Protocol in Helsinki in May 1989. The London Amendments of 1990 redefined the target as a complete phase-out of most ODSs by the year 2000, and the amendments adopted in Copenhagen in 1992 moved this deadline to 1996.

Why did countries make efforts to create an international policy regime? Political gains or economic benefits from international regulations of ODSs became salient only after negotiations had begun. And actors who eventually supported regulations did not do so in earlier stages. Companies came to support controls, but this was an act of capitulation after long years of firm opposition. Instead of trying to identify an actor who prevailed in interactions with other actors, it might be more useful to consider a background factor that may have affected the considerations of all actors. What could actors gain from controlling ODSs if it was against their political or economic interests initially? This question causes us to consider shared knowledge about the problem of ozone depletion and the content of scientific information.

Scientific Knowledge on Ozone Depletion

Following articles in scientific journals that suggested that human-made compounds destroy stratospheric ozone (Johnston 1971; Molina and Rowland

1974; Stolarski and Cicerone 1974), there was an explosion of research efforts in the 1970s to determine how the stratosphere reacts to an influx of pollutants of anthropogenic sources. At first, the concern was with water vapors and nitrous oxides from aircraft and space shuttles, a topic of a symposium of the International Association of Geomagnetism and Aeronomy in September 1973.[8] Then, two articles published simultaneously in 1974 asserted that chlorine may be a more serious destroyer of ozone than nitrogen. Richard Stolarski and Ralph Cicerone (1974) drew the attention to natural sources of chlorine: sea salt spray and volcanic eruptions that can inject chlorine directly into the stratosphere; Mario Molina and Sherwood Rowland (1974) focused on the possibility that human-made chlorofluoromethanes destroy ozone.

From the beginning, the formation and further evolution of the ozone regime went hand in hand with institutionalized scientific research. Decision makers at national and international levels solicited research and expert opinion, and political steps on the international level were taken after scientific input arrived. A CCOL was established in 1977 to coordinate national and international research and to take stock of all existing information on ozone. At this early stage, most ozone research was conducted in American scientific institutions. The National Academy of Sciences and NASA were considered the preeminent scientific authorities on ozone depletion (Stoel 1983, 67).

A broader multilateral research program was launched in 1984 that involved 150 scientists from eleven countries and began to produce regular reports on their findings. It was sponsored by the World Meteorological Organization (WMO), the UNEP, NASA, the National Oceanic and Atmospheric Administration (NOAA), the EC Commission, and the German Ministry of Science and Technology (WMO 1986). The 1985 Vienna Convention also established an advisory body, the Meeting of Ozone Research Managers, which consisted of government experts on atmospheric research and the effects of ozone depletion (Wettestäd 1999, 151–153). In 1986, yet another body, the Ozone Trends Panel, consisting of more than one hundred leading scientists, was established to sift through all ozone data in the world. And the first step after the Montreal Protocol was created to establish expert panels on science, technology, impacts, and economics. The resulting reports played an important role in the evolution of international policy, as parties to the Protocol negotiated amendments to the treaty that strengthened the regime.

Concerted research efforts gradually increased understanding of ozone depletion. Yet, the state of knowledge about the various aspects of the problem progressed very unevenly. There were clear contrasts in the level of scientific certainty about the extent, causes, and consequences of depletion. As the following inventory of scientific assessments elaborates, knowledge about the occurrence and *extent* of ozone depletion was unreliable until after the 1987 Montreal Protocol was created. Similarly, there were open questions about alternative *causes* of depletion and their relative contributions to the problem. Scientific consensus on the occurrence, extent, and anthropogenic causes of depletion emerged only in 1988. By contrast, knowledge about the *consequences* of the problem on human health and ecosystems was highly reliable and never disputed. From the beginning of public debates, scientists were unanimous that these impacts would be grave and transboundary, and political actors never questioned these claims. In short, there was shared and reliable knowledge about the shared consequences of the problem.

Sector I: Extent of Ozone Depletion

Problems with measuring ozone changes and attributing them to specific sources haunted research from the beginning and were never quite dispelled, despite the significant improvements made over the first decade. Initial optimism in 1975 that "the magnitude of [ozone] decrease can now be reasonably well predicted" (NRC 1975, 9) gave way to "the realization that the evolution of the atmosphere is more complex than had earlier been assumed" (NRC 1984, 15).

Whether depletion was actually occurring was a matter of controversy that persisted through the Protocol negotiations. Measurements of ozone depletion were considered unreliable until as late as the early 1990s (Parson 1993, 72; 2003). There were indications of increased quantity of substances that were believed to facilitate ozone depletion (WMO 1986) and general agreement that less ozone would mean more UV radiation (NRC 1979a, 6) but whether there was actual ozone change remained a question with no certain answers until after the Montreal Protocol was signed. NASA reported only evidence of increase in the gases that were believed to deplete ozone but not evidence of actual depletion. Just prior to the writing of the Montreal Protocol, a comprehensive international study concluded: "We are still data limited . . . the measurements are not adequate for critically testing the photochemical models" (WMO 1986, 13). NASA was even more explicit: "The question still remains concerning our ability to predict future concentrations of ozone and other atmospheric species" (NASA 1986, xii).

Uncertainty about the extent of ozone depletion derives from several factors that an early scientific report acknowledged (NRC 1976). First, atmospheric chemistry is enormously complex. At least 125 chemical reactions take place in the atmosphere, with speeds that were not known with certainty, and they produced a large cumulative uncertainty that "is unlikely to show rapid improvement in the future" (NRC 1979a, 9).

Second, ozone calculations could not be provided by studies of the atmosphere alone but had to involve virtually all natural sciences (WMO 1986).[9] Third, the constant motion of substances in the atmosphere changes the dynamics of atmospheric chemistry. Studies relied primarily on one-dimensional models that took into account only vertical movements of gases (NRC 1979a, 11–13; WMO 1986, 3).

Fourth, there are natural self-healing mechanisms in the atmosphere that can offset depletion. For instance, if ozone is depleted in the upper atmosphere, increased UV light penetrates deeper into the stratosphere, breaks up more oxygen and generates more ozone (NRC 1976, 12; Stolarski 1988). Such competing reactions may compensate for ozone loss from human sources. Fifth, predictions of ozone change were tied to anticipated rates of production of industrial ODSs, and those were contingent on a number of economic and social factors and were considered impossible to estimate (NRC 1979a, 6). Finally, apart from anthropogenic substances, there are a number of natural sources of substances that deplete ozone, and integrating those into the formula that predicts ozone depletion is still a challenge.

These difficulties were reflected in the substantive findings of research on ozone levels. An early report concluded: "while our knowledge of stratospheric ozone has become extensive during the past few years, it should be apparent from the discussion given above that significant uncertainties remain" (NRC 1976, 20). From then on, until the late 1980s, every report stated exactly that, in virtually the same words. The next report (NRC 1979a) was highly contingent on numerous stipulations and suggested that at 1977 release rates, the depletion would be between 5 and 28 percent (NRC 1979a, 5, 1979b, 5). "To make provision for possible tropospheric sinks we have, *somewhat arbitrarily*, reduced the most probable value [of ozone loss] to 16.5 percent" (NRC 1979a, 17; emphasis added). This "somewhat arbitrary" estimate was later reduced.

Two problems characterized findings from scientific assessments. First, estimates of ozone losses fluctuated considerably: 7 percent, 20 percent, 16.5 percent, 5 to 9, and 2 to 4 percent. Notably, the estimates of ozone losses were progressively declining. That is, each successive report showed higher and higher ozone levels, and less and less depletion expected at the middle of the next century. In 1978, the WMO estimated ozone depletion of 18.6 to 20 percent.[10] The best estimate of the National Research Council for total ozone loss was reduced from 16.5 percent in 1979 to 5 percent in 1982, and further to 3 percent in 1984 (respective NRC references).[11] Some early studies had even found an *increase* in total ozone between the early 1960s and the early 1970s, possibly attributable to the natural eleven-year solar cycles (Crutzen 1974). The persistent uncertainty about these assessments led the Council to abstain from quantification of confidence levels (NRC 1984, 12–14).

There were also significant discrepancies between model predictions and actual measurements. Actual observations indicated depletion that was even smaller than the ones predicted by models. In 1986, it was acknowledged that the actual quantities of ozone turned out to be 30–50 percent higher than the models estimated (NASA 1986, xiii; WMO 1986, 14). "In general, analyses for the trends in the total column of ozone show no statistically significant trend since 1970 in agreement with model predictions for the same period" (NASA 1986, xi). Even the amounts of ozone-depleting substances were smaller: concentrations of CFCs in the lower stratosphere were lower than the models predicted (NRC 1982, 2–3). If we assume that the models were reliable and served as a reference to decision makers, the declining estimates of ozone loss over the years prior to the ozone treaties still cast serious doubt that these estimates motivated the decisions. Instead, the successive reports were reducing the reason for such concern.

The Antarctic Hole: A Reconsideration

One widespread notion about the ozone story is that evidence of an Antarctic ozone hole created a powerful sense of urgency and facilitated negotiations on the Protocol (Litfin 1994). In fact, the first conclusive evidence of a hole appeared *after* the protocol was signed in Montreal. As Edward Parson (2003) recently noted, the role of the Antarctic hole in creating the original policy regime has been substantially exaggerated. Despite publicity in popular mass media, no one used a possible ozone hole as an argument in deliberations of the Protocol. At the time, evidence was unreliable and the hole was considered an inexplicable anomaly. Testimony of this was given by the leader of the Norwegian delegation, Per Bakken, and one of the chief American negotiators, Richard Benedick (Bakken 1989, 201; Benedick 1998, 18–20). The ozone hole did play a role, but only in the subsequent evolution of the regime.

In 1985, British scientists concluded a study that found significant decreases of ozone over Antarctica. The landmark "ozone hole" paper (Farman et al. 1985) attracted public attention and the interest of fellow scientists, and in 1986 NASA sent a National Ozone Expedition (NOZE) to McMurdo Station in Antarctica to make measurements. They found unusually high amounts of ODSs such as chlorine monoxide. At the same time, David Hoffman made measurements with balloons that showed that 35 percent of ozone between 7.5 and 12.5 miles of altitude was missing. These scientists hesitated in making conclusions, however, as they could not explain the results.[12] The 1986 NOZE operation triggered intense internecine disputes among scientists. Atmospheric dynamicists rejected the findings outright and intimated that the entire operation was a politically motivated fraud. Instead of bringing consensus the study raised even more disputes. The highly visible controversy only strengthened the stance of industry that could again point to the absence of scientific consensus on the problem (Cagin and Dray 1993, 315–317).[13]

To resolve the dispute, in 1987 NASA undertook a second operation that was meant to settle the issue by producing definitive results. This operation went to unusual lengths: scientists designed a special device for measuring chlorine monoxide and mounted it on a high-altitude, lightweight ER-2 plane that was flown repeatedly over Antarctica. The measurements showed a strict reverse correlation between levels of chlorine monoxide and ozone (Cagin and Dray 1993, 339–350). The *Washington Post* termed the findings "the first hard evidence that the critical environmental loss can be blamed on a man-made gas" (October 1, 1987). The report from the study was published only in 1989 (Anderson et al. 1989).

These results came too late to affect talks on the Montreal Protocol. The proof that CFCs were causing severe depletion over Antarctica came two weeks after the Protocol was signed on September 14, 1987. Scientists discussed the findings in a series of meetings through the fall of 1987 and reached consensus at a workshop in Dahlem, Germany, in early November (Cagin and Dray 1993, 352–354; Parson 2003, 152). Since these results and the consensus around them came after the policy agreement was reached, it is clear that reliable information about an Antarctic ozone hole was not part of the foundation for decision-making on the Protocol. The Antarctic hole was not discussed in the official WMO 1986 report. The executive summary contained only a passing remark about decrease in Antarctic ozone, but no figure was given (WMO 1986, 20).

Information of the extent of depletion explains neither the formation of the regime nor the content of the agreement. Participants in negotiations had explicitly decided to ignore as yet unconfirmed evidence of an Antarctic hole and purposefully did not bring it up during the talks (Cagin and Dray 1993, 357; Benedick 1998, 18–20). "All records of the negotiations, and the scientific advice being offered to them, are consistent with the widely reported claim that negotiators did not consider the Antarctic ozone hole or the unverified claims of global depletion" (Parson 2003, 142). Furthermore, the policy targets under the Montreal Protocol did not correspond with the scientific estimates. It was stated that if CFC growth was less than 1.5 percent per year, the effects on ozone would be relatively small, less than 3 percent over seventy years (WMO 1986, 19). Therefore, even a freeze of CFC or a small reduction would have sufficed, and the 50-percent cuts adopted in the Protocol were not justified by scientific data.

Uncertainty about the extent of ozone depletion was the hallmark of all reports until after the Montreal Protocol was signed. The first official confirmation of global decline in ozone levels (as opposed to regional depletion over Antarctica) came six months *after* the Montreal Protocol was adopted, in March 1988 (Watson et al. 1988). The Ozone Trends Panel released its findings at a press conference on March 15, 1988, one day after the U.S. Senate voted to support the Protocol (Parson 2003, 155). The executive summary of the findings stated that current ozone levels were already lower than those projected for the year 2050 by the scientific studies used as the basis of negotiating the Protocol. Depletion between 1969 and 1986 ranged from 1.7 percent over Florida to 4 percent in Australia and New Zealand. The ozone layer over the Northern Hemisphere had been reduced by up to 3 percent (Parson 2003, 155). By 1989, it was officially confirmed that "the research of the past few years has demonstrated that actual ozone loss due to the CFCs has already occurred, i.e., the Antarctic ozone hole" (WMO 1990). This improved knowledge affected the subsequent evolution of the regime and justified the stricter measures adopted with the London and Copenhagen Amendments to the Montreal Protocol (Parson 2003).

Sector II: Causes of Ozone Depletion

Natural variation of ozone levels was known to occur by year, by season, day to day, in latitude, and in altitude (Dürch 1974). Stratospheric ozone is under the simultaneous influence of a number of substances of human and natural origin, and there were several alternative explanations of ozone depletion that focused on natural phenomena. Sea spray ejects chlorine atoms from the oceans into the atmosphere, and chlorine acts as a catalyst for converting ozone into oxygen. Another theory drew attention to the role of ice particles on the surface of polar stratospheric clouds, and eleven-year solar cycles cause radiation to vacillate and ozone levels to fluctuate (Stolarski 1988).

Scientists found it impossible to determine the precise contribution of anthropogenic sources relative to natural factors. One major review of several groups of theories on the causes of depletion concluded that none of them can explain the Antarctic hole satisfactorily (Solomon 1988). As late as 1989, two years after the Protocol was signed, an international report stated that "the current record is too short to differentiate the effects of natural and human-induced processes on ozone," and that no attempt to do so was made (WMO 1990, ix). And into the 1990s, new suggestions about additional mechanisms that deplete ozone kept appearing (Cagin and Dray 1993, 360).

Even if decision makers ignored natural causes and focused on human-made ODSs, they encountered scientific uncertainty about the roles of individual chemicals. Compounds such as carbon dioxide and nitrous oxides from commercial aircraft could actually help *increase* ozone (NRC 1984, 12).

Space shuttles are also sources of ODSs but were excluded from consideration as early as 1976 because they were taken to be insignificant contributors of chlorine, in comparison to chlorofluoromethanes (NRC 1976, 17). The large number of natural and human causes of ozone changes made the indictment difficult: which substances were to be regulated?

Uncertainty about the *causes* of the problem greatly compounded the uncertainty about the *extent* of depletion. Even if evidence of ozone depletion was found, it could not be taken as proof that human activities were causing the depletion. "Because data on total global ozone cannot be analyzed to distinguish among causes of ozone changes, total ozone data alone cannot be relied upon for early detection of an anthropogenic change" (NRC 1982, 3). Uncertainty in one sector of knowledge thus amplified the effects of uncertainty in another sector. Opponents of regulatory measures could defend industrial chemicals by stating there was no hard evidence of either depletion or its causes.

Sector III: Consequences of Ozone Depletion

By contrast, the potential consequences of the problem were known with certainty and were never disputed by either scientists or policy makers. The detrimental effects of higher UV light were known from the very beginning of the political process and did not change essentially over the years of research and discussion. They were acknowledged in the first report (NRC 1975) and can be classified in three main categories: health effects on humans (skin disease, eye disorders, and immune system suppression), effects on terrestrial plants and bacteria, and effects on marine life. These effects were well documented even before multilateral talks on ozone depletion began, and the reliability of this particular knowledge grew over the years. The bibliography of an official 1982 report on biological effects alone ran thirteen pages (NRC 1982, 116–133). In 1986, UNEP published in three heavy volumes the proceedings of the International Conference on Health and Environmental Effects of Ozone Modification and Climate Change. Each article presented a comprehensive review of existing knowledge and covered many studies.

Health Effects

Effects of excessive UV exposure on skin cancers result from a well-known mechanism through which UV-B solar radiation inflicts damage to the DNA that becomes irreversible beyond certain critical levels. By the end of the 1970s, such impacts had been extensively documented (Rahn 1979; Saito et al. 1983). A number of nonmelanoma skin cancers have been "unequivocally associated with sun exposure," including premalignant actinic keratosis, basal cell carcinomas, and squamous cell carcinomas (Emmett 1986).[14] Sun-induced skin diseases constitute more than half of all skin diseases among fair-skinned people, including nonmelanoma and possibly melanoma cancers.[15] It was also known that in combination with UV exposure some chemicals in paints, dyes, and antibacterial products that were commonly used in households produced cancer. In addition, a number of other diseases are either triggered or exacerbated by UV exposure: albinism, herpex simplex, and nutrition deficiencies such as pellagra, porphyrias, and others (Emmett 1986, 138, 143).

Ultraviolet radiation can also damage several parts of the eye: the retina, the crystalline lens, the cornea, and the photoreceptors. The impact results in cataracts, visual aging, impaired visual development in children, and retinal degeneration—especially in infants and the elderly whose eyes are particularly vulnerable (Hiller et al. 1977). A review of the subject lists many studies from the late 1970s and early 1980s that demonstrate an association between cataracts and exposure to UV light (Waxler 1986).[16] The UNEP/EPA report stated: "Depletion of the ozone layer increases the ambient level of UV-B radiation and therefore also increases the risk of eye damage" (Emmett 1986, 152).

In 1987, EPA issued a five-volume report of 1,600 pages entitled *Assessing the Risks of Trace Gases that Can Modify the Stratosphere* (EPA 1987). It estimated that increased UV radiation over the next eighty-eight years would cause 12 million more eye cataracts, a growing number of immune system disorders, and 40 million additional cancers, 800,000 of them fatal (Cagin and Dray 1993, 310). Eminent scientific authorities confirmed health effects. The report was peer reviewed, and at a congressional hearing, the chair of the reviewing panel, Margaret Kripke, graded it as "an up-to-date document that accurately and fairly assessed the state of knowledge" (Cagin and Dray 1993, 310). Thomas B. Fitzpatrick, chairman of the Department of Dermatology at the Harvard Medical School, testified before the U.S. Senate that decreased ozone would undoubtedly increase future skin cancers.[17] He pointed out that a child born in 1930 when CFCs were invented had a 1-in-1,500 chance to get malignant melanoma, while in the late 1980s this risk was 1 in 135. The actual cases of melanoma in the southwestern United States had increased by 340 percent in a very short period, between 1975 and 1985.

The overall health impact is a function of lifestyle as well as the level of UV radiation in sunrays. The length of exposure and level of skin protection are important factors that depend on individual behavior. Natural UV radiation varies with latitude, altitude, time of day, season, and atmospheric conditions. People could absorb UV radiation not only from the sun but also from artificial sources: sunlamps, germicidal lamps, welding arcs, plastic and paint curing and drying processes, plasma torches, and ultraviolet lasers (Emmett 1986, 130). It was therefore difficult to provide a quantified measure of the overall impact on society—but there was consensus on the qualitative risks from increased radiation.

Effects on Plants

Between 1975 and 1985, several hundred studies documented the effects of UV radiation on plants (Teramura 1986b, 255). Two out of every three plants that were tested showed sensitivity to UV exposure (NRC 1982, 339). The resultant changes include reduction in leaf size and decreases in total dry weight and efficiency of water use by the plant. Photosynthesis in some plants was also decreased (Teramura 1986a, 170). Such alterations led to stunting of plant growth and a decline in plant productivity. The implications for agriculture are significant since the plant species found to be most sensitive to UV radiation were crop species: members of the bean, pea, cabbage, and squash families (Biggs and Kossuth 1978). Moreover, damage was most severe on plants in irrigated and fertilized areas, that is, in agricultural lands (Teramura 1986a, 167). Studies at the University of Maryland showed that 25 percent ozone depletion can lead to 20–25 percent decrease in the crop yield of soybeans (Teramura 1986a, 167).

Such high reduction of ozone is not anticipated today; what is important is the approximately one-to-one correlation between depletion and yield decline. There were some points of uncertainty but they did not concern the essential link between UV exposure and plants. For instance, scientists were not sure about the exact reason for plant sensitivity to UV light or about the combined effects of increased radiation and air pollution (Teramura 1986a, 168–169). "Despite these and other difficulties, our current uncertainty is not whether plants are affected by UV, but rather the magnitude of this sensitivity. Because only a handful of key species supply most of our agricultural needs, this potential susceptibility warrants great concern" (Teramura 1986b, 257).

Effects on Marine Life

Scores of studies converge on the conclusion that increased UV light inflicts damage to plankton and marine plants that are essential to aquatic food webs. As early as the 1930s, a number of experiments had shown detrimental impact of UV exposure on aquatic organisms (NRC 1984). These effects include increased mortality in adults, decreased survival of larvae, and decreased fecundity of survivors. The ramifications of this impact on phytoplankton are particularly sweeping because phytoplankton is at the bottom of the food chain and sustains the life and health of many other species.

There are also serious direct effects on zooplankton. Zooplankton is a biological term for the larvae and eggs of fish and small crustaceans, which means that virtually all marine animals other than mammals *are* zooplankton at their early stages of life. The larvae and eggs of species are translucent and allow deep penetration of UV light into the tissues. For some species such as the bay oyster, a 15-percent decrease of ozone could lead to a 30-percent increase in the number of abnormal larvae. For some species of economic significance, even a 1-percent decline may make the difference between economic viability and negative cash flow (Thompson 1986, 206). One laboratory test found that a 20-percent increase in UV exposure resulted in the death of 100 percent of anchovy larvae within fifteen days of exposure.[18]

All reports confirmed that increased UV exposure adversely affects their reproduction, growth, and survival. At the early stages, there was uncertainty about the quantitative measures of impact rather than the principal effects (NRC 1982).[19] The main problem was one of scale: it was difficult to quantify the overall impact on entire ecosystems due to the complexity of these systems. Scientists did not doubt the effects on individual species, but the dynamics of the system could either moderate or exacerbate their cumulative impact. Yet, even scientists who were concerned about these problems acknowledged that "clear and convincing evidence from research of the past decade indicates that UV-B radiation can injure the health of some marine organisms" (Kelly 1986, 238). Hence, there was certainty that higher UV radiation can damage microscopic marine life forms that are fundamental elements of marine ecosystems.

Quantification of all types of anticipated impacts grew in precision over the years. In reports from the 1970s, attempts to quantify impact were tentative: a 16-percent decrease of ozone was expected to result in several thousand more cases of melanoma cancer and several hundred thousand more nonmelanoma cases per year, and marine microorganisms and larvae would suffer "appreciable killing" (NRC 1979b, 6–7). Three years later, the measurements became more precise: a 2-percent increase in UV-B would give a 2 to 5-percent increase in basal cell skin cancer and a 4 to 10-percent increase in squamous cell skin cancer (NRC 1982, 9). Because of additional social factors such as increased longevity of populations, these estimates were raised even higher (NRC 1984, 164–167).

In summary, scientific knowledge about the consequences of ozone depletion—if and when it occurred—was rather solid and considered reliable. The only problems in this sector pertained to quantification of cumulative impact on entire ecosystems. The principal mechanisms through which increased UV radiation damages human health, terrestrial plants, and aquatic life were well understood and not disputed.

Knowledge and Action: The Impact of Information

The reliable and widely accepted knowledge about the consequences of the problem opened a zone of agreement that provided a constant background to political discussions. Throughout all the scientific trials and errors in ozone measurements, no one doubted the detrimental potential effects of ozone depletion, and this aspect of science was not debated. The chief negotiator of the United States notes:

> All of these possible effects were known to the negotiators of the Montreal Protocol, *and they were never seriously contested.* It was generally accepted that changes in the ozone layer pose serious risks to human health and the environment. The point of contention among participating governments was the extent of international action necessary to provide a reasonable degree of protection. (Benedick 1998, 22; emphasis added)

Reliable information about consequences was significant in two ways. First, it testified to the level of externalities involved: because the consequences of depletion were transboundary, the problem involved significant elements of interdependence among states. All countries would suffer the effects, regardless of the point of origin of ODSs, and unilateral policy action through national regulation would not preclude the possibility of damage from emissions abroad. Therefore, if regulatory action was to be taken, externalities required an international arrangement of reciprocal obligations.

Second, this particular type of information made possible cost-benefit calculations. Data about the detrimental impact of ozone depletion implied that the cost of inaction would have been considerable: the thinning of stratospheric ozone would jeopardize values of central importance such as human health and food security. At the same time, policy action to ameliorate ozone depletion would not be particularly costly. Production of these substances was a negligible part of national economies. CFCs accounted for only 2 percent of the revenues of the largest producer, DuPont (Wettestäd 1999, 135). The consumption of ODSs was also of relatively low social value. They were used as coolants in refrigerators, as propellants in the production of plastic foams, in firefighting, and since the 1970s, CFC-13 was also used as a solvent for cleaning computer microchips. In addition, halons were used by the military and by large banks and commercial airlines as firefighting foams. Uses of dyes, solvents, and coolants are not negligible, but none of them served basic social needs such as food or energy production or transportation.

By 1981, it was clear that substantial cuts could be achieved at low costs (Parson 1993, 73). In a risk assessment, the EPA estimated the global costs of 50-percent cuts in ODSs to be $27 billion, while their benefits for the United States alone would be $6.4 trillion (EPA 1986). Clearly, even rough cost-benefit calculations were in favor of regulations. The benefits were so significant that it would have been worthwhile for the United States to cover the global costs of a regime by itself (Parson 1993, 69). Such calculations were made possible by undisputed information about the consequences of the problem.

Information about the extent of depletion does not appear to have critically affected the basic political outcome (regime formation) as uncertainty in this sector of knowledge did not prevent the making of the treaty. This does not mean that such information is irrelevant or unimportant. Knowledge about consequences alone would not be sufficient because the anticipated impact of a problem is a function also of its magnitude. Consequences without any probability that they would take place do not provide reasons to worry about them.

The point here is that uncertainty and lack of conclusive evidence regarding this aspect of the problem did not hamper regime formation. Moreover, this type of knowledge influenced the subsequent evolution of the regime. After evidence of depletion became reliable and widely accepted, the regime was strengthened significantly—a move made easier by the now available alternatives to CFCs. At the first meeting of the parties to the Montreal Protocol in Helsinki in May 1989, 123 countries called for complete elimination of ODSs before the end of the century. Thus, the state of knowledge on the *extent* of a problem may be more important in affecting the particular design and strength of measures. Uncertainty about the extent of the problem may lead to disagreements about how much to do about it. Absence of reliable information about the magnitude of ozone depletion may help explain why the policy proposals of the United States and most of the European countries differed widely. This particular gap of information opened a wide area of disagreement on how much action should be taken.

Power and Knowledge

What made "solid knowledge" possible? An alternative explanation of the observed correspondence between the state of knowledge and outcomes would draw on the familiar theme "power and knowledge." According to that line of argument, knowledge is epiphenomenal: a construct by powerful political actors who generate and mold information to buttress their preferences. Hence, the argument would proceed, what really helps interpret the two cases is not the available information but the exercise of power that shaped such information.

The problem with this theory is that facts and logic get in the way. If knowledge were a puppet in the hands of powerful actors, one would logically expect such actors to "produce" information that suits their interests and to contest information that undermines their negotiating positions. This did not happen in this case. Powerful actors were not able to suppress information that runs counter to their preferences. The United States wanted a treaty and took the political and entrepreneurial leadership in the negotiating process. U.S. research institutions were the prime producers of ozone science and that should have provided good opportunity to massage information. Yet, the United States was not able to fabricate evidence about the *extent* of ozone depletion: the uncertainties were blatant and not eliminated until after the key agreement was signed. Moreover, American negotiators and policy makers did not deny the significant information gaps in that particular sector of knowledge. If power shaped knowledge, why was the United States unable to "produce" reliable information on this important aspect of the problem?

Conclusion

Attempts to clarify whether science was reliable and can help explain regime formation obscure important differences between the roles of several types of information. A close look at the available scientific knowledge about ozone depletion reveals that information on some aspects of the problem was abundant and reliable, whereas knowledge about other aspects of ozone depletion was far from complete. The formation of the international policy regime was accompanied by significant scientific uncertainty about the extent of ozone depletion and, to lesser extent, about its causes. There was, however, reliable information and consensus about the consequences of depletion—if and when it occurred. Multilateral research provided solid and undisputed evidence that the transboundary consequences of the problem would be grave. The principal mechanisms through which increased UV radiation damages human health, terrestrial plants, and aquatic life were well understood and never disputed by either scientists or negotiators. Correspondingly, the benefits from preserving the ozone layer were considerable and were seen as such by all actors.

This perception did not form automatically or quickly: techniques of persuasion, individual leadership, trade-offs, and other efforts to achieve equity all played a part. The evolution of the regime proceeded in incremental steps, and this gradualist approach allowed time for bargaining, persuasion, and reaching compromises. The Vienna Convention did not specify any targets, but it placed the issue on the political agenda and paved the way to the specific obligations under the subsequent protocol and its amendments. Consensual scientific knowledge about the negative consequences of depletion was an important enabling condition in this political process. It served as a constant background to discussions and opened a zone of agreement. It was significant not by itself but in conjunction with other factors, namely, it made possible utility calculations, and those were in favor of regulations because of the relatively low economic and social value of ODSs.

In the end, the international regime for protection of the ozone layer can be seen as a function of science, for several reasons. First, the issue of ozone depletion was brought up as a result of purely scientific research that was conducted out of curiosity. Second, the very first political moves on both national and international levels were to inquire into the available scientific information and to organize scientific workshops and research groups. Third, throughout the process of formation of the regime, comprehensive scientific assessments were conducted and reported to policy makers on a regular basis. Fourth, there was reliable and undisputed scientific knowledge about the detrimental impact of potential ozone depletion. It would be a mistake, though, to make a generalized conclusion that science was reliable and important. One particular type of information was indeed available and influential, but other seemingly highly relevant types of information (about the extent and causes of the problem) were neither complete nor consensual. This type of uncertainty did not stop decision makers from creating a policy regime.

Notes

1. *Linkages*, vol. 5, no. 9 (October 1, 2000). Available in electronic form at http://www.iisd.ca (February 11, 2005).

2. Scientists differentiate three ranges of ultraviolet radiation. UV-B is the most detrimental type, while UV-A is known to have largely positive effects.

3. Several other countries (Austria, Australia, Denmark, and Switzerland) were not part of the Toronto group but supported them in principle (Parson 1993).

4. The full text of the Montreal Protocol can be found in Appendix B in Benedick 1998.

5. Amendments to the Protocol could be made by votes representing 50 percent of global production. A task force had to be established one year before the first evaluation and to prepare a special report.

6. Similar developments had characterized the move to regulation of air and water pollution in the United States (Yandle 1989).

7. These developments confirm an observation made by Lynton Caldwell (1996) that the path to international environmental policy must be paved by prior national policies (pp. 35–37, 54–57).

8. The papers from the symposium were presented in a special issue of the *Canadian Journal of Chemistry* (vol. 52, no. 8).

9. The report noted: "Thus to really understand the processes which control atmospheric ozone and to predict perturbations we are drawn into a study of the complete earth system" (WMO 1986, 2).

10. Papers prepared for the WMO Symposium on stratospheric changes, Toronto, June 26–30, 1978; cited in Stoel 1983, 46.

11. Later the estimates rose again: the WMO reported in 1986 that models predicted that CFC-11 and CFC-12 at 1980 rates would reduce ozone at 4 percent in the tropics, 9 percent in temperate zones, and 14 percent in the polar regions (WMO 1986, 18).

12. In the words of one of the scientists involved in the project, Barney Farmer, "If you can't show how something works, then you don't have much of a case. Most scientists are extremely wary of not having a theory to go along with what they observe" (interview, cited by Cagin and Dray 1993, 315).

13. In its opposition, industry kept reiterating that actual depletion of ozone had not been measured. Scientists did not deny that, but argued that once actual losses are discovered, it may be too late to reverse the trend (Litfin 1994, 68).

14. Compared to nonmelanoma cancers, the evidence that UV radiation affects melanoma cancers is less consistent. This latter type of cancer is more deadly and is observed in people who sunburn easily and who have had repeated sunburns during childhood. *Lentigo maligna*, for example, accounts for 14 percent of melanomas and occurs on the sun-damaged skin of the face of older individuals. Such observations make it likely that melanoma cancer and exposure are related, but in the mid-1980s there was no technical proof of the link (Emmett 1986, 140–141). Melanoma cancer was not proved to be a result of UV radiation since the evidence was only circumstantial and there were other factors involved (NRC 1984, 168–190). Yet, it was not doubted that UV radiation is among these factors.

15. The risks vary with latitude, length of exposure, and type of skin. Most research was done on white populations because fair-skinned people are more vulnerable to UV radiation.

16. Each of the studies found that cataracts were associated with exposure to sunlight when the latter exceeded a total of 2,500 MEDs (minimal erythemal doses) annually.

17. U.S. Senate, "Effects of Chlorofluorocarbons on Stratospheric Ozone, Health Effects of Ozone Depletion, and Substitutes for Ozone-Depleting Chemicals," joint hearing before Subcommittees of the Committee on Environment and Public Works, 100th Congress, 1st. sess., May 12–14, 1987.

18. Testimony of Dr. Robert Worrest; U.S. Senate, "Effects . . . ," May 12–14, 1987.

19. "However, scientists are still not able to predict quantitative effects on crop plants or ecosystems" (NRC 1982, 6).

4

No Pie in the Sky: The Regime on Transboundary Air Pollution

Before we agree to act on a problem, we must agree that there is a problem.

—U.S. Secretary of State George Shultz, regarding acid rain[1]

IN THE EARLY 1970S, NO COUNTRY in the world had either a policy in place to combat long-range air pollution or scientific research programs to study the problem. By 1991, all European countries plus Canada and the United States were involved in an international regulatory regime to control emissions and had implemented national policies to comply with it. The regime on long-range transboundary air pollution (LRTAP) was created against powerful odds. The abatement costs were high since regulation would affect major industrial sectors, including the coal industry, power plants, and transportation.

Cheap technologies for pollution abatement were not available when regulation was being discussed (Wettestäd 1999, 97). Concerns about international economic competitiveness also increased states' reluctance to introduce controls. In short, abatement policies were against the interests of many powerful business groups. Yet, economic powerhouses such as the United States, the United Kingdom, and Germany made an about-turn and chose environmental protection over industrial stability. Even countries such as the United Kingdom, which would not benefit from international policy since they did not receive pollution from other countries, chose to protect the environment.

The case is remarkable for several other reasons. Despite high economic costs and a competitive dimension, many countries made unilateral commitments to reduce their emissions before the conclusion of multilateral agreements. Concerns with relative gains did not prevent major industrialized countries such as Germany, Sweden, and Norway from making commitments without assurance that others would reciprocate. Implementation has been remarkably strong even though the treaty provisions for compliance are weak. The international regime relies on self-reporting and not on independent verification of compliance. And disputes over implementation never arose: the dispute settlement mechanism of the regime was never utilized. Despite opportunities for noncompliance, countries not only did not take a free ride, they *over*complied with the major agreements. These characteristics make the case a fascinating subject of study.

The formation of the acid rain regime cannot possibly be understood without reference to scientific input and the shared knowledge that derived from it. This input was copious and most of the information was considered reliable. However, it would be fallacious to generalize that "science" was solid and influential because there were uncertainties about some aspects of the problem. Even though science was influential overall in policymaking, it is important to pay close attention to the status of different types of information and their respective roles in international policy deliberations.

The Problem of Acid Rain

Acid rain refers to the deposition of common industrial air pollutants emitted from power stations, large factories, and transportation vehicles. Once in the atmosphere, sulfur and nitrogen oxides undergo complex chemical processes and may dissolve in cloud and rain droplets to form sulfuric (H_2SO_4) and nitric acids (HNO_3). The oxides can be deposited either directly onto land and water (dry deposition), or indirectly through the derivative acidifying compounds that come down with precipitation (wet deposition). Dry deposition is more dominant in areas close to the source of emission, while wet deposition is more prevalent at greater distances. Emissions can reach high altitudes where high-speed winds can transport them rapidly over long distances. The average wind speed at a height of several hundred yards is 22 mph and is sufficient to transport gases from London to Stockholm within thirty-six hours (McCormick 1985, 17). When deposited, these substances can acidify soils, lakes, rivers, and underground waters.

Normal acidity in water plays a beneficial role in helping dissolve minerals that are important to plants and animals, but excessive acidity is detrimental. Acidification of the environment has many potential direct and indirect effects. It can damage aquatic and terrestrial life forms and pose health hazards to humans by activating toxic metals such as mercury, which can then infiltrate water supplies. Dry deposition attacks and corrodes buildings, affects plant growth, and can cause respiratory problems. Wet deposition acidifies lakes and streams and causes decline or extinction of fish and other species. Both types of deposition also facilitate acidification of the soils that can lead to loss of nutrients, agricultural crop decline, and damage to trees and other plant species. Soils have varying natural buffering capacity to neutralize increasing acidity, but that capacity can be overwhelmed beyond certain critical levels.[2]

In popular usage, the term acid rain has expanded to cover not only wet and dry deposition but also the role of other pollutants. Nitrous oxides and volatile organic compounds (VOCs) not only contribute to acid precipitation but also contribute to the formation of ground-level ozone, the most phytotoxic gaseous pollutant that is harmful to plants and humans. The greatest significance of nitrous oxides (NO_x) is in their role as precursor to ozone. Nitrogen dioxide can be broken down by sunlight and form a highly reactive oxygen atom that then combines with oxygen molecules to form ozone (O_3). Ozone, in turn, further contributes to acid rain by facilitating the conversion of sulfur and nitrogen oxides into acids. As of the late 1970s, half of the amount of nitrous oxides in the atmosphere was of anthropogenic origin— half coming from vehicles and the rest coming from stationary sources such as power stations (ERL 1983, 19).

Creating the Acid Rain Policy Regime

Internationally coordinated policy measures to reduce acidifying pollutants were negotiated and agreed on in more than one institutional setting. Parallel to the development of the international regime on LRTAP, European countries negotiated directives by the EC on large plant and vehicle emissions, beginning in 1984 and throughout the 1980s (Wettestäd 1999, 102–103). A third venue for international cooperation on acid rain are the bilateral agreements between the United States and Canada. The analytical focus of this study is on the LRTAP regime only.

The Early Stage

In the early 1970s, there were a small group of regulation advocates and a large group of countries that were either against controls or showed indifference to the issue. Sweden and Norway were the only states that considered acid rain a serious problem and they raised the issue at the international level in 1969 at a meeting of the Air Management Sector Group of the Organization for Economic Cooperation and Development (OECD). The meeting acknowledged that there was a "significant increase" in sulfuric compounds that could possibly travel long distances, and recognized that the problem "requires continuing study" (OECD 1972).[3] Sweden again introduced the issue on the international scene at the 1972 Stockholm Conference on the Human Environment, where its delegation circulated a special case study on the effects of sulfur emissions (Swedish Ministry of Agriculture 1972). During the preparatory meetings and at the Conference itself, they presented research results and asked for international controls. For much of the 1970s, however, Belgium, France, Italy, West Germany, and other European countries showed little concern about transboundary air pollution and no interest in international agreements (Wetstone 1987; Levy 1993).

Analysts relate the initial development of the regime to the political context of détente between East and West (Levy 1993; Munton et al. 1999; Wettestäd 1999, 85). In the 1970s, the Cold War warmed up as the two sides sought ways to reduce the antagonism between them. Environmental management seemed like a suitable domain for cooperation because it was a relatively new and less politicized issue area. The UN Economic Commission for Europe (UNECE) was asked to explore a variety of issues and to select an appropriate issue area. It considered eleven environmental problems, and chose acidifying air pollution because of its clearly transboundary character (Levy 1993). Yet, the formation of the acid rain regime cannot be explained as a functionalist development emerging from the international political context. The economic costs of implementing the resulting abatement policies were very high and the issue became highly politicized in domestic contexts. Because of the considerable obstacles that had to be (and eventually were) overcome, the LTRAP regime cannot be seen as a function of Cold War politics among leaders who were looking for a safe playing ground. The Cold War did affect the institutional setting that was chosen for talks on air pollution (they took place within the UNECE), but not the actual process and its outcome.

In 1979, most European countries, Canada, and the United States created the world's first multilateral treaty addressing atmospheric issues: the Convention on Long-Range Transboundary Air Pollution. The Nordic countries and the Communist bloc advocated binding regulations but did not succeed in obtaining them. As could be expected, the large emitters, West Germany and the United Kingdom, firmly objected. Germany opposed creating a legal agreement even after it became clear that the future treaty would not involve binding commitments: it wanted an agreement stipulating only multilateral research and nothing else (Wetstone and Rosencrantz 1983, 206; Levy 1993, 82). The Convention was signed by thirty-three signatories in November 1979 in Geneva and entered into force in 1983. Today it has forty-three members, including the United States, Canada, and all European states with the exception of Estonia and San Marino.[4]

The Convention is a general framework agreement: in its text parties recognized that transboundary air pollutants were a significant problem; parties pledge to limit and "as far as possible, to gradually reduce air pollution" (Article 2); and parties agreed to engage together in research and monitoring to improve understanding of the problem.[5] Although considered a binding agreement, the treaty had little problem-solving content as it did not single out concrete pollutants and did not specify targets and policy measures. Given the wide economic ramifications of regulations and various international asymmetries related to both costs and benefits of policy action, the prospects for binding and specific regulations were not bright at this stage.

Regime Overview

The substantial content of the policy regime was constructed through several protocols to the Convention that involved commitments to reduce emissions of several types of pollutants, with specific targets and timetables. Throughout the evolution of the regime, the political negotiation processes were open to a variety of actors, including NGOs and specialized international organizations: the WMO, the WHO, UNEP, and the FAO (Wettestäd 1999).[6]

The first regulatory step was the creation of the Protocol on the Reduction of Sulfur Emissions, signed by twenty-one countries in July 1985 in Helsinki. It specified 30-percent cuts in emissions and transboundary fluxes of sulfur dioxide by 1993, with 1980 as the baseline year. With the 1988 Protocol on Nitrous Oxides, twenty-five countries pledged to freeze the levels of nitrous oxides emissions at the 1987 levels by 1994. In addition, twelve of the parties issued a nonbinding declaration by which they voluntarily committed themselves to 30-percent reduction of NO_x emissions by 1998. A 1991 Protocol on Volatile Organic Compounds called for a 30-percent reduction of 1988 emission levels by 1999. Twenty-eight countries signed a second sulfur protocol in 1994. Instead of aiming at flat reductions of emissions, this latter agreement was based upon the concept of "critical loads" and specified individual reductions for each country according to calculations of ecological vulnerability of areas where particular emissions are deposited.

Today, the legal regime on transboundary air pollution continues to evolve. In June 1998, parties created two protocols on heavy metals and on persistent organic pollutants (POPs), respectively, and those were followed by a 1999 Protocol to Abate Acidification, Eutrophication and Ground-Level Ozone that imposes stricter emissions ceilings on all major pollutants: sulfur, NO_x, VOCs, and ammonia. These ceilings were negotiated on the basis of scientific assessments of pollution effects and abatement options. If the Protocol is fully implemented, Europe's total sulfur emissions in 1990 should be cut by at least 63 percent, its NO_x emissions by 41 percent, its VOC emissions by 40 percent, and its ammonia emissions by 17 percent.[7]

Evaluating the Regime

In terms of ecological results, the LRTAP regime may not be particularly effective in improving environmental quality. Forest surveys continued to reveal extensive damage for some time after the policies were introduced (Levy 1993, 126). From a political point of view, however, the LRTAP regime has been a success: states made binding commitments under international treaties and changed their behavior in complying with them. Gradually, the regime cast a wide net to control all major airborne transboundary pollutants. Despite far-reaching economic implications, there has been a steady development of a series of protocols that are progressively becoming more and more stringent and cover more and more polluting substances. Each of these protocols has entered into force by virtue of sufficient number of state ratifications.

Even if we use a stricter measure of success and go beyond regime formation to focus on implementation, the regime would still qualify as a success. A major review of implementation based on national data shows that most countries have *exceeded* the targets set by the treaties. The first sulfur protocol, in particular, is characterized by considerable over-compliance: parties have achieved an average of 48-percent reductions in sulfur dioxide, and Austria, France, the Netherlands, and all four Scandinavian countries achieved 70-percent reductions instead of the required 30 percent (ECE/LRTAP 1995). Although progress on the voluntary nonbinding declaration regarding nitrous oxides has been modest, nineteen of the twenty-five parties to the nitrous protocol have not only met the target of freezing emissions but have reduced them by an average of 9 percent. Based on implementation data, observers conclude that the LRTAP regime "must definitely be characterized as a high compliance regime" (Wettestäd 1999, 90).

Regime Evolution

Coordinated research and monitoring were strongly institutionalized in the LRTAP regime. The Convention places strong emphasis on improving scientific knowledge about acidification and establishes a system for gathering and disseminating data on emissions and flows of air pollutants. Along with the Executive Body and the Implementation Committee, its institutional structure includes a monitoring program, international cooperative programs (ICPs), working groups, and task forces on various research fields such as emissions monitoring, effects of acid deposition, policy strategies, and abatement techniques.[8] "Coordination of national research programs can be considered the bedrock of all LRTAP's activity" (Levy 1993, 87). The strong knowledge orientation of the regime is also evident in the fact that the first collective step after the Convention entered into force in 1983 was to adopt a protocol in 1984 to provide funding for the Cooperative Programme for the Monitoring and Evaluation of the Long-Range Transmission of Air Pollutants in Europe (EMEP) on a regular basis (Wettestäd 1999a, 86). "These [scientific research] processes proved to be the guiding force of the LRTAP dynamic" (Munton et al. 1999, 67).

The First Sulfur Protocol

A key moment in the early stages of regime formation was the dramatic shift of Germany's position. In 1979, German scientists submitted a major report to the nation's highest research agency that revealed extensive damage to German forests and argued that the cause is soil decline due to acid precipitation (Ulrich et al. 1979). In the early 1980s, further evidence of a dieback of the German forest (*Waldsterben*) created a public uproar, with scores of articles in popular newspapers and journals stirring debates and raising concern. In 1982, a committee of forty experts from the government and the scientific community concluded that 7.8 percent of Germany's forest area had been damaged (Ministry of Food, Agriculture and Forestry 1982). This issue became one of Germany's main domestic political issues. At a 1982 Conference on Acidification of the Environment in Stockholm, Germany made a complete U-turn and announced that it would support binding international commitments for control policies. Interior Minister Baum, who headed the delegation, announced the government's commitment to unilaterally reduce its SO_2 emissions from power plants and large factories by 60 percent by 1993 (Wettestäd 1999, 102). Further, Baum proposed Europe-wide sulfur reductions of 50 percent by 1985 (Levy 1993, 93). Since then, Germany has maintained strong leadership on the issue and remained one of the chief advocates for international regulations throughout the 1990s.

What followed was a progressive chain reaction in which country after country dropped its objections and joined the pro-regulations camp. Nine governments were in favor of 30-percent cuts in June 1993, eighteen in June 1984, and twenty by the end of 1984 (Levy 1993, 94). Subsequent negotiations on a binding agreement met opposition from major polluting states. The United Kingdom was firmly against and, unlike Germany, remained a laggard for a long time, earning itself the nickname "the Dirty Man of Europe." It was a net exporter: 65 percent of its sulfur emissions were transported beyond its borders (Levy 1993, 124). The expert opinion at the time was that Britain was not affected by other countries' emissions because of the prevailing wind patterns. Reductions of British emissions could, therefore, benefit other countries, but reductions in other countries were not expected to bring particular benefits to populations and ecosystems in Britain. At the same time, abatement costs in the United Kingdom would be considerable and highly concentrated: they would be borne by power stations and other specific and powerful industrial groups (Wettestäd 1998, 391).

At first, the policy preferences among those who supported regulations differed significantly. When a protocol was first negotiated in 1983, the countries could not write a draft document because of a lack of sufficient agreement regarding the objectives (Levy 1993, 93). Nordics pushed for a sulfur protocol with specific targets and timetables. Sweden, Norway, and several other countries were ready for 50 percent, but Canada was not. Austria, Germany, and Switzerland advocated adopting the best available technology for reducing pollution instead of reducing emissions. At a ministerial meeting in Ottawa, February 1984, thirteen countries issued a declaration committing themselves to 30-percent reductions of sulfur oxides. Finally, delegates in Helsinki adopted a compromise proposal put forward by the Nordic countries: 30-percent cuts in sulfur emissions by 1993, with 1980 as the base year. At the insistence of the Soviet Union, the protocol gave the option of reducing transboundary fluxes instead of industrial emissions.[9] Twenty-one parties signed the 1985 Protocol on the Reduction of Sulfur Emissions, and several prominent players, including the United States, chose to stay out. The United Kingdom, Poland, and Spain, which together accounted for 25 percent of sulfur emissions in Europe, did not sign (Wettestäd 1999, 89).

The Nitrous Oxides Protocol

Negotiating policy measures to control emissions of nitrous oxides began in 1985 as soon as the sulfur protocol was forged and it proved more difficult. Unlike sulfur dioxide emissions that came from a small number of large stationary sources such as power plants, nitrous oxides originated from a multitude of various nonpoint sources, including transport vehicles and ships. Because they involved the transport sector, respective regulatory policies would affect various actors and would have far-reaching social as well as economic implications. Moreover, scientific knowledge about the role of nitrous oxides in acid rain was not as well developed. One negotiator who participated in the deliberations reports that talks began without the necessary scientific basis. "The politicians decided to go ahead with actual negotiations several years before the necessary scientific basis had been established. . . . As a result, research funds had to be allocated to solve [scientific] questions vital to the continuation of the negotiations" (Bakken 1989, 202).[10]

Knowledge improvement took place within the regime and in parallel to political discussions. Scientific uncertainty about the problem and technological solutions was considerable, and countries launched a multilateral process for gathering additional information.[11] At the same meeting where the first sulfur protocol was signed, parties established a Working Group on Nitrous Oxides to advance knowledge on the sources and effects of NO_x. Because knowledge was not so well established, scientists had broad access to the negotiation process (Wettestäd 1998, 387). The Working Group served as the main venue of research, and the results were reviewed and evaluated by Designated Expert Groups, consisting of experts appointed by governments of all countries. The subsequent Protocol itself contains a clause stating that the agreement should be reviewed at regular intervals in light of updated scientific research and that member countries should start renegotiation on further measures six months after its entry into force.

The original plan was to copy the sulfur agreement and introduce 30-percent reductions of NO_x. Gradually, however, the ambitions were reduced due to the technological complexity of the issue and related political difficulties at regulating nitrous emissions (Wettestäd 1998). Any meaningful effort to reduce NO_x would require stricter vehicle exhaust standards. Germany did not have a problem with that because it produced larger cars on which it was easier to install catalytic converters and because converters were already required under 1983 national legislature. In contrast, British, French, and Italian automakers that produced smaller cars lobbied their governments to resist international regulations (Levy 1993, 95).

The environmentally minded coalition fell apart, and the lines between camps at the negotiation table were redrawn. Germany, Austria, Switzerland, the Netherlands, and Sweden advocated 30-percent reductions, while some enthusiasts on the sulfur protocol, such as Norway and Finland, now sided with the United Kingdom in supporting only a freeze of nitrous oxides emissions levels. Others such as Canada and the Soviet bloc were even more reluctant and joined the United States in skepticism (Wettestäd 1998, 384–385). When it became clear that there was not enough support for reductions, the enthusiasts' camp conceded to a freeze but advocated a freeze by 1990, while the skeptics preferred 1994 as the deadline. Here again, the skeptics won. In November 1988, twenty-seven countries signed the Protocol on Nitrous Oxides in Sofia, Bulgaria, that stipulated a freeze on either emissions or transboundary fluxes at the 1987 levels, beginning in 1994. The agreement also accommodated industrial concerns by allowing controls "based on the best available technologies which are economically feasible."

Remarkably, the reductions camp unilaterally committed themselves to reductions even though they had failed to convince other countries to do the same. A group of twelve European countries issued a separate nonbinding declaration in which they committed themselves to 30-percent cuts by the year 1998 (Munton et al. 1999, 170). The protocol also required continued negotiations on further reductions. Thus, the result was a compromise between the camps to meet halfway—but the meeting place was closer to the laggards' camp. Countries such as the United States and the Soviet Union that were initially unwilling to accept even a freeze did ratify the protocol.[12]

The Volatile Organic Compounds Protocol

The 1991 Geneva Protocol on Volatile Organic Compounds regulates emissions of a group of chemicals that come from motor vehicles, oil and gas industries, and the use of industrial solvents (Wettestäd 2000). When released in the atmosphere, VOCs contribute to the formation of ground-level ozone. Although stratospheric ozone plays a positive role in blocking harmful UV-B radiation, ozone near the surface of the Earth has negative effects on human health and causes respiration problems and nausea. Because both nitrous oxides and VOCs create ozone, in 1986 West Germany proposed treating them under a single protocol, but the idea was rejected. Just like the case of NO_x, there was an accumulation of knowledge within a relatively short time and within the institutionalized regime process. In 1988, a Working Group on VOCs was established, but research revealed complexities, and uncertainties remained.[13]

Most countries supported flat 30-percent reductions of VOCs outputs. The Soviet Union, Norway, and Canada, which did not suffer much from ozone, advocated controls only in regions generating emissions that could traverse borders; Eastern European countries could not make firm commitments because they were not sure whether they could implement them. The policy outcome was a complex agreement that gave three policy options instead of stipulating flat controls: to freeze emissions, to reduce them by 30 percent with a base year anywhere between 1986 and 1990, or to reduce emissions by 30 percent only in designated areas (Munton et al. 1999, 170). Twenty-one countries signed the protocol in Geneva. Some major polluters such as Russia and Poland opted out. The agreement nevertheless entered into force in 1997 and has been ratified by seventeen countries. Today, VOCs are further regulated by a 1999 protocol that relies on the concept of critical loads (see below).

The Second Sulfur Protocol

In 1994, countries adopted a second agreement on sulfur emissions: the Protocol on Further Reductions of Sulfur Emissions. The steady progression of successive agreements may create an overly optimistic impression of smooth progress in regime development. In reality, this negotiation process was rife with difficulties and bitter disputes. Rifts and differences among European states were difficult to bridge, and the EC states failed to form a common negotiating position. Greece, Italy, Portugal, and Spain were reluctant to further strengthen sulfur regulations because they had not experienced any additional damage from acid rain (Wettestäd 1999, 103).

The result was a binding agreement that was particularly impressive because it imposed uneven burdens on different countries. The "Second Sulfur Protocol" does not stipulate flat rate reductions but instead specifies individual targets for each country based on its abatement costs and the sensitivity of regions where emissions are deposited (Munton et al. 1999, 169). Not only were the commitments uneven but the deadlines for fulfilling them also were not uniform: for some it was 2000, for others 2005 or 2010. Perhaps the most notable feature of the agreement was that the policy targets were tied strictly to scientific estimates of ecological damage thresholds.

Central to the protocol was the concept of "critical loads" first developed by Scandinavian experts in the early 1980s and later successfully promoted in the LRTAP context (Nilsson 1986). A critical load is "a quantitative estimate of an exposure to one or more pollutants below which significantly harmful effects on specified sensitive elements of the environment do not occur according to present knowledge" (Levy 1993, 101–102). Critical loads vary by location because ecological sensitivity varies greatly depending on soil composition, climate conditions, biodiversity, and other factors. Mapping these was complex but feasible (Hettelingh et al. 1991). By the turn of the decade, the concept dominated the LRTAP agenda, and countries were busy mapping the ecological sensitivity of their territories (Levy 1993, 103).

Because the critical loads of any particular pollutant vary from location to location, the protocol would impose uneven burdens on different countries. It was known to all that some countries such as the Netherlands, Russia, Germany, and Norway would not need to modify their policies because already existing national plans would be sufficient to meet their obligations under the international protocol. Others such as France, Italy, Spain, and the United Kingdom would have to introduce new policies in order to comply with the agreement (Wettestäd 2000, 103). This disparity led to very confrontational negotiations, but eventually all agreed to join. Notably, by this time the United Kingdom was far from its original opposition and supported international policy. Wettestäd (1998) attributes this shift to several factors, including the recognition of domestic damages of acidification in Britain.

By adopting critical loads as a basis for designing policies, the process was more tightly linked to science. Countries accepted uneven obligations that were determined by purely scientific estimates of the amount of pollution that an ecosystem can tolerate without damage.[14] Moreover, the policy targets were set using the RAINS computer model developed at the International Institute for Applied Systems Analysis in Austria (Alcamo et al. 1991).[15] Countries thus relied on scientific methods to determine policy targets; those implied uneven burdens, and yet states chose to commit to the policy agreement. Analysts regard the Second Sulfur Protocol as a clear example of science-driven international policymaking (Levy 1993; Gehring 1994; Wettestäd 2000).

Explaining the Regime

The formation of the LRTAP regime is a striking example of international cooperation undertaken despite concerns with relative gains and economic competitiveness. It also offers one of the most clear-cut cases when environmental quality was placed above industrial interests, since policies for environmental protection were adopted despite considerable economic costs and social ramifications. How can we understand it? Did governments try to build their environmental profiles and create the regime to score points in domestic politics? This is clearly not the case because falling out of favor with the corporate actors outweighed political gains obtained from environmentalists at home. Costly policies would strike at major industries and affect the public through higher electric utility costs. The case cannot therefore be interpreted in terms of domestic politics.

Levy (1993) claims that the protocols' rules served as tote-boards and affected state behavior by generating internal as well as external normative pressures. Governments "changed their minds once the question became highly public and connected to normative principles" (p. 94). But why did states create these rules in the first place? Particularly in light of the high costs of regulations, the formation of the regime cannot be satisfactorily explained with simple bandwagoning motivated by norms. Action would strike at the two most fundamental socioeconomic sectors: energy production and transportation. It would affect industrial actors such as coal, oil, and electric utility companies as well as their many users.

The idea of controls went against such a powerful tide that we cannot explain regime formation solely or primarily with moral pressure or normative concerns. Indeed, some countries persisted in their opposition despite strong and consistent pressure from other states. The concerted campaigns by the

Scandinavian countries did nothing to sway Germany and later the United Kingdom and the United States, which stayed out of the legally binding sulfur protocol. The German government changed its position only after its own domestic public was alarmed with the effects of acid rain on its own territory. Later, the United Kingdom changed its position after evidence emerged that it, too, imports acid rain and therefore suffers consequences from foreign emissions.

Others look at the case in terms of trade advantages and other concerns with economic advantage. Boehmer-Christiansen and Skea, for instance, claim that Germany moved toward catalytic converters to impose trade barriers and contain Japanese car imports and to maintain its reputation of producing state-of-the-art efficient cars (1991, 279). This may be the case, but if those were the primary rationales of Germany and other countries, they would not have needed to use an environmental problem as an excuse and could have introduced new technologies without reference to acid rain. Even if such economic concerns played a role, they were not the main driving force and cannot explain the formation of the regime.

The regime can be better seen as a problem-solving exercise driven by concerns with the negative ecological impacts of acidification. Air pollutants were found to have numerous direct and indirect effects on aquatic and terrestrial ecosystems, human health, and buildings and materials. These consequences provided reasons to try to ameliorate the problem; because some of the pollution was transboundary, policy action had to be coordinated and reciprocal to be effective. To elaborate on this perspective, we have to examine the state of scientific knowledge about various aspects of the problem and the research activities undertaken to study the phenomenon.

Scientific Research on Acidification

That emissions from coal burning cause acid rain has been known for a century and a half. In the 1850s, a Scottish chemist named Robert Angus Smith discovered that coal burning causes levels of sulfuric acid in Manchester to rise. His book on the subject (Smith 1872) documented the phenomenon and discussed its detrimental effects on vegetation, fabrics, and buildings but failed to draw much public attention since at that time people were concerned with other types of pollutants. Eville Gorham, later a professor at the University of Minnesota, brought the problem back to the attention of modern scientists in the 1950s. He was the first to relate acid precipitation to distant rather than local air pollution and to point to effects on fresh waters (Gorham 1958; Wetstone 1987). Swedish researchers had begun monitoring the acidity of lakes in the 1940s, and by the 1960s had evidence that the levels were rising. Svante Oden (1968) published a study that for the first time revealed the transboundary dimension of the problem, by relating rising acidity to air pollution in other countries, particularly the United Kingdom and central Europe. Oden's ideas were highly unconventional at the time and met skepticism and opposition even within Sweden. The Swedish government was unconvinced and refused to fund his research further (Wetstone 1987, 165).

Continuing studies confirmed Oden's thesis and converted scientists and policy makers in Sweden and Norway. After their governments placed the issue on the table at an international political forum, multilateral monitoring and research began. Joint research was conducted through a conglomeration of national research programs and international coordinating centers that collected and harmonized the data. This protected the integrity and freedom of national research and increased governments' confidence in the results. In 1972, the OECD launched a monitoring program in which eleven countries participated: the Cooperative Technical Programme to Measure the Long-Range Transport of Air Pollutants. Its first report was published in July 1977 and submitted "strong evidence" that sulfur dioxide was causing acid rain. The report identified two countries as net exporters of acidifying compounds (Denmark and the United Kingdom), and several countries as net importers: Austria, Finland, Norway, Sweden, and Switzerland. The degree of accuracy of specific estimates, however, was said to be plus minus 50 percent, reflecting uncertainties about emissions data and dispersion models (Wetstone and Rosencrantz 1983, 136). Even at this early stage, however, there was not much controversy among scientists regarding the basic mechanisms behind the problem (Wettestäd 1999, 96).

Subsequently, an ambitious process for generating information was launched. Between 1967 and 1986, there were no less than 6,000 publications on acid rain (Schindler 1988, note 4). Much of the research effort was undertaken by "the most extensive monitoring program to accompany an environmental treaty" (Levy 1993, 132). This process began in the late 1970s, was continuously strengthened and expanded, and became more and more integral to political processes throughout the 1990s.

In 1978, the OECD program evolved into the EMEP, under the joint auspices of the UNECE, WMO, and UNEP. Its purpose is to supply governments with data on emissions, concentration, and deposition of pollutants and the long-range transport of pollutants. Research is conducted at the national level and data is then harmonized and used in computer models. EMEP combines data on emissions, air and precipitation quality, and atmospheric dispersion models to produce detailed estimates of each country's exports and imports of pollutants.[16] The results are matrices that show for each country the origins of its received pollution and also the destination of its own pollutants. Integral to the program is the so-called RAINS computer model that links emissions to impacts and also permits evaluation of economic costs and ecological benefits of alternative policy options. The EMEP network has 103 stations in thirty-three countries, with three coordinating centers, two in Oslo and one in Moscow. Its annual budget is assembled by parties to the Convention and in 1996 amounted to over $1,990,000.[17]

After the 1979 Convention came into existence, its member states set up an institutional structure in which the main units were the Executive Body and the Working Group on Abatement Strategies. The latter is a permanent negotiating body that receives on a continuing basis input from the scientific research groups, analyzes it, and prepares future protocols. In addition to these political/administrative bodies, there were two large groups of scientific bodies: the Working Group on Effects, and the EMEP monitoring network. The Working Group on Effects collects and synthesizes knowledge about the response of living organisms and materials to acidification and helps produce information on critical loads of acidifying pollutants. Under it are several International Cooperative Programmes (ICPs) and task forces, each of which is hosted by a particular country: on forests (Germany), freshwaters (Norway), materials (Sweden), crops (United Kingdom), and integrated monitoring (Finland), and a recently established task force on human health impacts.[18]

The State of Scientific Knowledge

Assessing the state of scientific knowledge on acidification is difficult because there is not just one ecological problem but a cluster of related problems. Transboundary air pollution involves a large host of human-made compounds that form an acid "cocktail": NO_x, SO_x, hydrocarbons, VOCs, and POPs. The VOCs group alone comprises hundreds of compounds. Emissions come from many and various types of sources, including power stations, vehicles, various factories, and ships. It is difficult to make generalized evaluations of the state of knowledge because information about these various culprits and their multiple effects is not evenly developed. Further, it is not easy to delineate the three sectors of knowledge (extent, causes, consequences), since some elements can be alternatively placed in two or more sectors of knowledge. For instance, is soil acidification to be treated as an effect of the problem or as a cause of damage to trees? As a result of these caveats, analyzing the role of scientific information in political processes and the extent to which this knowledge has weighed in on the formation of the regime is a challenge.

In the earliest stages in the 1970s, scientific knowledge on the acidification problem was not well advanced. Until then, little attention had been paid to the problem, there was scant scientific research on it, and reviews of the state of knowledge about it emphasized scientific uncertainties (Nriagu 1978). Knowledge related to sulfur emissions was more advanced partly due to longer history of sulfur research, but the NO_x and VOCs had more complex profiles. In addition to stationary sources such as power plants, NO_x emissions come also from inland vehicles and ships. The VOCs situation is even more complicated: the hundreds of compounds that qualify as VOCs are emitted from many types of industrial activities. Furthermore, their life spans, the distances they travel, and their relative contributions to ozone formation are uneven and subject to scientific uncertainty (Levy 1993, 68).

Yet, even in the early stages, there were pockets of information about aspects of the problem that was considered by scientists as reliable. In 1972, Norway organized a large multi-year, multidisciplinary research program on the effects of acid precipitation. After six years of work, the $15 million project culminated in a large international conference that involved three hundred scientists from eighteen countries in Europe and North America. Based on 140 research papers presented there, the conclusions of the conference were:

> Nobody denies that increasing acidity, for one reason or another, induces changes in assemblages of freshwater plants and animals, with the notable loss of salmonids. Further, there is no doubt that bodies of fresh water in parts of Scandinavia, the UK, Canada and the USA have become increasingly acid during past decades, and that the input of sulphuric acid from the atmosphere with precipitation and as dry deposition has increased considerably during the same period. (Drabløs and Tollan 1980, 10)

Knowledge improved and was increasingly accepted in the early 1980s. EMEP began generating enormous amounts of data and through increasingly sophisticated methods made it possible to calculate depositions in each country and to trace them to sources in other countries. "By this time . . . beyond doubt was the transboundary character of the problem, in which some countries gained whilst others lost" (Park 1987, 177). A 1987 NATO-sponsored scientific conference identified in its report the following areas of scientific consensus:

> 1. Atmospheric deposition (wet and dry fallout) has been anthropogenically acidified. 2. Runoff waters, streams and lakes, have been anthropogenically acidified. 3. The effects of this acceleration . . . can be observed in the chemical and biological parts of the ecosystems. . . . Potentially toxic substances have also been identified in acidifying lakes. . . . 4. These effects of acid deposition appear to be

proportionate to a) the rate of acid supply . . . and b) the acid buffering capacity
of the drainage system. (Hutchinson and Havas 1980, 626–627)

Increased acidification and its negative impacts were thus matters of consensus from early on.

To evaluate the state of knowledge in more detail, scientific information is
divided here into three sectors. The first one pertains to identifying and measuring acidification of precipitation, waters, and soils. The second pertains to
the causes of increased acidification: whether emissions cause it and whether
emissions could travel long enough to cross borders and acidify precipitation
in other countries. Finally, the third sector comprises information about the
various impacts of dry and wet deposition on aquatic and terrestrial environments as well as on human health.

Sector I: Extent of Acidification

Acidification of precipitation, freshwater, and soils could be measured accurately,[19] and the geographical distribution of acid precipitation was well
known even in the 1970s (Drabløs and Tollan 1980, 11). Conclusions from
many studies were firm: a rapid increase in acidification of waters had taken
place since at least the 1940s. The earliest records of lakes acidified through air
pollution came from Scotland in the mid-seventeenth century (Schindler
1988). Hannah Lake near Sudbury, Ontario, began acidifying immediately
after the opening of a nearby smelter in 1880 (Schindler 1988, note 21). Data
showed progressive increase in the acidity of lakes in southern Norway and
Sweden after the 1920s (Wright 1977), and that many lakes in the states of
New York and New Hampshire had become more acid since the 1920s and
even since the 1950s and 1960s (Patrick et al. 1981). In affected areas in Norway, Sweden, England, and Scotland, pH levels in lakes were observed to fall
from 5.0–6.5 to 4.5 (ERL 1983, 15).

Later, further evidence showed that the number and extent of areas that are
geologically vulnerable to acid precipitation are much greater than originally
thought. Sensitive areas existed not only in Scandinavian countries, the
United Kingdom, and eastern North America but also extended to Belgium,
the Netherlands, Denmark, Ireland, Italy, Switzerland, West Germany, and
western North America (Schindler 1988). "It is now clear that acid rain has already caused widespread acidification of many aquatic ecosystems in the
northeast United States, Canada, Norway, Sweden, and the United Kingdom"
(Schindler 1988, 150). Evidence from four very different types of sources
(geochemical theory, analysis of long-term trends, comparison of chemical
records, and paleoecological analyses) consistently demonstrated increased

acidification of lakes and streams in North American and European areas that
received acid precipitation (Schindler 1988, 150). Even the chief British scientist (of the U.K.'s Nature Conservancy Council) submitted conclusions in a peer-reviewed article that air pollution had caused acidification in British freshwaters, with resulting damage to flora and fauna (Woodin 1989).

Sector II: Causes of Acidification

The state of knowledge on the causes of acidification was a mixed bag. On the one hand, the chemical reactions that convert oxides into acids were a matter of scientific fact and emissions could be measured or estimated accurately. On the other hand, acidification could be caused by several natural as well as anthropogenic causal factors, and their relative contributions were not known with certainty. Sulfuric and nitric acids contribute to acidification in a 70/30 percent ratio (ERL 1983, 5). Sulfur dioxide emissions were steadily increasing until the 1970s and then fell 15 percent between 1973 and 1983 (ERL 1983, 7). They could be accurately measured and also could be estimated reliably on the basis of fuel consumption data (Levy 1993, 89). The first report from multilateral research was the 1977 report of the OECD monitoring network. It submitted that (1) air pollutants not only could but did indeed travel long distances; (2) eleven countries received pollution from abroad; and (3) five of them (Austria, Finland, Norway, Sweden, and Switzerland) received more foreign than domestic pollutants (OECD 1977; Levy 1993, 80). Over 90 percent of SO_2 emissions and 50 percent of NO_x emissions in Europe were of anthropogenic sources (ERL 1983).

There was principal understanding that VOCs create ground-level ozone that is harmful to humans and vegetation. There was uncertainty as to the relative contribution of various VOCs to ozone formation. For one thing, there are many compounds whose ozone-creating potential varies significantly (Levy 1993, 99). Furthermore, VOC emissions are difficult to measure since they derive from a wide variety of activities, including dry cleaning, fuel combustion, and use of industrial solvents. Several months before the VOC protocol was signed, only five countries had inventories of their emissions (Levy 1993, 99).

One area of uncertainty involved the so-called dose/response relationship, the link between one unit of emissions and the amount of resulting change in acidity. Opponents of regulatory action, such as the UK's Central Electricity Generating Board, argued that the conversion of oxides into acids is so contingent on weather conditions that it is not certain whether emissions acidify the environment; therefore reducing emissions may not reduce acidification proportionately (McCormick 1985, 19). The "linearity" debate went on for a while. The ERL report stated that there is lack of consensus on whether sulfur deposition and ozone formation are linearly related to SO_x and NO_x, respectively (ERL 1983, pp. 5, 10).[20] This was clearly a matter of controversy, yet linearity was a viable possibility. A panel of the U.S. National Research Council, for instance, concluded that contrary to industry claims, a 50-percent reduction in emissions of sulfur and nitrogen gases would produce approximately a 50-percent reduction in acid deposition downwind of the emissions source (NRC 1983). The only catch was that they could not predict the exact locations where deposition would diminish because the models that simulated atmospheric transport were not accurate enough. In any case, it appears that there was agreement on the strong connection between emissions and deposition, whether this relationship is linear or not.

What increased acidification of lakes was also a matter of some controversy. Lakes could be acid because of natural ecological conditions or because of anthropogenic interference (Patrick et al. 1981). Two competing hypotheses were proposed in Scandinavian research of the 1960s and 1970s. One attributed lake acidification to atmospheric acidification and acid rain; the other focused on purely local causes such as aluminum inflows and afforestation (Wettestäd 1999, 121, note 41). Increasingly, evidence led to strengthening the link between transboundary pollution and acidification, but information on the relative contribution of different causes remained incomplete: "Acidification from acid precipitation is often small compared to acidification from other natural and man-made sources" (ERL 1983, 10). For instance, 65–80 percent of acidification of agricultural lands was due to fertilization with nitrous compounds, and only 5–20 percent was due to acid precipitation (ERL 1983, 11). The uncertainty about natural processes of acidification was not so important since naturally formed acids are weak, while those related to anthropogenic influence are strong and can incur much more damage (ERL 1983, 10–12).

Sector III: Consequences of Acidification

Acid precipitation is known to have a large number of negative impacts on terrestrial and aquatic environments. Environmental damage caused by acid rain was recognized very early on (Smith 1872; Gorham 1958). Mediated by factors of geology, climate, and biology, acid rain could acidify sensitive lakes and streams, mobilize toxic aluminum, and deplete nutrients (Krugg and Frink 1983; Beament et al. 1984). Under conditions of lower pH (higher acidity), many chemicals exert a higher oxygen demand. As a result, lakes with higher acidity become poorer in oxygen and that affects all species in them (Patrick et al. 1981). Acid precipitation also causes acidification of soils and mobilizes toxic metals. The potential impact on forests was established early on and was a subject of a 1978 NATO conference (Hutchinson and Havas 1980). Later reports attributed changes in vegetation to high nitrogen deposition resulting from emissions of nitrous oxides and ammonia (Woodin 1989).

By 1980, scientific knowledge about the effects on aquatic ecosystems was solid and not disputed, but there was more uncertainty about terrestrial ecosystems (Drabløs and Tollan 1980; Hutchinson and Havas 1980). At a 1978 international conference at the NATO Advanced Research Institute, "It was emphasized that there is little solid evidence to date of the occurrence of visible or even detectable damage to terrestrial ecosystems caused by the acid precipitation events of the past twenty years. This provides marked contrast with that of lake ecosystems where substantial effects have been recorded" (Hutchinson and Havas 1980, 617). Another large international scientific conference two years later reached virtually the same conclusions:

> From contributions in this volume, it is evident that serious changes have been detected in aquatic ecosystems, and there is no longer any doubt that most of these changes are related to incoming precipitation. . . . It must be pointed out that effects upon the growth and well-being of terrestrial plants, either directly or indirectly through the soil, have not been proven. (Drabløs and Tollan 1980, 10)

Nevertheless, even in the 1970s it was well known that high concentrations of sulfuric and nitrous oxides and acids are toxic to plants—the only difficulty was in quantifying the exact threshold levels (Drabløs and Tollan 1980, 11).[21]

Information about the response of fish to acidification is extensive, and evidence of damage to aquatic life was rich and consistent (Magnuson et al. 1984; Schindler 1988). The EPA sponsored a critical assessment of acid rain effects in the United States. The peer-reviewed study discussed potential versus known effects and attempted to evaluate the certainty of information. The resulting report concluded that when acidification occurs, fisheries have been damaged by loss of fish and reductions in populations of invertebrate species. "Experiments in the laboratory and the field have established a direct cause-and-effect relationship between acidification and adverse effects on fish."[22] Where pH levels fall to 4.9 or lower, most fish species, almost all molluscs and some groups of invertebrates were expected to disappear (Magnuson et al. 1984).

Higher acidity was known to damage the sodium balance of the gill membranes of fish, and some fish species were more resilient and adaptive than others. Fish decline in Norway was first noticed in the 1920s, and became severe in the 1950s and 1960s. Some degree of damage was documented in an area of 33,000 square kilometers, 13,000 square kilometers of which were completely devoid of fish. Several major salmon rivers lost all the salmon stocks. Moreover, the loss of populations increases with increased acidity (Muniz 1984). More than half of the fish stocks in southern Norway had been lost between 1940 and 1980 in an area covering 20,000 square kilometers. In Sweden, fish were lost in 3,000–4,000 lakes (ERL 1983, 15). Streams were known to be even more vulnerable than lakes because of typically less diverse biodiversity. Because most studies focused on adult fish instead of on the more sensitive juveniles or species lower in the food web, and on lakes rather than streams, estimates of biological effects on aquatic organisms were said to be underestimations (Schindler 1988, 151). In addition, changes in populations of phytoplankton were dramatic and remarkably similar in all acidified areas. "Clearly, we know enough about the effects of acid rain on aquatic ecosystems to make a strong case for regulating emissions of sulfur oxides" (Schindler 1988, 153).

The cause-effects relations in terrestrial systems were more complicated and more difficult to verify compared to those in aquatic systems (Schindler 1988). In addition to acid rain, other factors can cause the same negative effects, and the relative contribution is difficult to establish. In some circumstances, natural processes of soil formation are more important in determining the acidity of lakes than acid precipitation (Krugg and Frink 1983). Identifying overall forest decline, let alone attributing it to particular causes, remained a challenge even after the agreements were concluded (Pitelka and Raynal 1989). Even scientists who maintained that acid rain is the main cause of tree damage considered that other factors also contribute to tree decline: disease, fragile soils, drought, and inappropriate forest management (Pitelka and Raynal 1989). Proceedings of a 1982 international workshop highlighted gaps in current knowledge on soil processes and difficulties encountered in attempting to predict soil-mediated impacts of air pollutants (Ulrich and Pankrath 1983). As late as 1989, some scientists drew cautious and somewhat contradictory conclusions.[23]

There were also controversies on the exact mechanisms through which acid precipitation exercises its negative impacts on land, with numerous competing hypotheses linking forest decline to causal agents. Bernhard Ulrich, a German soil scientist, advanced the hypothesis that the main cause of forest damage is that acid precipitation induces aluminum attacks on tree roots. Others maintained that the primary cause is the direct impacts of sulfur oxides, nitrous oxides, and ozone. Still other theories emphasized the direct effects of acid mist and rain (Woodin 1989, 753). "Although it is likely that acidic deposition has some effects on forest ecosystems, research to date has not documented significant *direct* effects on plants" (Pitelka and Raynal 1983, 6; emphasis added). The prevalent scientific opinion was that acidification causes forest decline indirectly by affecting the soils. "While forest damage is far from being completely understood, a consensus that air pollution may be but one factor among many contributing to a complex set of damage syndromes" (Boehmer-Christiansen and Skea 1991, 40). Thus, uncertainty existed about the quantitative extent of impact as well as the relative contribution of causal factors.

Aside from disputes, there were two areas of agreement. There was widespread consensus about the principal cause-effect links and the *potential* impact of acidification. Knowledge on the effects of acidification by sulfur and nitrogen compounds in particular was generally accepted as certain. The second area of agreement was that the contribution of acidification as a causal factor was significant. "Nevertheless, the scale of the damage and the spatial and temporal manner of its occurrence strongly suggests that acid precipitation and/or ozone are likely being the principal causes" (ERL 1983, 13). In the early 1980s, effects of sulfur dioxide and ozone were already seen as the most likely cause of forest decline—even in research of the U.K. Forestry Commission (Binns and Redfern 1982). There was also some limited evidence that acidic deposition may affect negatively terrestrial wildlife such as water birds and frogs and other amphibians through loss of habitat or food resources (Schreiber and Newman 1988).

The effects on agricultural crops were less well established, although seriously considered. On the one hand, there were few observations of actual yield decline, and it was known that any loss is highly dependent on idiosyncratic climate, soil type, and crop species.[24] One study in the United Kingdom concluded that acid rain is unlikely to affect crop production (Woodin 1989). On the other hand, no one disputed that high levels of ground-level ozone were harmful to plants and can cause loss of yield between 5 and 40 percent. Studies in the United Kingdom and the Netherlands suggested that high concentrations of SO_2 can also reduce yield. Furthermore, data showed increased levels of ground-level ozone (ERL 1983, 14). One conclusion submitted to the EC was couched in tentative terms but was alarming nonetheless: "It is apparent that crop damage *potential* from acid pollutant/ozone may well be significant in almost all EEC Member States" (ERL 1983, 14). According to one analyst, the potential damage to crops, although not proven, affected the political process: "The scientific consensus now is that ozone is just as harmful to forests and agricultural crops as sulfur deposition. It is also a public health problem in many urban areas. All this was accepted during negotiations of the nitrogen protocol. There was dispute over the magnitude of the damage, though" (Levy 1993, 94).

The impact of acidification on human health was potentially serious, but evidence was somewhat mixed. A number of studies documented the detrimental effects of interactions between acid rain and metals (Schindler 1988,

153). As precipitation becomes more acid, larger quantities of these become soluble in water, mist, and fog. Aluminum, for instance, constitutes 5 percent of the earth's crust and is present in vast quantities in the soils. Under normal conditions it is not soluble in water and remains harmless, but acidification makes it soluble and thus creates a toxicity effect (Krugg and Frink 1983; Abrahamsen 1984). As late as 1974, aluminum was believed to be nontoxic to humans but afterward was discovered to cause dementia, and a number of studies from diverse parts of the world linked it to a variety of neurological disease including Lou Gehrig's disease (Maugh 1984).

Acid precipitation was known to increase the solubility of highly toxic metals such as lead, cadmium, mercury, and aluminum. That acid rain increases the leaching of these metals into soils and water supplies was not disputed even early on (Hutchinson and Havas 1980, 618). It was certain that acidification of water supplies leads to increases in concentrations of toxic metals in the water. As a result of acid rain, "the concentration increase of dissolved aluminum in lakes is absolutely massive."[25] Acidic water was known to leach other toxic metals from water pipes, the soil, and lake sediments. In addition, it could free carcinogenic asbestos fibers from cement-asbestos pipes used in some water systems (Maugh 1984). Even skeptics who stressed uncertainty granted that acidification has created problems in the past.[26]

Apart from the indirect impacts of acid rain, the direct health effects of high concentrations of SO_2 were considered as a "conventional" local pollution problem rather than as a part of the transboundary acid rain problem (ERL 1983, 1). These effects were very serious nevertheless and provided strong reasons for controlling acidification. To take one example, a study of six hundred people in Japan established a very strong correlation between severe lung disease and exposure to sulfuric acid aerosols; all patients lived close to a plant with such emissions, the incidence decreased with increased distance from the plant, and dropped sharply when the plant installed equipment to control emissions (Maugh 1984).

Synopsis on Science

On balance, it is difficult to evaluate the state of knowledge in a straightforward way. Knowledge on aquatic impacts was more developed than knowledge on terrestrial ecosystems. It seems fair to conclude that there was good principal understanding about the essential cause-effects relations and the potential impacts of acidification. Areas of uncertainty pertained only to the quantitative measures of impact, as well as the relative contribution of acidification vis-à-vis other possible causal factors.[27] At the same time, no one in the scientific literature appears to have disputed the potential negative consequences of acid rain for soils, vegetation, aquatic life, and human health. One comprehensive assessment of the state of knowledge on the problem, prepared for the European Commission, summarized the results in a manner reflective of this ambiguity:

> However, it has not been unequivocally established that these environmental impacts are caused by acid pollutants emissions, nor is the relative importance of other factors properly identified. . . . Nevertheless circumstantial evidence would suggest that acid emissions and their subsequent chemical transformation and precipitation are at least a partial contributory cause to these observed effects and may be giving rise to yet unidentified impacts, some of which could be irreversible. (ERL 1983, vii)

Knowledge and Action: The Impact of Information

Analysts characterize the regime as "consistently science- and ecosystem-driven" (Levy 1993, 110) and consider the strong scientific component as one of its most distinct features (Wettestäd 1999). Particularly since the late 1980s, "various types of scientists are drawn into the LRTAP decision-making process in a perhaps hitherto unprecedented manner within the realm of international environmental co-operation" (Wettestäd 2000, 109). It is worth emphasizing that working groups were progressively organized around types of environmental damage rather than types of pollutants (that is, around *consequences* rather than causes of the problem). This left the regime open-ended and made it possible for any pollutant to enter its scope on the basis of evidence of ecological damage (Levy 1993, 110–111). If we look at the overall evolution of the regime, the input from these groups was the avant-garde of the political process of negotiating international policies. Gradually, more and more compounds became subject to agreements, and the selection of VOCs and later POPs was based on science.

Before the establishment of EMEP, the vast majority of countries did not accept the idea that air pollution could cross borders. Austria, Finland, the Netherlands, and Switzerland had vulnerable ecosystems but were unaware of their acidification and their initial positions were that acidification was not a problem. Their participation in EMEP involved them in measuring acidification, assessing damage to forests, freshwaters, and buildings. Results of coordinated research within EMEP revealed the extent of acidification, countries accepted it and the debate was over by the early 1980s (Levy 1993). As a British official conceded: "EMEP drew us into the 1979 convention."[28]

Political consensus was greatly strengthened during a 1982 Stockholm Conference on Acidification of the Environment, organized by Sweden and attended by most European countries. Its purpose was to hear a series of research presentations, consider the state of existing knowledge, and consolidate understanding of the problem. More than one hundred experts from twenty nations produced a summary of the state of knowledge on the acidification problem. The conclusions pointed to scientific certainty about the causes and effects of the problem: that increased acidification was primarily due to industrial sulfur and nitrogen emissions, that it caused negative changes in ecosystems, and that the reducing emissions would lead to roughly proportionate reductions in acidification (Wetstone 1987, 186). The final statement of the meeting included the following conclusion: "The acidification problem is serious and, even if deposition remains stable, deterioration of soil and water will continue and may increase unless additional control measures are implemented and existing control policies are strengthened" (Swedish Ministry of Agriculture 1982).[29] One important event during the same conference was the dramatic U-turn that Germany made in announcing its support for regulatory action.

All evidence suggests that information about the negative consequences of acidification played a particularly important role at both national and international levels. In Norway, the first scientific input to the political process on sulfur reductions came first and primarily from the "damage scientists" who studied the negative impact of acidification on Norwegian lakes. Their research was used also in other European countries to mobilize public pressure (Wettestäd 1998, 408–415). It later turned out that most damage associated with long-range transport of NO_x occurred in Central Europe (Wettestäd 1998, 409). The "hottest" input at the 1982 Stockholm conference was evidence of forest damage in Central Europe where 100,000 hectares of forest were dying and 1,000,000 hectares were at risk (Levy 1993, 93).

National research reports kept pouring in during the 1980s and submitted evidence of damages due to acid rain. During a 1983 public hearing on acidification at the European Parliament Committee on the Environment, Public Health and Consumer Protection, "all agreed that the adverse effects of acid rain were clear, and the debate centered not on whether or not to reduce emissions but on how it should be done and who should pay for it" (Park 1987, 174). Finally, the importance of effects information is evident in the concept of critical loads that formed the scientific foundation for determining each country's individual obligations under the 1994 and 1999 Protocols. This concept centers on the *impact* of acidification: critical loads is the maximum level below which no ecological damage occurs.

After getting involved in research, governments became more aware of existing evidence of damage from acidification, more concerned about addressing the problem, and more willing to support regulations (Levy 1993, 120–121).

The transboundary sources of pollutants implied the need for international obligations for mutual benefit. States that chose to join the first sulfur protocol had accepted the scientific evidence. Those who chose to stay out (such as Poland and Spain) did not deny the science but explained their opposition with other considerations such as the large economic costs of regulation. Only the United States and the United Kingdom claimed that more research needed to be done (McCormick 1985, 85), a line that appears to be part of the standard operating procedures of U.S. delegations at all international environmental discussions. Eventually, driven by accumulating scientific knowledge, the regime evolved to cover pollutants and damages that were not on the radar in 1979 when the Convention was established. The overall connection between mandated scientific research and protocol creation is clear. Yet, the specific policy measures under this particular were not scientifically derived. The 30-percent reductions target, as well as the particular base year (1980), was decided politically (Haigh 1989).

Ecological problem-solving was indeed the core rationale behind the regime, but it was only one of the reasons for international coordination. In the early stage of agenda setting and the initial development of the Convention, other considerations motivated participation as well. The agenda setting was, to a large extent, related to Cold War politics and the desire to strengthen détente through East-West cooperation. Into the 1980s, this kept countries involved in deliberations even when they were nonchalant about the environmental problem. Some Eastern European countries signed onto the Convention to increase contact with the West and to not antagonize the Soviet Union (Levy 1993, 92). Canada and the United States joined the European regime for reasons unrelated to the ecological problem. None of the European emissions of the regulated substances were believed to affect North America (Levy 1993). And some countries joined the regime because it would not pose additional costs for them. France, for instance, calculated that its nuclear program would reduce sulfur emissions anyway (Levy 1993, 93).

It would be an exaggeration to claim that the international treaties were created only because of the transboundary consequences of acidification. Concerns with local effects of one's own emissions were equally important, but unilateral national actions to reduce emissions would decrease international economic competitiveness. An international agreement for coordinated action was seen as a way to equalize the costs of action and reduce asymmetries by making sure that others reciprocate. Here, economic considerations supplemented environmental concerns. This played a particular role in the negotiation and adoption of EC directives on vehicle emissions and large combustion plants. "Germany adopted strict national standards out of concern with its own forests, and sought to extend those standards to other members to equalize the terms of economic competition" (Levy 1993, 108). It is important to note, however, that while the regime may have served to even the playing field *within* Europe, it also reduced the competitiveness of European countries vis-à-vis outsiders such as Japan. Because of this effect, concerns with economic competitiveness primarily offered reasons against regulations. The regime was a function primarily of environmental concerns and not of economics.

Power and Knowledge

Scientific knowledge was an important formative influence. Was the available scientific information itself a product of the exercise of political power? The idea that power shapes knowledge presupposes that the powerful have preexisting interests and produce knowledge in ways that serve those interests. In our case, however, government and corporate actors did not have a prior interest in reducing emissions and therefore had no reason to fabricate knowledge about a problem that would justify action. Quite the opposite: they had every reason to avoid emissions controls. Political efforts to suppress information and to misrepresent scientific knowledge were made—but did not succeed. Research findings consistently went against the current preferences of governments and refuted their positions.

In some cases, the powerful did not resist knowledge, and research output led to a dramatic shift in government's positions. Evidence of widespread damage to German forests, for instance, compelled Germany to turn from being a laggard to being a strong advocate of regulations. In other cases, government agencies (in the United Kingdom and the United States in particular) made efforts to contest scientific claims but eventually failed.

Even back in 1976, British officials acknowledged that emissions from the United Kingdom could indeed reach Scandinavia (Wetstone 1987, 169). Later on, British scientists published on the negative effects of acid deposition (Beament et al. 1984). Important research activities in the United Kingdom, such as a Surface Waters Acidification Programme, were funded by large businesses such as the British Coal Board (Wettestäd 1998, 391). But a House of Commons Environment Committee (1984) dismissed assertions by the Ministry of Agriculture, Fisheries and Food that there was no evidence of damages to agriculture as "complacent and founded upon little other than conjecture."[30] The U.K. Forestry Commission initially stated that there was no evidence of forest decline in Britain, but the results of the 1987 and 1988 tree surveys indicated that the health of British trees is as poor as that in other parts of Europe, including Germany, where the widespread decline was already a matter of significant concern (Woodin 1989, 753). Even studies that were sponsored and organized by industries spun out of political control and produced findings that were uncomfortable to corporate actors. A study funded by the U.K.'s national utility industry, the Central Electricity Generating Board, provided conclusive evidence that acid deposition was killing fish in the freshwaters of southern Norway (Levy 1993, 125). Such mounting evidence helps explain why the United Kingdom joined the second sulfur protocol in 1994, although it had stayed out of the first one in 1985.

Government actors in the United States, too, denied evidence and emphasized scientific uncertainties. Research findings consistently undermined these claims, and this research came not only from other countries but from American researchers at the National Research Council. Early on, the EPA itself published a report on the extent and magnitude of the problem and its consequences (EPA 1979). A later report by the U.S. National Academy of Sciences was a thinly veiled slap in the face of the Reagan administration: "Although claims have been made that direct evidence linking power plant emissions to the production of acid rain is inconclusive . . . we find the circumstantial evidence for their role overwhelming" (NAS 1981).[31] Joint Canadian-American work groups reached consensus on the existence of severe damage to aquatic systems and attributed their increased acidification primarily to sulfur emissions in the U.S. Midwest (Wetstone 1987, 173). When the U.S. National Academy of Science and the Royal Scientific Society of Canada created a Joint Scientific Committee on Acid Precipitation, the U.S. administration refused to let them conduct joint peer reviews of multilateral research and insisted that the peer review be conducted unilaterally by the White House Office of Science and Technology. Surprisingly, even the U.S. committee concluded that "the phenomenon of acid deposition is real and constitutes a problem for which solutions should be sought" (cited in Wetstone 1987, 175). Thus, the efforts by U.S. government actors to obstruct research and to perpetuate impressions of scientific uncertainty eventually failed. Even government-sponsored reports by American scientists consistently pointed to a serious problem and contradicted the U.S. government's preferences.[32]

Nor could communist governments, with their proverbially close control over scientists, alter the scientific findings and the consistent conclusions that pointed to a serious problem. Eastern European researchers were not allowed to publish data at home (and could only send it abroad to LRTAP bodies). The Convention's provisions for collective research at the international level fostered research at the national level that may not have been funded otherwise, and British and Czechoslovakian researchers found it easier to obtain government funding because their research was now a matter of international commitments.[33] Governments in Eastern Europe "were seeking to *suppress* knowledge of environmental damage, yet were lured into *creating* it because of their

entanglement in LRTAP" (Levy 1993, 115). Thus, even authoritarian governments did not have power over knowledge. Evidence from the acid rain case
strongly suggests that existing scientific information cannot be explained with
reference to power and therefore should not be treated as epiphenomenal.

Conclusion

The LRTAP regime was established not because of but despite economic concerns, and states altered their behavior not because of stringent enforcement
mechanisms but because of a genuine desire to reduce acid rain. The amount
of research on the problem was overwhelming and the quality of information,
as well as the degree of scientific consensus, was high in all three sectors of
knowledge: extent, causes, and consequences of the problem. Lingering uncertainty pertained to the quantitative measures of the critical threshold levels of acidification as well as to the relative contribution of anthropogenic
emissions vis-à-vis natural acidification. However, all the principal cause-
effect relations were well understood and not disputed. Knowledge about consequences was particularly influential. Findings of actual damage from acid
rain brought along opponents like Germany and the United Kingdom to actively seek binding sulfur reductions, and the acceptance of science only increased over time. The science-politics interface was especially strong during
the creation of the second sulfur protocol: states agreed to commit to uneven
obligations to meet uneven targets by different deadlines—all of which were
based on ecological thresholds of damage calculated by computer models.

The policymaking and the research processes were well integrated. Policy
makers actively sought scientific input, established and funded a broad set of
institutionalized research programs, and accepted their substantive findings—
even when that meant incurring large economic costs. A number of research
programs were initiated within the framework of the regime *in order to* provide an information basis for negotiations. Countries initiated concerted multilateral scientific research that engaged them in a learning process that led
them to reconsider their interests and dramatically alter their preferences regarding policy action. The established networks for coordinated research
stimulated investigation of the domestic effects of acid rain and eventually
generated knowledge about the negative impacts of acidification. The subsequent policymaking process went closely hand in hand with institutionalized
scientific research. Policy commitments were adjusted in accordance with current scientifically derived knowledge: the targets under the NO_x protocol were
reduced from 30-percent cuts to a freeze due to recognition of scientific uncertainty (Wettestäd 2000, 100–101).

Notes

1. Cited by Munton et al. 1999, 246, footnote 41.

2. Soils that are deep and rich in lime or other alkaline substances have a strong neutralizing capacity. In contrast, thin and sandy soils such as those in Scandinavian countries have a weak buffering capacity and most precipitation would reach lakes and underground waters with its acidity mostly unaltered (McCormick 1985, 21).

3. Cited in Munton et al. 1999, 166.

4. As far as the pollutants regulated under LRTAP are concerned, the environmental problems in North America are unrelated to the problems in Europe. Canada and the United States are members of the regime even though the emissions from Europe do not affect them. Levy (1993, note 11) interprets their decision to join with the expected benefits from scientific collaboration and with the existing linkages between the LTRAP process and the bilateral conflict between the two countries over acid rain.

5. The texts of the Convention and its protocols are available in electronic form at http://www.unece.org/env/lrtap/welcome.html (February 11, 2005).

6. All LRTAP meetings, including meetings of the working groups, were open to NGOs with consultative status with the UNECE; these actors were excluded only from the actual negotiations among governments (Wettestäd 1998, 386).

7. See LRTAP's official website at http://www.unece.org/env/lrtap (Febuary 11, 2005).

8. A diagram with the institutional structure can be found in Wettestäd 1999, 87.

9. The Soviet Union did not want to commit to cutting its emissions and, with prevailing winds blowing east, it could argue that its emissions do not affect European territories (Levy 1993, 92).

10. It has been suggested that politicians had acknowledged that acid deposition is caused by many pollutants and that the sulfur protocol would not be sufficient to ameliorate the problem—and that this recognition is the reason why talks proceeded without sufficiently precise scientific information (Wettestäd 2000, 100).

11. Wettestäd (1998; 2000) emphasizes scientific uncertainty about nitrous oxides and its "sobering" effect on the decision makers who reduced their regulatory ambitions. However, based on his data, it appears that the uncertainty pertained not to the ecological aspects of the problem but instead to the feasibility of technological solutions and the effectiveness of policy options. In the United Kingdom, for instance, scientists revealed technological and political complications in achieving reduction targets but, at the same time, accumulated more and more evidence of environmental damage from acid rain (Wettestäd 1998, 396).

12. A list of signatories and ratifications can be found in Table 4.2 in Munton et al. 1999, 176–177.

13. "The science had not advanced sufficiently by the end of 1991 to establish [critical] loads" (Levy 1993, 100).

14. Countries agreed that they could not reduce sulfur deposition below critical levels and instead decided to seek to reduce by 60 percent the gap between critical loads and current levels (Wettestäd 2000, 102).

15. RAINS is an abbreviation of Regional Acidification Information and Simulation. It combines data on emissions, long-range transport of pollutants and environmental effects of acid deposition. On that basis, different abatement strategies can be compared. In addition to the RAINS model, some countries had their own computer models and those produced dissimilar recommendations. According to Sweden's model, the United Kingdom would have to reduce VOCs by 88 percent, while the U.K.'s own model indicated a need for 76-percent reductions (Wettestäd 2000, note 18).

16. EMEP can also serve for monitoring compliance but has not been utilized for that, and verification is left largely to self-reporting. Updates are provided every year and major overall reviews of policies are conducted every four years (Levy 1993, 90).

17. Green Globe Yearbook 1996, 98, cited by Wettestäd 2000, 105.

18. A diagram of the LRTAP organizational structure and information about all working groups can be found on the official website at http://www.unece.org/env/lrtap/conv/lrtap_o.htm (February 11, 2005).

19. The degree of acidity of a liquid is measured on a pH scale that ranges from 0 (most acidic) to 14 (most alkaline), with 7 being neutral. The scale is logarithmic, meaning that every single unit increases or decreases acidity by ten. This means that water of pH 4 is ten times more acidic than water of pH 5. Pure rain is believed to have a pH of 5.6, but in normal conditions that could range from 4.9 to 6.5 (McCormick 1985, 18).

20. "It is probable that there is not a linear relationship between SO_2 emissions and SO_4^{2-} deposition as the supply of oxidants/catalysts may be a limiting factor. Opinions differ on the degree of this effect for wet deposition" (ERL 1983, 5).

21. "In general terms, the reactions of acid with soils are well-known, but the quantification of rates and processes are in need of further study" (Hutchinson and Havas 1980, 621).

22. Cited in a preliminary publication authored by participants in the assessment (Magnuson et al. 1984, 511).

23. "It is reasonable to suspect that acidic deposition plays some role in some of the current unexplained instances of forest decline. Acidic deposition can have effects on soil chemistry, and there is a growing consensus in Europe that soil nutrient deficiencies are responsible for much of the forest decline observed there. However, there is little compelling evidence to indicate that acidic deposition alone is a major cause of decline" (Pitelka and Raynal 1989, 8).

24. In calcerous soils, which constitute the majority of soils to be found in EEC Member States, neutralizing base metal cations was believed to prevent significant acidification. In many neutral and acid soil areas that are often used for agriculture and coniferous forestry, acid precipitation is not naturally neutralized in soil (ERL 1983, 10).

25. Pamela Stoke, of the University of Toronto, cited in Maugh 1984.

26. Morton Lippman of the New York University Medical Center was reported saying: "At this point in our studies, I think it is clear that we cannot adequately describe the nature and the extent of the effects of the inhalation of acidic pollutants on human health. We just don't know enough. . . . We do, however, know a great deal about some

aspects of the problem. We know, for example, that acidic air pollutants have created health problems in the past" (cited in Maugh 1984).

27. "It is harder to identify the extent to which environmental damage/change is caused by acid precipitation in relation to other possible factors" (ERL 1983, 10).

28. Interviewed in 1990 by Marc A. Levy (1993, 84).

29. Cited in Wetstone 1987, 186.

30. Also cited in Wettestäd 1999, 101.

31. Cited in Wetstone 1987, 176.

32. The overall impotence of power to control knowledge is captured in a statement by Wetstone: "Although one government might lose interest in the joint studies, and even seek to obstruct them, the integrity of participating scientists could, in the end, preserve the credibility of the exercise" (1987, 175).

33. Interviews conducted by Marc Levy (1993, 88).

5

Lost in the Woods:
International Forest Negotiations

You'd see meetings of thousands of people discussing a problem, assuming
that the problem is there.

—Rob Rawson, International Tropical Timber Council

IN THE LATE 1980S, A FORESTER DESCRIBED the international forestry agenda as
"a series of loudly trumpeted non-events" (Westoby 1989, 165). Today, it
could be more accurately portrayed as a series of loudly trumpeted events
with no policy output. Countries participated in numerous global and regional initiatives to devise international policies for sustainable forest management, but negotiations have consistently failed to produce a forest policy
agreement, despite a consensus among governments that the rate of deforestation is unsustainable. Few governments dispute that forests are important,
and all agree that action should be taken, but many countries oppose the idea
of coordinating forest management under an international treaty.

The repeated failure to reach a forest policy agreement is particularly notable because of the prominence of deforestation as an environmental problem. Forests are popularly known as the lungs of the planet and have become
emblematic of the natural environment. They have been in the center of public attention, and their destruction has long been a matter of concern to a variety of political actors. Domestic as well as international environmental
norms have grown over the last century (Meyer et al. 1997). In an age of
strengthening norms of joint environmental management, one might expect
that if obscure ecological problems such as persistent organic pollutants can

trigger treaty formation,[1] then forests, with their symbolic value and command of public attention, would have a good chance at being addressed through an international agreement. Yet, forestry deliberations have become notorious in diplomatic circles for their futility and lack of progress.

To what extent can the absence of a global forest treaty be explained with shared scientific knowledge about deforestation? It would be difficult to draw a meaningful connection between science and the failure of negotiations if we treat science holistically and discuss scientific forest research in general. Scientific research on forests is extensive and deeply institutionalized in the policy-making processes at national and international levels. Scientists and policy makers alike accept the abundant data about deforestation. Indeed, there is no scientific controversy that could explain the hesitation of states to cooperate in forest policy. Because of these features, it may seem implausible to explain the political outcome in terms of scientific knowledge. However, if we disaggregate the concept of scientific knowledge and distinguish between types of information, a different picture unfolds. Multilateral scientific assessments of forest resources submit abundant information about the extent and causes of deforestation, but there is a remarkable paucity of data on its transboundary *consequences*. Because it is not clear how logging in one country affects other countries, few states see a reason to enter a legally binding treaty on sustainable forest management. At the same time, the costs of "green" policies are very high since forest utilization is a cross-sectoral issue that involves a number of socioeconomic interests.

Insufficient knowledge about the cross-border consequences of deforestation has been a major obstacle in negotiations. The following section reviews the history of international efforts to create international forest policy. I then explore multilateral global assessments and evaluate the state of scientific knowledge about deforestation. The final section analyzes how gaps in knowledge have affected the dynamics and outcome of international negotiations on a forest convention.

Efforts at International Regime Formation

Deforestation and forest degradation are well-known problems that figure prominently in public discourse. The forest cover of the planet is known to be dwindling due to a number of human activities including commercial logging, clearing of agricultural land and pastures, and construction of roads and dams. The international agenda that addresses the forestry problematic is decentralized and greatly fragmented. It consists of a number of bilateral, regional, and global initiatives that involve a variety of actors: governments, international organizations such as the FAO, the UN Environment Programme, the UN Development Programme (UNDP), and the World Bank. In addition, NGOs such as the Forest Stewardship Council and the International Union of Forest Research Organizations fund forestry projects and actively engage in forest-related research, education, and training. While there are elements of soft law such as Chapter 11 of Agenda 21 as well as tools for private forest governance operated by nonstate actors (Cashore et al. 2004), a forest policy regime based on hard international law is absent. At a major session of the UN Intergovernmental Forum on Forests (IFF), governments officially acknowledged that there is no global legal instrument that deals with forests in a comprehensive and holistic way (E/CN.17/IFF/1998/L.1).

Existing Relevant Agreements

The global institution that is most directly relevant to forests is the International Tropical Trade Agreement (ITTA), established in 1983 and renegotiated in 1994 (Humphreys 1996; ITTO 1996; Gale 1998). The design of the ITTA makes it far from adequate for protection of forests, for three reasons.

First, the agreement is limited in geographical scope.[2] It covers only tropical forests, while temperate and boreal forests supply 80 percent of industrial timber on the international market (cited in VanderZwaag and MacKinlay 1996, 12).

Second, the ITTA is narrow in thematic scope. It is a commodity agreement, a centerpiece of a trade regime that regulates trade in tropical timber. The 1994 amendments did add provisions for sustainable development and established the Bali Partnership Fund to assist countries with sustainability projects. It is difficult, however, to reconcile this objective with the primary objectives of the original treaty: to increase processing of tropical timber, to promote the utilization of wood, and to boost wood exports (Article 1). Countries even rejected a proposal for certification of tropical timber from sustainably managed forests (VanderZwaag and MacKinlay 1996, 16).

Third, the agreement has no monitoring and compliance mechanisms, and the ITTC has no authority to conduct independent reviews of national forestry practices.[3] In the end, the agreement's policy contributions to sustainable forest management are negligible. A key insider confided, "The money spent on projects is insignificant ($230 million over 10 years) . . . ITTO's impact on the ground is minor, minor."[4]

Apart from the ITTA, there are several legal treaties that are not focused on forest issues but include provisions that could be used to introduce forest-related policies: the United Nations Framework Convention on Climate Change (UNFCCC), the Convention on Biological Diversity (CBD), and the

Convention to Combat Desertification (CCD). Article 4 (1) (d) of the UN-FCCC requires the promotion of conservation of sinks and reservoirs of greenhouse gases, including forests. However, the Global Environmental Facility that finances implementation projects does not channel funds to forest projects (Tarasofsky 1995, 14). International reports on forests recognize that the UNFCCC has had a minor impact on forestry since there is a wide range of forest-related issues that lie beyond its scope (FAO 1997, 104). The CCD relies on regional annexes for implementation, and Article 8 (3)(b)(i) of the African annex requires the development of national action plans to sustainably manage natural resources, including forests. Yet, forest policy does not figure in the main text of the agreement, even though forests are of central importance in combating the advance of deserts. In addition, the convention is considered impotent because no funding mechanism was established. The only legal treaty for sustainable forest management is a small regional agreement, the 1993 Central American Forest Convention, which, however, has not entered into force.[5]

Toward a Forest Treaty

The chronology of international forest-related events (box 5.1) is a relentless series of failures to produce policy output. The political move toward a global forest convention emerged in the late 1980s. In the context of proliferating environmental agreements and strengthening environmental values, the absence of global policy on forest preservation was growing conspicuous and generated public pressures on governments. At a 1990 meeting in Houston, Texas, the group of industrialized countries (G-7) discussed the problem, and at a press conference U.S. President George W. Bush proposed to start negotiations on a global forest convention (Kolk 1996, 145). The FAO Committee on Forestry supported the idea and introduced it in the preparations of the 1992 UN Conference on the Environment and Development (UNCED) at Rio de Janeiro. International deliberations on forest management have taken place within three institutional settings: at the 1992 UNCED in Rio de Janeiro; in four sessions of the Intergovernmental Panel on Forests (IPF), between 1995 and 1997; and during four rounds of the IFF, between 1997 and 2000.

Forest Discords at Rio

The plan to include negotiations on a forest convention on the agenda of the 1992 Earth Summit in Rio de Janeiro was abandoned at the preparatory stage due to sharp disagreements among states on the need for such a treaty.[6] The United States, Canada, and European countries emphasized the principle

---

Box 5.1.   Chronology of forest-related international events

1983	International Tropical Timber Agreement negotiated
1990	Industrialized countries propose negotiations on a global forest treaty
1992	Forest treaty negotiations lifted from the agenda of the Earth Summit
1992	Nonbinding "Forest Principles" adopted at the Earth Summit
1994	International Tropical Timber Agreement amended
1995	Intergovernmental Panel on Forests (IPF) created
1995	United States reverses its position and opposes a forest treaty
1997	Intergovernmental Forum on Forests (IFF) launched to replace IPF
1998	Malaysia reverses its position and supports a forest treaty
2000	IFF concludes with the decision not to pursue a global forest treaty
2001	A UN Forum on Forests (UNFF) created, without policymaking or implementation mandate
2001	A Collaborative Partnership on Forests established among eight international organizations to coordinate relevant activities

---

of global responsibility in preserving forests, but developing countries stressed their sovereign right to use their natural resources as they saw fit. Countries with large forests, Malaysia and India in particular, viewed proposed international policies as methods of raising trade barriers: a treaty would put limitations on their timber exports and/or oblige them to engage in sustainable forest management that makes harvesting more expensive (Humphreys 1996). At the second preparatory meeting, held in Geneva in April 1991, it was agreed that the minimum goal would be the adoption of a nonbinding declaration (Kolk 1996, 154).

The Rio conference generated neither a legal treaty on forests nor new funds for forest policies, and instead produced a set of nonbinding Forest Principles: the Non-Legally Binding Authoritative Statement of Principles for a Global Consensus on the Management, Conservation and Sustainable Development of all Types of Forests.[7] They reaffirm the sovereign rights of states over their forest resources (Principle 2 [a]) but state that the costs for forest conservation are to be shared by the international community (Principle 1[b]) and call for additional funds to be made available to developing countries. The document omitted references to global or regional benefits of forests, and previous references to the interests of the world community were replaced with "values to local communities" (Preamble [f]). Its insignificance as a legal instrument is reflected in the very small group of states that cared to engage in negotiating the text (Kolk 1996, 158–159).

Malaysia and India blocked the inclusion of a recommendation for a future legally binding convention. On that score, the only concession to Northern pro-Convention countries was paragraph (d) of the Preamble that mentions further cooperation pending assessment of the adequacy of the nonbinding principles. The rich countries did succeed, however, in deleting from the draft text references to their responsibility for destroying extensive areas of their own forests and to compensation for forest destruction in developing countries during colonial times (Kolk 1996, 158).

Initiatives after Rio

A number of other initiatives were launched after Rio. Parties to the ITTA considered expanding the scope of the treaty to include boreal and temperate forests. The United States and the European Union (EU) firmly objected, stressing that they considered changes in the character of the treaty unacceptable (Kolk, 1996, 161). Developing countries considered such position as duplicity: the North was pressing them to take costly action to protect tropical forests but was unwilling to reciprocate with temperate and boreal forests. Given that boreal forests in Russia alone are nearly twice as large as the Brazilian Amazon forests and that the rate of their depletion also is twice higher than that of Amazonian deforestation (Myers and Kent 2001, 176), focusing on boreal forests indeed made sense from an ecological perspective but posed obvious political difficulties.

In the meantime, activities of NGOs were beginning to alter forest practices worldwide and to affect governments' preferences regarding forest policy. Environmental groups such as the Forest Stewardship Council, established in 1994, began to encourage sustainable forest management by issuing eco-labels to certify forest products from sustainably managed forests. They embarked on a double-track campaign to lobby companies such as furniture manufacturers to buy only timber harvested from certified forests and to encourage individual consumers to buy eco-labeled products from such companies. People responded favorably, and the companies saw the opportunity to attract environmentally minded consumers. The new market for certified forest products began to affect the dynamics of international timber trade. In 1998, Malaysian logging companies lost half their European market. As a result, Malaysia changed its position on a forest treaty, and began to view it as an opportunity to counter the NGO offensive. It believed that international standards negotiated by governments would be less stringent than standards promoted by NGOs (Porter et al. 2000, 206–207).

Failed Negotiations at IPF and IFF

During debates at the UN Commission on Sustainable Development in April 1995, countries recognized the need for an international dialogue dedicated exclusively to forests. To this end, they established a temporary ad hoc forum for discussion called the Intergovernmental Panel on Forests (IPF), and asked several international institutions to form an Inter-Agency Task Force on Forests (ITFF) to provide information and technical advice. The ITFF was chaired by the head of the forestry department of the FAO and included the World Bank, UNDP, the International Tropical Timber Organization (ITTO), UNEP, and the Secretariat of the Convention on Biological Diversity (Grayson and Maynard 1997).

The IPF convened four times between 1995 and 1997 and produced a list of proposals for action on cooperation in financial assistance and technology transfer, forest research, criteria and indicators for sustainable forest management, and trade. Yet, states could not agree on major issues such as the need for a global forest convention or financial assistance for forest policies in developing countries.[8] At the UN General Assembly, they decided to continue the policy dialogue and established an ad hoc IFF, widely perceived as a mere continuation of IPF.[9]

By far, the most controversial issue pertained to what international policy arrangement to introduce and whether to do it at all. The major policy options under consideration were: coordinating existing treaties, strengthening existing nonbinding agreements, establishing a permanent governmental forum on forests, and creating a comprehensive global forest convention. At IFF's second session in 1998 (IFF-2), Canada and Costa Rica began a separate initiative to promote the idea for a global forest convention. The Costa Rica–Canada Initiative consisted of two global and eight regional expert meetings that involved six hundred experts from more than forty countries and organizations.[10] Divisions remained, and the initiative failed to achieve political consensus on the desirability of a treaty.[11]

The bargaining process at IPF and IFF was characterized by stagnation.[12] Throughout the eight global conferences, the positions of individual countries as well as the arguments offered on each side remained unchanged. A large group of countries advocated a treaty: Canada, Scandinavian countries, France, Switzerland, the Russian Federation, Malaysia, Turkey, South Africa, Senegal, and the Czech Republic, among others. Stressing the absence of a holistic international approach to forest management, treaty advocates emphasized that existing instruments do not adequately address the problems confronting the world's forests and supported the initiation of negotiations on a "legally binding instrument."[13] Switzerland underscored the regional differences in forest resources and policy needs and suggested creating a global framework convention with detailed regional protocols to be negotiated separately.[14]

The motivation of treaty supporters was most likely mixed. There were speculations among delegates that the federal government of the Russian Federation saw a treaty as a lever for wresting control over forest resources from the hands of its regional governors. Some developing countries, as well as Eastern European countries, hoped that a treaty would channel development assistance into their forestry departments. Canada and Malaysia were betting on the prospect of a weak treaty that would fend off environmental criticism while giving the green light to their logging industries by legitimizing environmental standards that would be lower than those upheld by NGOs. All other treaty advocates were from Europe where deforestation is not a problem, since forest cover has been steadily increasing for the last sixty years. For European governments, therefore, an international agreement would entail zero policy costs and, at the same time, reap domestic and international political benefits.

On the other side of the fence, the United States and Brazil were leaders of an antitreaty coalition that included Australia, New Zealand, Japan, the United Kingdom, Mexico, India, Indonesia, China, and most other developing countries, which negotiated jointly as a group (the G-77). This camp advocated a "nonbinding arrangement" that would not entail any concrete policy obligations. Brazil repeatedly upheld the nonbinding Forest Principles of Rio as a sufficient instrument and reiterated that there was not enough consensus to launch a negotiating process. The United States had made a U-turn since the early 1990s that could be seen as part of its general redeployment away from multilateralism in international relations. When negotiating text documents, the U.S. delegation, together with New Zealand and Brazil, rejected references to an international policy "agenda" and preferred to speak of the less committal "dialogue." At IFF-2, the United States even opposed a proposal for an international framework for monitoring forest conditions.

The division between the two camps was not based on either North-South lines or on types of forests. Each camp included rich and poor countries, some with tropical and others with boreal forests. Motivation for supporting a treaty varied, from a genuine desire for sustainable forestry, to obtaining money for policy implementation, to domestic politics. Justifications for opposing a treaty also ranged from protecting sovereign rights, to focusing on implementation, to taking action under other instruments. New Zealand and the United States argued that negotiating a treaty would impede action and suspend forest policies for years. Indigenous peoples feared that a treaty would further impinge on their rights to a forest-based culture and livelihood.

The treaty debate was closely related to the issue of finance. Developing countries were afraid that if they committed to a binding agreement, the North would not provide resources for its implementation. Many delegations, including those of South Korea, Peru, Colombia, Nigeria, and Gabon, stated that it was premature to discuss a treaty given the lack of consensus on financial resources for policy implementation. At IFF-2 and IFF-3, China supported the idea of an international arrangement but stressed the need to include financial mechanisms for its implementation. At IFF, African countries such as Zambia and Nigeria indicated that they would consider joining a treaty only if a global forest fund is created. On the last day of IFF's final session, the speaker on behalf of developing countries (the G-77) finally threw the cards on the table and openly stated: "We do not have a principal objection to a treaty if the money is provided to implement it."[15]

All industrialized countries were adamant in their refusal to provide additional money. At IFF-3, the EU opposed references to financing forest conservation in the decision text of the meeting. Even strong supporters of a treaty, such as the Scandinavian countries, curtly stated that money was already provided on bilateral and multilateral bases but, they argued, this money was not being used properly and efficiently by recipient countries. Canada attempted to use the finance issue as a trump card, suggesting throughout IFF sessions that a fund is contingent on creating a treaty. It was obvious, however, that Western countries refused to pledge new funds for international forest policy.

One of the remarkable aspects of the story is the position of environmental NGOs. Most NGOs present at the negotiations bitterly opposed the creation of a global forest treaty. At UNCED in 1992, they had been enthusiastic supporters of a convention but their position had begun to evolve by the mid-1990s. They had gained confidence in their own ability to affect the behavior of governments and consumers of forest products. In formal statements at IFF, coalitions such as the Global Forestry Action Project emphatically called for reliance on existing binding and nonbinding initiatives (Humphreys 2004).[16] During coffee breaks, they actively lobbied delegates with whom they were on first name basis after years of working together at similar meetings.

The position of NGOs was motivated by two considerations. First, they maintained that negotiations would divert attention from existing initiatives and suspend sustainable forest policies because actors would wait for the resulting convention.[17] Second, they were deeply skeptical about the content of any resulting treaty. Witnessing the deep disagreements among governments and their refusal to commit new funds for forest policy, the NGOs came to believe that an eventual treaty would be weak and would serve to legitimize the exploitation of forests. As one of their representatives stated: "NGOs have been against a convention. It won't include anything we would like, and at the same time [treaty negotiations] would suspend policy progress for ten years."[18] Publications of the International Union for the Conservation of Nature (IUCN) and the World Wildlife Fund offered extensive analysis of the problematic to argue that it is premature to begin negotiations on a convention (Tarasofsky 1995; 1999).

The Outcome: the Monty Python Paragraph

The denouement of the negotiations came at IFF's last session (IFF-4) in early February 2000. Consensus could not be reached after long hours spent trying to reconcile opposing positions, and the final decision amounted to rejecting the idea of a forest convention. Countries decided to create a permanent UN Forum on Forests (UNFF) for nonbinding discussions, and a collaborative partnership among relevant international organizations and secretariats of existing treaties, to enhance cooperation and coordination among its members. In order to appease the pro-treaty coalition, the plenary adopted what NGOs dubbed the "Monty Python paragraph": after five years of work the UNFF would evaluate its own effectiveness and would then "consider with a view to recommending the parameters of a mandate for developing a legal framework on all types of forests."[19] The awkward wording was product of linguistic acrobatics, negotiated over the course of an entire night until it was made sufficiently obscure as to allow both sides to save face. One delegate remarked that, "In five years' time, a vast array of lawyers will spend large amounts of public money trying to interpret what the negotiators meant." The final text also indicated that the Forum did not reach consensus on whether to establish a global fund to facilitate the implementation of forest policies.

The United Nations Forum on Forests

The futility of efforts to devise international forest policy became even more apparent at the new UNFF. The first session of this institution was held in June 2001 in New York.[20] Although countries agreed to disagree on all substantive policy matters, when it came to the particular mandate and design of the UNFF, they cooperated in eviscerating the new institution. Treaty opponents and proponents worked together to strip the international arrangement of substantive content. Arguments about the unique policy needs of each country were used to ensure that states would not be bound by any decision of the UNFF. The United States tried to portray the UNFF as a success in order to undermine arguments for a legal treaty. At the same time, the ·U.S. delegation did their best to deprive UNFF of any capacity to generate policy. Throughout discussions, they insisted on deleting key paragraphs from draft texts, including references to financial provisions, policy targets and timetables, and concrete responsibility for monitoring and reporting. Developed countries together succeeded in removing trade issues from the program of work. In this way, the North reserved its right to import timber products from developing countries while blaming the South for cutting trees.

The decision texts that describe the Plan of Action and the program of work of UNFF are masterpieces of Machiavellian diplomacy.[21] With meticulously chosen words, they contain all the right ideas but commit no one to do anything about them. The adopted documents allow countries to set their own priorities and do not require them to report on policy implementation. In short, the UNFF is purposefully designed to be an empty eggshell: it has no mandate for decision-making, leaves everything for countries to do, lets them choose what they want to do, does not provide them with financial assistance to do it, and has no right to hold them accountable for the results of their (in)action.

Recent sessions of UNFF have become notorious in diplomatic circles for their lack of purpose. They produce resolutions that are negotiated meticulously over long days but merely reiterate already existing proposals for action without specifying means of implementation. Delegates privately confide in the corridors that the resolutions are only intended to show signs of life in UNFF. When occasionally a new proposal is tabled, countries such as the United States (self-proclaimed enthusiasts) remind the Forum that UNFF is not a body that can engage in action. High-level officials such as the head of the Canadian delegation call UNFF a "circus," while others question the rationale behind its existence in more diplomatic ways.[22] Insiders confide that "The UNFF is not designed to do anything, there is no policy in it whatsoever. It is just a place one could go. This way countries can say 'Look, we are doing something internationally.'"[23]

This raises the question of why an international arrangement was created if it leaves everything for countries to do, lets them choose what they want to do, does not provide them with financial assistance to do it, and has no right to hold them accountable for the results of their (in)action. The creation of a hollow UNFF is not the focus here but presents a fascinating theoretical puzzle that can be explained with a global norm of environmental multilateralism (Dimitrov 2005). When the decision to establish the UNFF was taken at IFF, no one seemed particularly enthusiastic about it. It was simply the only alternative to doing nothing at all. Few countries have interest in an institution "with teeth," yet no government can afford to give the impression that they are not addressing a prominent and popular environmental issue such as deforestation. Some delegates at IFF-4 said in consternation that the sole reason for producing a final text with recommendations was to justify to their publics and governments the expensive three-year process of international deliberations. Thus, the UNFF is the institutional excuse of governments to their publics for not having an international forest policy.

The Last Straw

The last session of UNFF in May 2005 was a particularly embarrassing failure. It had been eagerly anticipated for years, since the meeting was mandated to evaluate the Forum's achievements and consider the need for an alternative international arrangement (read: treaty). A promising starting point of the session was a near-consensus that the status quo is unacceptable. Even the United States now publicly conceded that UNFF is seriously lacking. The EU came ready for a showdown and threatened to abandon the process if they do not receive guarantees for significant changes. They arrived in New York determined to obtain policy commitments under a "code of practice" and insisted on quantifiable and timebound global and national goals. In the ensuing fight, demands for "quantifiable" global targets were dropped, national commitments became "voluntary," and targets at neither level had to be achieved, only pursued. When these major concessions were not reciprocated on other issues, negotiations collapsed. The meeting neither produced a new international arrangement on forests nor strengthened the current one. The inability to prepare even a weak political declaration was an embarrassment for all. The session did not produce even a statement, only a nominal document of three paragraphs to show that the meeting took place, with an appendix containing the charred remains of the draft negotiated text.

Explaining Failure

After years of formal debate and intersessional meetings, there remains strong resistance to international action under a policy agreement. The collective decision not to create a forest treaty can be explained by a number of factors that work against international policy coordination in sustainable forest management. These obstacles include the large number of actors involved, the distribution of power across negotiating coalitions, concerns with relative gains, material interests in commercial logging and agriculture, the policy impact on economic sectors, and the distribution of costs and benefits among domestic actors. In his work, Dauvergne (2001) documents the deeply entrenched corporate interests in logging. Humphreys (2003) and Lipschutz (2001) argue that global forest politics is dominated by neoliberal principles of capitalism and free trade that impede sustainable forest management. Examining the early stage of forestry negotiations, Davenport (2005) focuses on the hegemon's interests and the unwillingness of the United States to build a pro-treaty coalition in the early 1990s. The socioeconomic costs of protective policies are high since forest utilization is a complex cross-sectoral issue that affects a number of socioeconomic realms.[24] Concerns with relative gains and losses are acute because the geographical distribution of forests is uneven and a global treaty would impose unequal obligations on states, with countries having extensive forest cover bearing a heavier burden. All these factors impede progress in the policy deliberations and help explain why states have not introduced common policy.

One fundamental obstacle that, in conjunction with other factors, has made regime formation particularly difficult is the insufficient information about key aspects of the problem of deforestation. In particular, gaps in existing knowledge about the consequences of the problem create uncertainty about the benefits from a treaty. As the following section will articulate, most of the known impact of deforestation is confined to the local and national levels, while information about the cross-border consequences of deforestation is scant and incomplete. Because the known negative consequences of deforestation are primarily local and national, the working definition of the problem does not invoke interdependence or generate concern about unintended effects of a country's policy on other countries.

Scientific Research on Deforestation

A distinct feature of global forestry discussions is the virtual absence of scientific controversy. Unlike other environmental cases such as climate change, forest degradation is not a subject of conflicting research results and competing scientific views. Similarly, policy makers of various countries do not debate the existing research-derived knowledge. This is not to say that this knowledge is complete. Rather, there are significant gaps of information on important aspects of the problem, and all assessments converge on recognizing them. These gaps are well known in scientific and policy circles alike and are not a matter of debate in international deliberations.

Forest science is a well-established academic discipline, and forest research is institutionalized in policymaking on national and international levels. In Europe, the first foresters were gendarmes of the landed property and were focused on growing and protecting trees for timber production and agriculture. Knowledge was integrated and strengthened through systematic research, specialized publications began to appear in Europe in the seventeenth century, and the first forestry school was established in 1768, in Ilsenburg, Germany (Westoby 1989, 77–81).

Today, research reports on forest resources come from a variety of sources, including national governments, environmental NGOs, and international institutions that organize and coordinate multilateral scientific assessments of forest conditions on a regular basis. National surveys are inconsistent in their approaches, measures, and concepts, while reports sponsored by NGOs have come under criticism for using speculative methods (Myers 1989). Assessments by international organizations have their own limitations but are nevertheless credited as the most reliable (Westoby 1989, 92; Kolk 1996, 64). At present, several multilateral scientific programs are under way for assessing and monitoring forest resources in order to provide the international community with appropriate information.[25] Although each of these scientific programs is well designed and rigorously pursued, only the FAO's projects provide truly global assessments of all types of forests in all ecological zones.[26]

Comprehensive global assessments of all types of forests began only recently. Not until 1990 was a multilateral study carried out on a global scale (FAO 1995a). FAO has carried out assessments since the 1940s, but until the 1980s none of the studies looked at deforestation over time (see Persson 1975; FAO 1976; Sommer 1976). In 1982, the FAO and the UNEP organized the first comprehensive study of *tropical* forests (FAO 1982, 99).[27] In 1987, the Forestry Department of FAO initiated preparations for a global assessment of all types of forests. The resulting Forest Resources Assessment (FRA) of 1990 covered 179 countries to provide reliable information on the state of global forest resources and the extent of changes since 1980 (FAO 1995a, 1).[28] It used remote sensing via satellites in outer space, and the use of infrared photography also makes it possible to survey forests that are constantly under cloud cover. The exercise was repeated and improved ten years later, in 2000 (FAO 2001).

The State of Scientific Knowledge

The series of international reports provide plentiful and precise information about the extent of deforestation,[29] as well as its causes. However, they offer remarkably little information about the consequences of the problem. There is general discussion of the effects of deforestation, but reports do not provide specific estimates of damage and acknowledge that global effects on climate change and biodiversity cannot be measured with any degree of precision. The FRA hardly contributed anything to knowledge about the consequences of the problem. Multilateral research efforts have focused most on identifying the extent of deforestation as well as its causes. Correspondingly, knowledge on the rates and causes of deforestation is detailed and reliable, but knowledge about the cross-border consequences that would illuminate elements of interdependence is tentative and unreliable.

Sector I: Extent of Deforestation

Knowledge about global rates of deforestation and the extent of the problem is generally considered reliable. Assessments provide extensive data with a high degree of precision.[30] The FRA 1990 study concluded that between 1980 and 1990, global forests and other wooded lands had decreased at an annual rate of 0.02 percent (FAO 1995a, 7–8).[31] Apart from the global level, the study found strong regional characters in the process of change. The rate of change over the decade was 6.6 percent in Africa, 5.9 percent in Latin America, and a much higher 11.3 percent in tropical Asia. In Europe, there was a net increase in forest area of almost 2 million hectares, a continuation of a steady trend that began in the middle of the twentieth century (FAO 1995b, 30).[32] The next and most recent global assessment, FRA 2000, was the first to use a consistent methodology and a common definition of forest cover (FAO 2001).[33] As a result, the study was able to produce the first global forest map based on satellite data (figure 5.1).

At the beginning of the twenty-first century, forests cover 3,869 million hectares or about 30 percent of the world's land surface (FAO 2001). Their distribution is highly uneven: three countries account for more than 50 percent of all forest area: the former Soviet Union, Brazil, and Canada (FAO 1995b, 27). At the global level, net deforestation for the period 1990–2000 was 9.4 million hectares per year, at an annual rate of 0.02 percent and 3.6 percent for the entire decade (FAO 1995a, 7–8; 2001, 1).[34] The lost forest area was smaller than the 11.3 million hectares for the period 1990–1995 and 13.0 million hectares for the period 1980–1990 (FAO 1995a). Although noting that the estimates are not fully comparable because of the dissimilar definitions on which they rely, the assessment concluded that the rate of deforestation has slowed down since the 1980s (FAO 2001, 11). Regionally, net deforestation rates are highest in Africa and South America; the forest cover in industrialized countries remained essentially stable whereas afforestation significantly offset the loss of forests in Asia.[35]

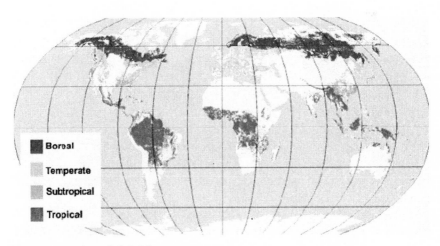

Figure 5.1.   Map of global forest cover.
Source: Food and Agriculture Organization, *Forest Resources Assessment 2000* (FAO 2001).

According to present estimates summarized in table 5.1, 12 percent of the world's forests are in protected areas, and another 2 percent (80 million hectares) are certified for sustainable management. More broadly, 89 percent of forests in industrialized countries and 6 percent of those in developing countries are under some type of management plan. Because of widely recognized problems with policy implementation and compliance, we do not know how much of these are actually managed sustainably (FAO 2001, 346). "Paper parks" that exist only in theory are not uncommon. The "sustainably managed" Tongass Forest of Alaska, part of the U.S. National Forests system, is being depleted through logging more rapidly than most forests in the Amazon or Indonesian Kalimantan (Myers and Kent 2001, 171–172).

Sector II: Causes of Deforestation

The causes of forest changes can be divided into natural and human. Natural factors include repeated fires, attacks by insects, disease, plant parasites, and destruction by cyclones that can cause considerable damage to large tracts of forests, particularly in the Caribbean, Central America, and Southeast Asia. At an international expert meeting on forests, no one mentioned natural causes of forest degradation.[36] There is general agreement that the main causes are human activities: commercial logging, agriculture, pasture, colonization programs, mining and hydroelectricity projects such as the construction of dams, and military activities.[37] In tropical countries, 11 million hectares were harvested annually during the 1990s. In industrialized countries, annual felling of timber was 1,632 million cubic meters and actual removal was 1,260 million cubic meters, implying significant waste and harvest losses (FAO 2001, 78).[38]

TABLE 5.1
Forest cover and forest cover change (1990–2000).

Region	Land Area	Forest Area 2000		Change 1990–2000		Forest 1995	Change 1990–95
	Mln ha	Mln ha	%	Mln ha/yr	%/yr	Mln ha	Mln ha/year
Africa	3,008	650	17	−5.3	−0.8	520	−3.7
Asia	3,167	542	14	−0.4	−0.1	503	−2.9
Oceania	849	201	5	−0.1	n.s.	91	−0.1
Europe	2,276	1,040	27	0.9	0.1	933	0.5
North/Central America	2,099	539	14	−0.6	−0.1	537	−0.3
S. America	1,784	874	23	−3.6	−0.4	871	−4.8
World Total	13,183	3,856	100	−9.0	−0.2	3,454	−11.3

Source: Food and Agriculture Organization, Global Forest Resources Assessment 2000 (FAO 2001).

Different studies converge in their estimates of the role of particular human-induced causes. For instance, according to a World Bank study, agricultural settlement is responsible for 60 percent of the loss of tropical moist forests (World Bank 1991, 31), and another study found that clearing land for agriculture accounts for nearly two-thirds of tropical deforestation worldwide (Rowe et al. 1992). More recently, FRA 2000 confirmed that the main global causes of deforestation are agricultural activities: it found that most of the conversion of forests was into agricultural land and pastures. There is more ambiguity about some background factors behind deforestation. Until recently, the FAO emphasized the impact of population growth and density on deforestation (FAO 1995a). In its most recent assessment, however, it revised its position and concluded that existing studies show a weak and oversimplified connection between forest area and demographic factors (FAO 2001).

The activities that contribute to the depletion of forests are conditioned by a large complex of broader socioeconomic factors such as government policies, population growth, poverty, and unemployment. Because timber exports are important to economies, many governments encourage logging through subsidies, investment incentives, and conducive tax provisions (Repetto 1988, 15–37). Direct and indirect government subsidies come in many forms: tax breaks, low-interest loans, reduced royalties, underpricing for loggers, and incentives given to people to settle in forested areas. The total subsidies to the forest industry in Canada's British Columbia range between 2 and 5.9 billion Canadian dollars. In the 1970s and 1980s, subsidies covered half of the costs of a typical ranch in the Brazilian Amazon (Myers and Kent 2001, 165). The World Bank estimates that two-thirds of deforestation in Indonesia was a result of activities either sponsored or encouraged by the government (World Bank 1991). In these incentive structures, not only are the environmental functions of forests ignored, but even their timber value is not adequately reflected. In countries as diverse as the United States, Indonesia, the Ivory Coast, China, and Brazil, governments do not have revenue systems that capture profit from logging for the public treasuries. To take one example, in 1993 the Indonesian government captured only one-third of the economic rent from timber concessions (cited in Myers and Kent 2001, 163). Furthermore, poverty and social inequality leave large populations without land and this leads them to clear forests in order to cultivate crops. In some developing countries, few job opportunities exist that would draw local populations away from clearing forests for land and fuel.

Just as different regions experience unequal rates of forest change, the principal causes for these changes also vary across regions. Data analysis reveal that the single most important cause of forest change in Africa was subsistence farming, linked with rural population pressure.[39] In Latin America, the main causes were centrally planned operations such as resettlement schemes, large-scale cattle ranching, and hydroelectric projects. In Asia, there was a balance between the various driving forces (FAO 1996, 58–60; FAO 1997, 20). The regional differences with regard to the main causes of deforestation are conditioned in part by differences in the role of the state as proprietor.

Ownership of forests varies across regions. In Latin America, the Caribbean, and Asia, most forest lands belong to the state. In the late 1970s, the state owned practically all forests in Bolivia and Peru, over 80 percent in Brazil, Colombia, and Venezuela, and between 80 and 90 percent in Asia as a region. Accordingly, the control and administration of forests is in the hands of forestry and agriculture departments. In contrast, little of the forests are legal property of governments in English-speaking countries in tropical Africa and the Pacific.[40] In Papua New Guinea, as in most countries of the Pacific, clans and tribes own forests, and the government must negotiate with them in order to use forest resources in any manner. In some countries, it is difficult to determine who owns the forests and has control over their utilization because the relationship between customary and written laws is unclear. Even when the state does hold legal rights over forest land, in many countries local populations exercise usage rights in state-owned forests where they can hunt, gather vegetable products, collect wood for fuel and building, and graze their animals.

These differences have implications for international policy proposal deliberations. Because the causes of deforestation are not the same everywhere, policy action cannot be the same either, and this makes it even more difficult to devise a system of uniform international obligations. Many states are reluctant to take on international obligations for policies, for either one of two reasons. First, a state may not have the authority to control the use of forests since the ownership of forests may be private or communal. Second, because much deforestation is caused by local communities and individuals rather than by state-controlled activities, states may be unwilling to take on responsibility for forest conditions. The cooperation of local communities is essential. "Nothing lasting will be possible in this field without the cooperation not only of those others responsible for rural development . . . but also above all those principal protagonists, the communities living in and around forests: without their direct participation there is no hope of reaching harmonious balance in the use of land" (FAO 1982, 101).

Whether the state does or does not have the authority and capacity to manage forests, the social and economic costs of policy innovations are high. The use of forests is a cross-sectoral issue, a pivotal point in which many socioeconomic issues meet each other. Revenues from timber exports are considerable, and logging is an important part of economies not only in developing countries but also in countries such as Canada and the Russian Federation.

The FAO places their economic value at $400,000 million per year, or 2 percent of global GDP, and provides extensive tables with figures for each country (FAO 1997, 21–25). Forests are also being cleared to open up land for agriculture, to produce wood for household fuel, or to construct dams for flood control and hydroelectric energy production. Because the factors that condition forest utilization reach into a number of social sectors, effective policies for forest management affect many realms and impinge on various interests. Consequently, undertaking international obligations for sustainable forest management would have wide ramifications for societies.

Sector III: Consequences of Deforestation

The consequences of forest degradation derive from the loss of the ecological functions that forests perform. The first ostensible attempt to assess the global nonwood benefits of forests was made during FRA 1990. In response to a questionnaire, national experts listed the following forest functions: wood production, protection, water conservation, hunting, nature conservation, and recreation. Remarkably, the respondents did not mention the roles of forests in regulating climate or in maintaining biodiversity. Furthermore, for most of the nonwood benefits that were listed, countries did not provide concrete figures that would throw light on the negative effects of deforestation at national levels.[41]

No one questions the local benefits of forests. They provide food items, tradable products, and employment, and play ecological functions that support agriculture (Pimentel et al. 1997, 106). Maintaining forest cover on critical watersheds is essential for safeguarding water supplies for irrigation systems, and trees provide windbreaks for agricultural fields, protecting them from wind erosion and direct wind damage. Forests are also sustainable sources of a number of "minor forest products" such as fruit, seeds, mushrooms, fibers (rattan, bamboo, and reeds), rubber, gums, resins, waxes, pharmaceutical and cosmetic products, and ornaments (FAO 1982, 64).

However, there are little concrete data on these nontimber values of forests. One review of existing research unequivocally concludes that such information is at a primitive level and that the problems with estimating nonwood forest services are overwhelming (Nilsson 1996). To take one local effect of deforestation, there is information on the extent of soil erosion, but multilateral assessments do not quantify the connection between the loss of soil and deforestation. According to one estimate, 10 million hectares of arable land are lost because of erosion (Pimentel et al. 1997, 106). Erosion is also related to numerous other problems: siltation of harbors, disruption of sewage because of siltation, eutrophication of waterways, flooding, and increased water treatment costs (Pimentel et al. 1997, 107). It is known that forest degradation under-mines these functions, yet there are few estimates of its precise contributions to soil erosion. One of FAO's reports includes a scant two-paragraph comment on soil erosion as a result of timber harvesting and offers no data or discussion of the socioeconomic consequences of such changes (FAO 1995a, 54).

In 1995, the FAO submitted a report stating that there was no inventory of nonwood forest products and services (FAO 1995c). FAO's first attempt to provide one was made during FRA 2000 when it collected all available infor-mation from all countries, only to conclude that

> Information on the resource base and on subsistence use of [non-wood forest products] is non-existent. . . . Despite their real and potential importance, na-tional institutions do not carry out regular monitoring of resources or evalua-tion of the socioeconomic contribution of [non-timber products] as they do for timber and agricultural products. (FAO 2001, 95, 81)

Individual countries provide figures on exports of particular products, but developing and developed countries alike lack comprehensive inventories. Few reliable estimates on nonwood products exist for most European coun-tries (UNECE/FAO 2000). And Canada could not provide comparable data for one of its main products, maple syrup.[42] Only Asian countries have main-tained national statistics for decades and were able to supply more data.[43]

Livelihoods and Food Security

There is an ambiguous relation between forestry and food security. On one hand, the clearing of forests provides new agricultural land for subsistence of the hundreds of millions of impoverished people worldwide. On the other hand, healthy forests generate employment, provide food items and tradable products, and play ecological functions that support agriculture (Hoskins 1990; FAO 1997, 43–44; Pimentel et al. 1997). In the 1980s, people employed in forest-based en-terprises in Jamaica, Thailand, Honduras, Sierra Leone, and Bangladesh, for in-stance, averaged 12.3 percent of the population (FAO 1987). Large segments of developing country societies depend on wood fuel for their energy needs. Burn-ing wood meets 7 percent of the energy needs of the world as a whole, 70 per-cent of the needs in thirty-four countries, and more than 90 percent of energy consumption in thirteen countries, most of which are African (FAO 2001, 34).

Cross-Border Consequences

The greatest uncertainty pertains to the global and regional effects of de-forestation. Scientists and policy makers alike consider knowledge to be the least reliable when it comes to the impact of deforestation on biodiversity and climate change. Forests are rich in biodiversity. Tropical forests in particular cover only 7 percent of the land surface but provide habitat for half of all known species. The general recognition of the importance of forests contrasts with the absence of concrete and reliable data on the number of existing species, the impact of deforestation on biodiversity, and, most importantly, the impact of biodiversity loss on human communities.

The FAO reports recognize the uncertainty: "The magnitude of such losses or the extent of degradation of biodiversity is unknown" (FAO 1997, 41). As incredible as it may sound, no country has data on the total number of its tree species. FRA 2000 reports that there is no global list of trees and no data on other biological species that reside in forests. The FAO concludes that "there is no accepted methodology for linking these changes [in forest area] to their impacts on forest biological diversity. . . . This is especially evident when information is aggregated at the global level" (FAO 2001, 47–48). At present, scientists and policy makers can only assume negative socioeconomic impacts of forest-related biodiversity loss but cannot estimate them. "On a scale of 0 to 10, we are somewhere between 0 and 1.5. That's how poorly we understand biodiversity."[44] As to the impact of biodiversity changes on societies, "They can only speculate on that."[45] Thus, the ecological role of forests as habitats of species has not been addressed.

Forests can either mitigate or contribute to climate change. On the one hand, when forests grow, they withdraw carbon dioxide from the atmosphere. On the other hand, the burning of forests releases carbon dioxide and other greenhouse gases such as methane, nitrous oxides, and carbon monoxide (FAO 1995a). The FRA 1990 assessment did not generate data on its own but cited an independent study that found that between 1980 and 1990 deforestation and degradation caused a release of 900 million tons of carbon (Dixon et al. 1994). Deforestation and forest degradation were estimated to accounts for 23 percent of human-induced carbon dioxide emissions (IPCC 1996).

The scientific uncertainty about the effects of the problem is so overwhelming that the newest assessments do not even try to address this aspect of the issue. The FAO's FRA 2000 does not include any information whatsoever on the consequences of deforestation. A study of the forests' ecological functions was not part of the assessment. And the science of forests' role in climate change is still considered incomplete. The senior science and technology officer for the Convention on Climate Change summarized, "If you chop a tree, you know what happens to carbon—but what this is causing is largely unknown."[46] Ironically, global warming is expected to have a highly positive impact on the productivity and volume of forests: middle scenarios predict a

20–25 percent increase in net primary production, with a benefit to the forest sector of $10 to $15 billion (Nilsson 1996, 34).

Evaluating Forest Science

In summary, some aspects of deforestation are understood better than others. International assessments provide reasonably good information about global forest cover and the rate of deforestation, as well as undisputed principal understanding of the causes of deforestation. However, there is a marked paucity of information about the nonwood benefits of forests and about the consequences of deforestation. The least reliable knowledge is on the transboundary effects of deforestation. Most of the socioeconomic and ecological benefits of forests are local and national in character.

Forest assessments conclude that it is hard to draw conclusions from the available data (Koch and Linddal, 1993, 226–248), and the FAO recognizes that "the essential needs of researchers and policymakers cannot be met satisfactorily" because of gaps in information and the considerable variation of data between countries (FAO 1995a, 41). Even pro-environment publications reveal that we do not know in specific terms how important forests are.[47] Comprehensive studies on the state of knowledge conducted by the International Union of Forest Research Organizations reveal serious lack of data. One overview of existing research concludes that in view of efforts to set international forest policy,

> It is rather astonishing that so much data and knowledge are still missing. International organizations such as the FAO and the World Bank and aid organizations such as USAID, CIDA, SIDA, and Finnida [sic] have pumped billions of dollars into forestry activities over the decades, and yet we cannot answer some of the most basic questions concerning global forest resources and their functions. (Nilsson 1996, 55)

Not only do we not know, but scientists tell us that we are not going to know any time soon. The global synthesis report noted the difficult problem of placing values on the different functions of forests and stated that in the absence of viable methods, "it is highly unlikely that it will be possible, in the near future, to make comprehensive inventories of non-wood goods and services on a global basis" (FAO 1995a, 30).[48] FAO reports weave caution even into general statements: "Forests supply many global benefits: they store carbon; maintain diverse, unique and rare forms of life; store biotic potential; and encompass natural phenomena *that have yet to be understood*" (FAO 1995a, 21; emphasis added). The FAO pointed squarely at a contradiction between the policy emphasis on deforestation in the global forest agenda and the shortage of reliable information (FAO 2001, 11).

Knowledge and Action: The Impact of Information

From Information to Knowledge: What Decision Makers Know

Interviews with policy makers and negotiators reveal that their own perceptions closely reflect the state of existing scientific knowledge. Government officials and negotiators tend to think of forests in terms of their local and national benefits and are dubious about cross-border effects of forest degradation. All of the interviewees, both advocates and skeptics of international forest policy, point out that the global roles of forests in climate change and biodiversity are uncertain. Many of them question the link between forests and climate change. The U.K.'s senior forest official for international policy commented, "Deforestation is seen as an international problem but in fact the links are not so easy to establish. . . . The connection between deforestation and carbon [emissions] still has to be confirmed and clarified."[49] Leaders of environmental NGOs also openly state: "The impacts [of deforestation] are not global; there is no threat to health and human well-being. The consequences are local and national. Both the causes and the consequences are in the locale."[50]

Most remarkably, even political actors who advocate strong international policy openly recognize existing uncertainties. Canada ardently advocates for a forest treaty, yet, when asked about the scientific knowledge about the shared consequences of deforestation, a Canadian policy maker said: "Oh, it is all speculative. To my knowledge, there is no government that tries to ascertain them."[51] Another noted, "The link between forests and climate change is somewhat weak, the knowledge is very much under construction."[52] High-level officers in international forest institutions also acknowledge gaps of knowledge. The head of the Secretariat of IFF commented, "There is a lot of mythology in [discussions of] biodiversity, a lot of fiction and few facts."[53] And the coordinator of NGO activity at forest negotiations remarked: "With forests, science is all conjecture. Both the causes and consequences of deforestation are debatable."[54]

The lack of knowledge is recognized at international meetings, where most participants in policy deliberations understand that scientific knowledge is incomplete. In its official final report, the Intergovernmental Panel on Forests notes:

> Much attention is still given to timber and forest cover, whereas other goods and services provided by forests, such as fuelwood, the sustainable use and conservation and the fair and equitable sharing of benefits of biological diversity, soil and water protection functions, and carbon sequestration and sinks, as well as other social, cultural and economic aspects, are rarely covered and need to be considered. (E/CN.17/1997/12, paragraph 80)

During discussions on forest research at sessions of the IFF, a number of delegates recognized the difficulty in evaluating nonwood goods and services such as biodiversity and recreation, and agreed on the need to strengthen research to inform policy. The group of developing countries (G-77)[55] and China called for research to develop valuation methodologies that take into account environmental, socioeconomic, ethical, and cultural considerations.[56] Suriname said that research priority should be on the functions and benefits of forests. New Zealand argued the need to develop an approach to identify both the costs and benefits of sustainable forest management, and all delegations concurred that such an approach is missing.[57]

The Impact of Information

The gaps in information about the cross-border consequences of the problem hamper international policy action in two ways. First, they deprive the issue from elements of interdependence and hamper the formation of common interests. Because the known effects of forest degradation are local, they do not justify the need for reciprocal state-to-state obligations under an international agreement. How would country A benefit from forest protection in country B (and C, D, etc.)? Answers to this question remain unsubstantiated by existing knowledge. For that reason, the utility of a treaty that would impose international obligations remains unclear.

The absence of reliable information about the transboundary consequences of deforestation has helped shape bargaining positions of states and has affected international debates at various stages. At the Rio conference, the G-77, including China, Brazil, and India, have maintained that because the problem is essentially local in nature, it is subject to national policy and legislation and not to be a matter of international obligations (Grayson and Manyard 1997, 27). The Brazilian minister of the environment, José Goldemberg, stated that Brazil saw no need for an international convention unless the uncertainty about greenhouse gas emissions was dispelled. Consequently, the text of the Forest Principles omitted references to global or regional benefits of forests. Previous references to the interests of the world community were replaced with "values to local communities" (Preamble (f)) (Kolk 1996, 156–159). Many countries continue to reject the idea of forests as a public good. Everton Vargas, principal negotiator for Brazil at IFF-4, curtly stated: "Forests are not global commons, they are national resources." Notably, no delegate objected to this statement. The U.S. delegate to the expert meeting in Ottawa, and later a negotiator at IFF-4, stated as a matter of fact that "Forests are inherently local, they are not global commons. The net effects [of deforestation] are too disaggregated."[58]

This type of shared perception helps explain the failure of treaty proponents to make a strong case for the need for a convention. In private conversations, some delegates at IFF shared the belief that "there are no serious reasons to have a forest treaty" and that "if someone comes up with a really good reason to have a treaty, we would consider it."[59] Yet, few concrete arguments for a treaty were offered. Even the most ardent proponents of a treaty acknowledge that forest issues could be handled effectively through unilateral action. When asked whether forests could be handled exclusively through national policies, a Canadian negotiator answered: "Absolutely."[60] And a coordinator of NGO initiatives stated that some countries have no reason to join a treaty because they can effectively manage their forests by themselves.[61]

An additional obstacle in international deliberations on forest policy is the existence of international treaties that are tangentially relevant to forests. Even if one argues that there are indeed negative transboundary effects on biodiversity and climate change, there are already treaties to address these two problems: the Convention on Biological Diversity and the Framework Convention on Climate Change. Because these legal instruments are tangentially relevant to forests, they dilute incentives for creating a separate forest treaty and reduce the momentum that some countries are trying to maintain. Throughout discussions at IFF-4 and at the Ottawa meeting of the Costa Rica–Canada Initiative, actors who opposed a treaty repeatedly pointed at existing treaties as potential avenues for action and used them to argue that there is no need for a separate treaty.

Second, lack of information about consequences impedes cost-benefit calculations regarding policies for forest protection. If natural water management provided by forests is important, how important is it relative to timber production? Is the maintenance of biodiversity in two hectares of forest more important than the timber that can be extracted from it? To even begin weighing such questions, decision makers must have information about consequences of deforestation, and such data must have some degree of specificity.

The severe shortage of reliable scientific information about the environmental benefits of intact forests does not permit evaluation of the benefits that can be expected from forest protection. Because the information on ecological services and other nonwood benefits from forests is lacking in precision and reliability, these benefits cannot be evaluated in relation to commercial profits from timber. The cost of policies is high due to the economic importance of activities that cause deforestation. At the same time, the benefits from such policies remain unclear. Even experienced and concerned foresters point out "a lack of clarity about which tropical forests should be saved, how much, *and for what reason*" (Westoby 1989, 167).

Moreover, even when traditional cost-benefit calculations are made possible, they appear to favor forest exploitation. As speculative as they are, the few attempts to assess the economic values of standing forests imply that logging is more profitable than preserving forests. The wood products industry is worth over $400 billion per year, with forest products trade accounting for 3 percent of all global trade in 1995 (World Resources Institute 1999, 31). The environmental and social costs of lost forests are far lower in comparison. According to one estimate sponsored by the International Institute for Sustainable Development, losing 1 percent of forests would cost $47 billion, that is, nine times lower than commercial benefits from it (Myers and Kent 2001). Given that the official rate of global deforestation is only 0.2 percent, the cost-benefit ratio would be even more strongly in favor of logging.

Cost-benefit analysis may be an extremely narrow and restrictive way to discuss forests because they have values that cannot possibly be captured in numeric terms. Their esthetic value cannot be quantified, yet it is the most important one for many people. Economists use concepts such as "existence value" and "option value" (Adger et al. 1995). Some people like to know that forests exist and are available for them to enjoy—even if they never actually go to see them nor derive any economic benefits from them (existence value). And forests may have potential uses that are yet to be discovered and applied ("option value"). These are very important, yet virtually impossible to estimate. Norms-oriented approaches are better equipped to analyze how such concerns figure in decision-making on forest management. The point here is that the lack of information makes difficult even the seemingly more tangible economic values of forests.

Conclusion

After years of research, intersessional meetings, and formal debate, there remains strong resistance to the creation of a global forest convention. Every international initiative on forests produced a last-minute agreement to keep talking. At UNCED, countries adopted nonbinding Forest Principles. The Intergovernmental Panel on Forests was renamed and continued as the IFF, which produced a recommendation to establish a permanent forum for discussion of forest issues, the UNFF. Governments agreed to disagree on key questions of finance, technology transfer, trade, and the need for a legal convention.

This state of political affairs is not surprising, given the existing scientific information and the corresponding knowledge that is shared by policy makers around the world. Information on the effects of the problem is incomplete

and does not portray the issue as one involving interdependence. The consequences of deforestation that are known with certainty are not transboundary
but local and national. Therefore, it is not known if deforestation in one country affects other countries. Few dispute that forests are important, and all
agree that action should be taken. They are not convinced, however, that coordinated policy under an international treaty would have added value. Existing knowledge on deforestation does not clearly justify the need for a system
of mutual obligations.

Several additional factors that pertain to the nature of the problem hamper
efforts to establish a treaty on forest management. For one, the socioeconomic
costs of protective policies are very high since forest utilization is a conglomeration of cross-sectoral issues that involves a number of economic and
broader social interests: commercial logging, international trade, agriculture,
food security, energy consumption, and water management. Second, because
the geographical distribution of forests is uneven, a global treaty would impose uneven obligations on states, with countries with extensive forest cover
bearing a heavier burden. In this context, concerns with relative gains and
losses become acute. Third, in some countries, states do not have full control
over forest practices since they do not own the forest resources. The respective
governments are reluctant to enter obligations under a treaty since they do
not have the authority to implement policies.

Notes

A different version of the forest case study appeared in Radoslav Dimitrov, 2004, "Lost
in the Woods: International Forest Policy." In Neil E. Harrison and Gary C. Bryner
(eds.), *Science and Politics in the International Environment*, pp. 173–202. Boulder,
Colo.: Rowman and Littlefield.

1. 2001 Stockholm Convention on Persistent Organic Pollutants. For the text of the
treaty and additional information, visit http://www.pops.int (February 11, 2005).

2. In the text of the treaty, tropical timber is defined as "non-coniferous tropical
wood for industrial uses, which grows or is produced in the countries situated between
the Tropic of Cancer and the Tropic of Capricorn" (ITTA, Article 2[1]).

3. Rob Rawson, member of the International Tropical Forest Council and Assistant-
Secretary of Agriculture, Fisheries and Forestry, Australia, Forest Industries Branch. Interviewed December 5, 1999, in Ottawa.

4. Manuel Sobral Filho, executive director of the International Tropical Timber Organization. Interviewed November 2002.

5. The text calls for compulsory environmental impact assessments of development
projects, recovery of deforested areas, and reorienting resettlement policies in forest

areas (Tarasofsky 1995, 17–19). A search on the Worldwide Web did not reveal information on the treaty.

6. An account of the forestry deliberations during the UNCED process is provided by David Humphreys (1996).

7. The full text of the Forest Principles can be found in Appendix A in the Canadian Council of International Law, *Global Forests and International Environmental Law* (London: Kluwer 1996).

8. The final text is available at http://www.un.org/documents/ecosoc/cn17/ipf/1997/ecn17ipf1997-12.htm (February 11, 2005).

9. Resolution 1997/65 of ECOSOC.

10. Final Report of CRCI, on file with the author.

11. Information on the final CRCI meeting and on IFF-4 is based on direct observation; the author was a rapporteur for the Canadian government and for the Earth Negotiation Bulletin, respectively.

12. A complete account of forest-related international negotiations, including statements by delegations, is provided by the *Earth Negotiation Bulletin* at their website at http://www.iisd.ca/process/forest_desertification_land.htm (February 11, 2005). The *Bulletin* is an excellent resource on current and recent environmental negotiations.

13. Statements and interventions by these delegations at all IFF sessions were seemingly endless reiterations of this line of argument.

14. Statements of Switzerland at IFF-4. Daily coverage of the meeting from New York can be found at http://www.iisd.ca/forestry/iff4/index.html (February 11, 2005).

15. Statement of Nigeria, official spokesman of the G-77 at IFF-4, February 11, 2000.

16. IFF and similar UN meetings are open to NGOs who are allowed to make formal statements and to attend negotiations in working groups but not to participate in them.

17. Interviews with Stuart Wilson, Forests Monitor, and Bill Mankin, Greenpeace, former Director of Global Forestry Action Project, a collaborative initiative of Sierra Club, Friends of the Earth, and the Natural Wildlife Federation.

18. Stuart Wilson, Forests Monitor, interviewed May 2004, Geneva.

19. Final Report of IFF to the UN Commission on Sustainable Development (E/CN.17/IFF/2000/14), available at http://www.un.org/esa/sustdev/ecn17iff2000-sprep.htm (October 2004).

20. The account on UNFF sessions is based on direct observation.

21. The Plan of Action and the Programme of Work are contained in E/CN.18/2001/3/Rev.1.

22. In its opening statement, the Swiss delegation at the third session of UNFF stated: "The outside world is looking with some confusion onto what is going on within the UNFF process. Presently, it is unclear whether the UNFF will indeed play its role as the director of the international forest orchestra, or whether it will simply become irrelevant."

23. Alastair Sarre, ITTO. Interviewed November 2003, in Yokohama.

24. In addition to timber production, forests are cleared for agriculture, to supply wood for household fuel, or to construct dams for flood control and hydroelectric energy production.

25. The Forest Resources Assessment (FRA) conducted every ten years by the FAO; the LANDSAT Pathfinder Tropical Deforestation Project, a collaborative research effort under the auspices of the NASA Goddard Space Flight Center, the University of New Hampshire, and the University of Maryland; and Project TREES by the Joint Research Committee of the Commission of the European Union. To learn more about the LANDSAT Pathfinder Project and access its database, you can visit http://geo.arc .nasa.gov/sge/landsat/landsat.html (February 11, 2005).

26. The LANDSAT Pathfinder Project carries out complete mapping of the areas it studies but it concentrates on only two zones of tropical forests—wet and very moist—and has only one forest class: forest cover. FAO's FRA includes all ecological zones and has ten categories of forest types, but it uses statistical sampling as a method. Thus, the LANDSAT project can be characterized as more intensive, while the FRA is more extensive and aims at detailed description and quantification of processes of land cover changes for the entire tropical areas. It also helps understand the dynamics and mechanisms of these change processes. For the above reasons, the FRA is considered the most comprehensive existing study. Abundant information about the FAO and electronic versions of the reports of its assessments can be found at http://www.fao.org/ forestry/Forestry.asp (February 11, 2005).

27. The assessment was a multilateral effort by several dozens of experts from forty-five countries who used already existing information from national governments and research institutions, supplemented with satellite imagery. Its authors pointed out that it is impossible to have a complete picture of global forest cover with the absence of a similar study on temperate forests. An earlier study of deforestation in the tropics (Myers 1980) did not offer a quantitative assessment.

28. The data for temporal and boreal forests were to be provided by the FAO/ECE Agriculture and Timber Division in Geneva, and the data for tropical and subtropical components were to be provided by the FAO Forestry Department.

29. Deforestation is defined as complete clearing of tree formations. Thinking only in terms of deforestation is simplistic since deforestation is only one of the types of changes in forest cover. Other types include forest degradation defined as decrease in density or increase of perturbation, fragmentation defined as a loss of two-thirds of original forest area, and amelioration (implying increase in forest area and/or biomass (FAO 1993, 38).

30. FRA 1990 consisted of two phases that used different methods: analysis of existing information from national inventories, and a statistical sample survey that used new multidate data from high-resolution satellite imaging. The results from the two phases of the assessment turned out to be highly consistent. The correlation coefficient of the two estimates of forest cover was 0.96, a correlation "so high to be almost identical" (FAO 1993, 78). Thus, two assessments using different methodologies arrived at highly similar measures of forest cover and forest change.

31. While assessments measure the quantity of forests, no precise estimates exist of their quality. The increase or decrease of forest area does not necessarily correspond to

qualitative changes. During the 1990s, 1.5 million hectares of natural forests were converted to plantations each year, a trend that indicates a reduction in forest quality, since plantations have lower biodiversity than natural forests (FAO 2001, 343). Although this may have implications for their ecological functions, the FAO reports that "it was not possible to make objective estimates of the extent or severity of [forest degradation] for most countries because of data limitations. Qualitative changes are reported in country reports and briefs, but it was not possible to derive globally valid statistics" (FAO 2001, 7).

32. Globally, there was a 230-percent increase in the harvested forest area between 1961 and 1990, and 265-percent increase in the volume harvested. The distinction between volume and area can be rather significant. The area harvested in Asia was only 89 percent of that in Latin America between 1986 and 1990, but the volume of logs produced annually in Asia was 3.7 times that of Latin America (FAO1995b, 30, 52–54).

33. The FRA 2000 considered a forest any area whose vegetation cover was at least 10 percent of the observable land area. In other words, when observed from above, at least 10 percent of the land is covered by forest canopy. This definition was agreed upon at a workshop in Kotka, Finland, and is now uniformly used in global assessments (Nyyssönen and Ahti 1997). The FRA 2000 was also the first study to provide a consistent methodology for assessing forest change between two assessment periods. It relied on satellite imaging as well as on surveys of countries, and used statistical random sampling (10 percent) of the world's tropical forests that was employed through 117 sample units and observation of three points in time over the twenty-year period 1980–2000 (FAO 2001).

34. Net deforestation is the difference between gross deforestation (estimated at approximately 14.6 million hectares per year) and expansion of natural forests and plantations (5.2 million hectares per year).

35. Ninety-five percent of the total forested area is natural forests and 5 percent is plantations created either through artificial afforestation or conversion of natural forests. FRA 2000 found significant increases in forest plantations and in regrowth of natural forests. There was an expansion of natural forests of 3.6 million hectares per year and deliberate afforestation of 1.6 million hectares per year. Plantations grew more than tenfold in two decades: from 17.8 million hectares in 1980 to 43.6 million in 1990 to 187 million in 2000. Today, China is the leader in plantation development, accounting for 24 percent of the global plantation area (FAO 2001, 27).

36. An expert meeting of the Costa Rica–Canada Initiative, Ottawa, Canada, December 6–10, 1999. Personal observation.

37. One example is the Vietnam War during which 1.25 million hectares were spread with defoliants, and more than 4 million hectares were damaged by shells (FAO 1982, 90).

38. Because the data for one region are on harvest area and the other on harvest volume, the two cannot be compared.

39. The use of various forest classes in FRA 1990 had made it possible to analyze causes of forest changes. For instance, since the category "short fallow" is land under subsistence agriculture, changes from closed forest to short fallow imply that the driving force behind the change is small-scale agriculture.

40. Local ownership is more common in English-speaking African countries. In French-speaking countries, forest law is based on Roman law, according to which any unoccupied land without ownership documents belongs to the state.

41. See for instance, FAO's general discussions on nonwood benefits (FAO 1997, 39–46; FAO 1995b, 18–21).

42. Canada submitted that production of maple syrup was valued at US$44.9 million in 1993 and measured 15.3 million liters in 1995 but could not provide both the quantity and the value for either year. Table 10-8 in FAO (2001, 95).

43. The average value of world trade in bamboo products is $36.2 million, and trade of morel mushrooms is worth between $50 and $60 million per year. Rattan is used in many regions of Southeast Asia for making furniture, fish traps, mats, hammocks, and brushes (FAO 2001, 81–87).

44. Evelyn Trines, Science and Technology Program, Secretariat of the Framework Convention on Climate Change. Interviewed December 10, 1999, Ottawa.

45. Evelyn Trines, interview.

46. Evelyn Trines, interview.

47. Authors of one NGO-sponsored publication noted, "Remarkably, in light of what is at stake overall, there have been scant attempts to come up with aggregate evaluations of forest outputs" (Myers and Kent 2001, 184).

48. The absence of suitable methods is evident also in the following statement: "The forestry community has a responsibility to supply policymakers, planners, managers and others . . . with the information they need for rational decision-making, and this comprises more and more elements that cannot be obtained by traditional forest inventory methods. The challenge is to devise and put into operational [*sic*] new methods to gather such information" (Myers and Kent 2001, 31).

49. Mike Dudley, head of International Division, United Kingdom Forestry Commission. Interviewed December 10, 1999, Ottawa.

50. William Mankin, director of Global Forestry Action Project, a collaborative initiative of Sierra Club, Friends of the Earth, and the Natural Wildlife Federation (interviewed December 9, 1999) and Stuart Wilson, Forests Monitor, interviewed February 2, 2000, New York.

51. Mike Fullerton, Canadian Forest Service, Division for International Affairs. Interviewed December 9, 1999, Ottawa.

52. Richard Ballhorn, head of the Canadian delegation at IFF-4. Interviewed December 10, 1999, Ottawa. Decision makers from Finland, France, the United States, and the United Kingdom stated similar views.

53. Jag Maini, head of the Secretariat of the Intergovernmental Forum on Forests. Interviewed December 9, 1999, Ottawa.

54. Mankin, interview.

55. Approximately 120 countries are members of the G-77. They usually make joint statements at UN conferences and negotiate as a coalition.

56. Joint statement at the second session of the IFF, in Geneva, Switzerland, from August 24–September 4, 1998.

57. Statement by New Zealand at the third session of IFF, in Geneva, Switzerland.

58. Jan MacAlpine, senior forest officer, U.S. State Department, Office of Ecology and Terrestrial Conservation. Interviewed December 11, 1999, Ottawa.

59. Rob Rawson, co-chair of the International Tropical Forest Council and assistant secretary of Agriculture, Fisheries and Forestry, Australia. Interviewed December 5, 1999, Ottawa.

60. Michael Fullerton, interview. Ironically, he reasoned, "For an issue to trigger an international (policy) response, there have to be global dimensions, there has to be a problem that is shared . . . common impacts. . . . Forests don't affect everyone in the same sense."

61. Mankin, interview.

6

At Sea: International
Coral Reef Management

The broader ecological consequences of reducing biodiversity remain essentially uninvestigated for coral reefs.

—Nancy Knowlton, prominent coral reefs scientist

THE "TROPICAL FORESTS OF THE SEA," as coral reefs are sometimes referred to, are the ecosystems richest in biological diversity and are considered a focal point of interaction between marine ecology and coastal socioeconomics. Beginning in the 1980s, coral biologists, scuba divers, and environmentalists have increasingly raised concerns over the plight of coral reefs, and in policy circles and scientific communities today it is commonly recognized that corals are being degraded by land-based water pollution, mining, destructive fishing practices, and climate change. According to a recent global assessment, 20 percent of the world's coral reefs have been destroyed (GCRMN 2004). In the mid-1990s, a number of unilateral, bilateral, and multilateral state initiatives were established to address this problem. Yet, despite symbolic gestures such as declaring 1997 as the International Year of the Reef, states are unwilling to introduce a formal policy agreement on coral reef management.

Given claims about the global importance of coral reefs and numerous appeals for remedial policy action, why is an international treaty for reef management absent from the global political agenda? Coral reef decline is not the only ecological problem that is left ignored by international law, but the absence of a legal regime on reefs is particularly puzzling for several reasons.

First, there are no interest groups who oppose remedial policy action.[1] On the contrary, businesses such as pharmaceutical companies and tourist ventures have vested interests in reef preservation, and one would expect them to be active proponents of regulation.

Second, policy options for reef preservation have been described as win-win situations since measures to protect reefs bring additional benefits such as promotion of tourism, reduced water pollution, and health benefits from improved sewage systems (Bryant et al. 1998, 5; GCRMN 2000).

Third, the major superpower, the United States, has taken the political leadership and has been supported by other influential states such as France and Japan in establishing an International Coral Reef Initiative (ICRI). The supportive involvement of powerful state actors is yet another condition that should facilitate progress in international policy and yet there is no policy coordination.

Fourth, the small number of state parties involved should make it easier to reach a formal agreement. Nearly one hundred countries have coral reefs, but over half of all coral reefs are under the jurisdiction of six states: Australia, Fiji, Indonesia, the Maldives, Papua New Guinea, and the Philippines. Indonesia and Australia combined possess 35 percent of reefs (Hempel and Morozova 1999; Spalding et al. 2001).

Finally, it should not be difficult to gain popular support for reef preservation since reefs are charismatic and their degradation is not an obscure problem known only to scientists. Strong political leadership, the absence of opposition, the presence of supporting business interests and public appeal, and the small number of actors involved are all favorable factors that make it particularly puzzling why there is no formal state agreement on policies to alleviate coral reef degradation.

Existing knowledge-based theoretical approaches to the study of international policy are not well equipped to handle coral reef politics. An analysis that focuses on the role of epistemic communities of experts would be thwarted here because scientists are actively engaged in the main political forum for discussions, natural scientific research is extensive, and this input is well institutionalized (Hatziolos et al. 1998). In fact, research is the main substantive activity handled at the international level, and scientists are the largest and most visible group at international meetings of ICRI. Hence, the absence of international policy on coral reefs cannot be explained through the lens of the epistemic communities literature with the absence of mobilization of experts. However, it is useful to focus instead on the *content* of scientific knowledge and to pay attention to the absence of particular types of information.

The remainder of the article is organized in four sections. A brief primer on coral organisms is followed by an overview of international political initiatives related to coral reef issues. The third section presents an inventory of existing research-derived information on the extent, causes and consequences of coral reef degradation. Finally, I consider alternative theoretical approaches, and show that neither the distribution of power, nor economic considerations, nor epistemic communities can adequately explain the case. I offer a modified knowledge-based explanation for the absence of an international coral reef treaty. The main argument advanced here is that the information base is too weak to support an international legal regime. In particular, knowledge about the transboundary effects of the problem is virtually nonexistent and could not justify the need for international obligations.

The Problem: A Primer on Coral Reefs

Corals are living organisms, tiny polyps that concatenate and form colonies of thousands. Apart from soft corals, there are 835 known species of hard corals that form calcium carbonate skeletons. The concretion of vast numbers of these skeletons results in rock-like physical structures called coral reefs that can extend hundreds of miles (Veron 1995; Knowlton 2001). Many reefs are about 8,000 years old (Wilkinson and Salvat 1998) and some are as much as 2.5 million years old (Bryant et al. 1998, 5). Their labyrinthine structures provide habitat for a vast number of marine organisms, including many fish species. Coral reef ecosystems have the largest biodiversity per unit of area on Earth. Although only 93,000 coral reef species have been catalogued, one scientist estimates there are at least 950,000 and possibly up to nine million. In comparison, tropical forests, the second richest in biodiversity of ecosystems, have two million species but occupy an area twenty times larger than that of reefs (Reakla-Kudla 1997, 93–94).

No definition of a reef is universally accepted across disciplines. Among biologists, the most widespread definition is a rigid, wave-resistant framework constructed by large skeletal organisms (Wood 1999, 4). Corals are not to be equated with reefs, since living coral organisms can be found in a broad range of habitats other than reefs; at the same time, some reefs are built by other organisms, including calcifying algae. Reefs can be found in a wide variety of settings: in tropical, temperate, and even Arctic waters, at depths sometimes greater than thirty meters (Wood 1999, 3-7). *Coral* reefs are a narrower category, communities of stony coral species that develop in clear tropical and subtropical waters.

Coral organisms form a symbiosis with various algae that cover them, provide them with nutrients, and give them the bright colors for which they are known. While corals themselves are relatively resilient, the algae on them are sensitive to environmental conditions such as the water temperature and transparency. In climate-related bleaching, corals expel most of the algae, and thus lose their own supply of nutrients. However, they can survive without algae for several weeks and usually the remaining algae can repopulate the coral later on and restore its color (Keith 2000; Knowlton 2001).

Corals reefs have come under increasing stresses that contribute to their degradation.[2] At the same time, they are highly dynamic ecosystems that can effectively respond to considerable fluctuations in their environmental conditions. They are subjected to daily, seasonal, and annual and interannual variations of natural origin such as El Nino, an oscillation of the ocean-atmospheric dynamics that occurs in the tropical Pacific every three to five years (Wood 1999, 139–142). Hurricanes, too, can inflict catastrophic damage to reefs and the recovery takes between five and forty years (Scoffin, cited in Wood 1999, 142). Furthermore, constant disturbance is believed to be necessary for reef growth and for the functioning of coral reef communities. While scientists agree that coral reefs show a "formidable array of acclimatization processes" (Wood 1999, 164), they also point out that at present reefs are under human-induced environmental stress that is potentially disastrous.

International Policy (In)Action

Although problems have been known for decades, there is little coordinated policy action to protect coral reefs. Concerns over the conditions of coral ecosystems have been expressed in various international forums, in the context of the Convention on Biological Diversity, the Framework Convention on Climate Change, the Convention on International Trade of Endangered Species, and the Global Conference on Sustainable Development of Small Island Developing States.[3] Discussions in such institutional settings have not led to collective remedial policy action. As one observer noted: "I prefer to use an analogy of a patient visiting his doctors and being told through increasingly sophisticated diagnosis that the condition is bad and getting worse, without any treatment procedures being implemented" (Kenchington 1998, 12). Some 660 marine protected areas contain coral reefs, but more than 150 of them are less than a square kilometer in size, and many are "paper parks" that exist only in theory (Bryant et al. 1998, 44; Spalding et al. 2001). Dissatisfied with short-age of governance, concerned stakeholders continue to trumpet calls for action such as the 2004 Okinawa Declaration in which participants of the 10th International Coral Reef Symposium "declare in the strongest terms that additional destruction of coral reefs must be avoided and more effort is necessary to prevent further reef demise. Conservation and restoration of coral reefs should be made without delay in each nation acting individually and in concert through closer international cooperation."

The most significant policy development at the global level is the ICRI, which grew out of concerns expressed at a conference of small island states in Barbados in 1993.[4] The United States took the leadership in a process that quickly drew in Australia, France, Jamaica, Japan, the Philippines, Sweden, and the United Kingdom, and the U.S. Department of State hosted the first Secretariat of the initiative. ICRI is a loose partnership of governments, international development banks, NGOs, scientists, and the private sector. It has involved representatives of eighty governments, as well as international organizations such as the World Bank, UNEP, UNDP, UNESCO, and the International Union for the Conservation of Nature (IUCN) (Kenchington 1998).

ICRI is neither an international governance structure nor a policymaking body. Its expressly defined goal is to identify and promote needed action without directly engaging in policymaking. This loose institution is an informal network of interested parties, an open forum for like-minded political actors to discuss coral reef issues, share information, promote research, identify priorities, and facilitate policy action. The initiative does not have a permanent bureaucratic structure or organization and does not engage in action: it neither formulates, nor funds, nor implements policy. It only encourages stockholders to establish projects at the local community level by sharing information on the health of reefs, by increasing political support, and through capacity building (GCRMN 2004). In summary, ICRI is an arrangement that is meant to serve as a temporary catalyst for action.

Officials that run ICRI see it as "an advocacy group"; it is deliberately intended as an informal arrangement, and most governments want to keep it that way (Kenchington, personal communication). From time to time, there have been discussions on whether to formalize the initiative, but members have unanimously preferred to stay with a flexible and informal mechanism rather than engage in the burdensome task of making institutional and financial arrangements. The logic behind this is that ICRI would be more effective in influencing national governments and relevant international institutions if it is a flexible informal mechanism instead of a competing agency.[5] France is the only country that has a preference for a more bureaucratized structure, but they too want it to be nonbinding (Wilkinson, personal communication; Colwell, personal communication).[6]

The first activity under ICRI was a four-day international workshop that took place in 1995 in Dumaguete City, the Philippines, and involved participants from forty-four nations, intergovernmental organizations, NGOs, the science community, and the private sector. The conference produced two documents. One was a "Call for Action," which recognized that coral reefs are in serious decline due to human activities and urged actors to focus on coastal management, research and monitoring, and capacity-building. The second document was a "Framework for Action," which outlined activities that governments could undertake to mitigate the plight of coral reefs.[7] ICRI's main policy recommendations pertained to integrated coastal management, education, strong environmental laws, ecologically sound land-use practices, sustainable fisheries management, and developing a network of marine protected areas. The next phase comprised six regional workshops in the Caribbean, East African seas, South Asian seas, East Asian seas, the Western Indian Ocean, and the Pacific region. The express purpose of these workshops was to translate the global Framework for Action into agendas for regional action. The coordinating role was passed from the United States to Australia in 1996, the ICRI Secretariat moved to France in 1998, and was jointly run by Sweden and the Philippines between 2001 and 2003 and by the United Kingdom and the Seychelles between July 2003 and June 2005.[8]

Much of the current international agenda on coral reefs consists of generating scientific information. In response to the perceived shortage of data, ICRI partners established the Global Coral Reef Monitoring Network (GCRMN) to provide an information base for further discussion. The monitoring network has been the main operational unit and key component of ICRI, intended to monitor reef conditions and provide the necessary data for effective reef management (Wilkinson and Salvat 1998, 17). A second unit is the ICRI Network whose purpose is to facilitate the flow of scientific information to decision makers. Finally, ICRI established the International Coral Reef Action Network (ICRAN) whose mandate is to assist in capacity building for reef management in developing countries. ICRAN was funded in March 2001 with $5 million by the UN Foundation to establish demonstration conservation sites (Wilkinson, personal communication, August 2001). Thus, ICRI activities focus on the generation and dissemination of expert information.

Scientific Knowledge on Coral Reefs

Local-scale research on coral reefs began in the 1960s, but concerted documentation of their global decline began in earnest only in the mid-1990s. Scientists conducting research on coral species have networked through the International Coral Reef Symposium that has met every four years since 1969 and has served as a focal point for exchanging and releasing information on coral reefs. Yet, no large-scale studies were conducted, and various review documents in the mid-1990s indicated that comprehensive knowledge on the health and values of coral reefs was virtually absent ("Strategic Plan"; Bryant et al. 1998). A meeting of scientists and managers held in Miami in 1993 considered isolated stories of problems with reefs but acknowledged that there was insufficient data to draw conclusions about regional or global patterns (GCRMN 1998; Wilkinson and Salvat 1998, 17). In 1993, the International Center for Living Aquatic Resources Management and the World Conservation Monitoring Centre (WCMC) established a global database on coral reefs called ReefBase. In 1996, WCMC published the first global map of shallow reefs (Bryant et al. 1998, 5), and, together with UNEP, produced the World Atlas of Coral Reefs in 2001.

Before 1998, the only information on the global status of reefs was a widely cited estimate "based on guesswork by a number of scientists and on anecdotal evidence" (Bryant et al. 1998, 7) that 10 percent of reefs were dead, and that another 30 percent were likely to die within ten to twenty years (Wilkinson 1993).[9] In response to the need for data, in 1996 the Intergovernmental Oceanographic Commission (IOC), the UNEP, the World Bank, and IUCN formed a partnership to establish a Global Coral Reef Monitoring Network. Its goal is to collect, synthesize, and disseminate information on coral reef health, and to help communities and states build research capacity for coral assessment (Strategic Plan). The GCRMN employs hundreds of researchers and formed a partnership in 1998 with Reef Check, a network of 5,000 volunteers whom scientists train in monitoring and assessment techniques (Wilkinson, personal communication). The results are then fed into ReefBase, the most comprehensive database on coral reef distribution, conditions, and vulnerabilities. The research coordinators draw data from seventeen operational nodes in six regions[10] and incorporate it in biannual global reports.[11]

The first global assessments of coral reefs appeared in 1998. Coincidentally, three separate reports were released that year: GCRMN's first report, *Status of Coral Reefs of the World: 1998* (GCRMN 1998); a joint report by the World Resources Institute (WRI) and UNEP called *Reefs at Risk* (Bryant et al. 1998); and a report from a multilateral study on coral reefs and climate change, conducted by a working group of the International Geosphere-Biosphere Programme (IGBP) and the NOAA Coastal Ocean Program (IGBP/NOAA 1998). What are the products of these research activities and what are scientists able to tell us about the extent, causes, and consequences of coral reef degradation around the world?

Sector I: Extent of Coral Reef Degradation

At this early stage of multilateral scientific research, estimates of the extent of the coral reef degradation fluctuate considerably. WRI/UNEP's *Reefs at Risk* did not contribute information on actual reef conditions and was quick to indicate that, "We still lack comprehensive estimates regarding the status of, and the magnitude of threats to, these aquatic ecosystems" (Bryant et al. 1998, 7). The study drew on fourteen databases on human settlements, development, and population, and used a model to estimate potential, rather than actual, threats to coral reefs. Its authors reiterated that, "Our results serve as an indicator of the threats to these ecosystems, not as an actual measure of degradation. Scientists do not know the actual condition of the vast majority of the world's reefs" (Bryant et al. 1998, 7).

The report submitted that 58 percent of reefs worldwide are potentially threatened by human activities. The Pacific Ocean that contains one-fourth of all mapped reefs was characterized as the least threatened, while 80 percent of reefs in Southeast Asian waters were estimated to be at high or medium risk (Bryant et al. 1998, 6, 20, 22). The authors noted that in some cases reefs mapped as at risk are in fact relatively healthy, while in other cases the indicator underestimates actual degradation (p. 19). In conclusion, the report stated that, "Scientists and managers have only rudimentary, incomplete data on the status and health of coral reef ecosystems. For example, we still lack a complete global map depicting reef location, and the vast majority of coral reefs are unassessed" (p. 38).

The first global assessment of actual reef conditions was GCRMN's first report, *Status of Coral Reefs of the World: 1998*. It drew data from three hundred sites and was considered to be the first reliable estimate of global reef conditions. Interestingly, instead of ringing an alarm bell, it sounded fairly optimistic notes. In the executive summary, the authors announced that "most of the world's reef corals are in good or excellent condition, because they are either remote from human populations, or are under good management." According to the report, only 10 percent of reefs had been severely degraded. Reefs were found to be healthy in most areas: in the Red and Arabian Seas; off the coasts of Australia, including the Great Barrier Reef; in large parts of the Indian Ocean; and in 9 percent of the Southwestern and Eastern Pacific Oceans, as well as the Caribbean reefs that are richest in biodiversity.

Furthermore, the GCRMN report indicated that already damaged reefs have high chances of recovery: "Fortunately most reefs have high capacity for recovery, and if pressures are reduced or removed, many damaged reefs will rebound to a healthy status." The report was alarmist about a bleaching of coral reefs in 1997–1998, particularly in parts of the Indian Ocean, but stated that many of the reefs recovered within one or two months and that "full recovery is the norm." The document also noted that large parts have remained unaffected, and that "patterns are unclear, with many exceptions."[12] Today, approximately 40 percent of the reefs that were seriously damaged by the 1998 bleaching have either recovered or are recovering well (GCRMN 2004). Such findings are in line with results of the IGBP/NOAA study that concluded that corals have a variety of robust adaptive mechanisms that gives them long-term resilience in coping with stresses.

Estimates of the extent of reef decline vacillate: only two years later, GCRMN's second report took a much more pessimistic tone. *Status of Coral Reefs of the World: 2000* concluded that 27 percent of the world's reefs were lost, that in 1998 alone 16 percent were destroyed, and that "probably half of those will never adequately recover." It also made predictions that 40 percent of reefs will be lost by 2010 and another 20 percent twenty years after that. According to the most recent global report, 20 percent of the world's coral reefs have been destroyed and another 24 percent are under imminent risk of collapse under human pressures (GCRMN 2004). Such results contrast with the relatively optimistic conclusions drawn a few years earlier. Furthermore, now the regional picture differed from the previous report: whereas in 1998 the plight of corals was said to be the worst in Southeast Asia, in 2000 the problem was said to be most severe in the Middle East, where 35 percent were reported lost with a low chance of recovery, and in the wider Indian Ocean that lost 59 percent of reefs. Southeast Asian reefs were still "probably under the greatest threats from human activities," but in term of actual degradation the report had shifted the emphasis to other regions. The GCRMN reports pointed out that more monitoring and greater coordination of assessment efforts are needed.

Two problems hamper efforts to quantify the extent of coral decline: difficulties with data collection and incomplete understanding of coral adaptation. The shortage of reliable data is conditioned by shortage of funding. Detailed assessment of reefs can be made using aerial photography or sensors mounted on ships, boats, or submersibles, but all of these methods are very expensive. It costs around $10,000 to operate a research vessel for a day (Bryant et al. 1998, 40). Existing satellite imagery can be used at low additional cost but is not of sufficient detail, and the resulting mapping is rather coarse. For these reasons, the main sources of information are scuba divers. However, the number of scuba diving scientists is small, and the sampling approaches vary across regions and over time, thus limiting the comparability of results. This is why GCRMN formed a partnership with the volunteer-based monitoring program Reef Check and focuses its efforts on training scuba divers in data collection (GCRMN 1998).

Apart from difficulties in collecting data, limited ability of modern science to study highly complex systems prevents it from drawing firm conclusions about eventual reef responses to anthropogenic stress. The IGBP/NOAA (1998) report, *Coral Reefs and Global Change*, noted fundamental uncertainties and stated in its conclusion that "inadequate understanding of [corals' adaptation] and of the critically important calcification mechanisms, severely limits our ability to predict and manage the future of reef systems."

GCRMN's *Status of Coral Reefs: 2000* also indicated that the degree of eventual destruction is uncertain and that the results are not conclusive because reefs may recover, but how much recovery would occur was uncertain. "It remains unclear whether coral reefs as we know them will succumb to global warming because coral-algal symbioses do have some capacity to increase their ability to withstand stresses such as high temperatures" (Knowlton 2001, 5420). One global assessment referred to corals as "generally self-repairing systems" but stated that "It will be several years before we can state that reefs will recover, or whether there will be local loss of species"(GCRMN 2000).

Sector II: Causes of Coral Reef Decline

The scientific knowledge on the causes of the problem could be evaluated as moderately sufficient. Scientists involved in coral research share a general consensus on a cluster of factors that contribute to coral reef decline (Knowlton 2001). At the same time, the relative contributions of the particular causes remain undetermined. Different scientific assessments give conflicting rankings of the causes of reef degradation, with a general shift away from local causes and toward regional and global factors.

The factors behind coral reef decline can be grouped in three categories: natural, indirect human, and direct human causes. Coral reefs can be damaged by severe natural stresses such as hurricanes, typhoons, underwater earthquakes, seabed volcanoes, disease, and pest outbreaks. Corals recover from such natural damage within ten to twenty years (Wilkinson and Salvat 1998, 16–17). Reports speculate that different stresses act synergistically, with human factors exacerbating the effect of natural factors in reef degradation, but here, too, the evidence is said to be "anecdotal" (Bryant et al. 1998, 15). Second, there are quasi-natural causes behind which human influence could be at least speculated. These include: changing ocean chemistry, global warming, sea level rise, and increased ultraviolet radiation resulting from ozone depletion. Until 2000, these causes did not receive much attention either.

All multilateral scientific assessments focus on the third category of causes: direct human, or anthropogenic, factors. Those causes occur on a relatively small scale and have minor to moderate impact, but because they are widespread, chronic, and persistent, they lead to the steady decline in the health and distribution of corals (Wilkinson and Salvat 1998, 17). *Reefs at Risk* considers four such categories of human causes: coastal development, overexploitation, inland pollution and erosion, and marine-based pollution. Coastal development involves coral reef mining for construction materials, anchoring, the dredging of harbors, and construction in shallow waters, all of which directly destroy reefs. People in local communities break off corals with crowbars and use them as construction material: they grind them to produce lime to be used as plaster or to mix with cement to reduce the construction costs (Cesar 1998, 166). The government of the Maldive Islands ordered large areas of coral reefs to be destroyed and used to build coastal defenses against rising sea levels (McWilliam 1997).

"Overexploitation" includes destructive fishing practices such as blast fishing. In many areas of the world, fishermen detonate small bombs in shallow reefs in order to kill entire schools of fish. The bombs are made of dynamite or artificial fertilizer, and the blasts shatter corals and other organisms (Cesar 1998, 166). Another destructive practice is "poison fishing," a method of capturing food and aquarium fish in which fishermen dive with *hookah* tubes attached to air compressors on boats and squirt cyanide from bottles into coral formations in order to stun the fish residing in them. In the process, the poison may kill corals. According to one estimate, Filipino fishermen squirt 125,000 tons of cyanide per year into their reefs to meet the high market demand for live fish (McWilliam 1997, 18). In North America and Europe, some aquarium species bring up to $350 per individual, while in Southeast Asia restaurant consumers are ready to pay up to $300 per plate for certain rare reef-dwelling fish such as Napoleon wrasse and certain kinds of groupers (Barber and Platt 1998, 39, 49).

This high demand stimulates cyanide fishing in countries such as Indonesia (accounting for 50 percent), Fiji, the Maldives, Papua New Guinea, the Philippines, Vietnam, and other countries of Southeast Asia, and the Indian and the Pacific Oceans. The total supplies of reef fish are estimated to be 20,000 to 25,000 metric tons per year, valued at $200 million per year (Barber and Platt, 1998, 40; Cesar 1998, 165). The use of cyanide has been made illegal in virtually every country of the Indo-Pacific region, but lax enforcement renders the measures impotent (Barber and Platt 1998, 41). *Reefs at Risk*, however, downplays the role of poison fishing, noting that it is not a widespread threat and that it is based on anecdotal evidence (Bryant et al. 1998, 12, 15).

Water pollution from various land sources is another major cause of reef decline. Because corals are dependent on light, any change in the clarity of water affects them. Cutting trees destabilizes soils and releases sediments that flow into rivers and then into the coastal seas, block sunlight, and affect the health of corals. So do industrial toxic effluents, hot-water discharges from power plants, and mine runoff. Finally, nutrient pollution from sewage releases and agricultural runoff stimulates algae growth either on the reefs or as plankton in the waters above. As a result, corals are both shaded and outcompeted. Thus, siltation, toxic and nutrient pollution all act to contribute to the decline of coral reefs (Cesar 1998, 163–164). In addition, marine pollution from passing ships poses "an unknown, but probably less significant, threat to coral reefs" (Bryant et al. 1998, 14).

Although the overall list of causes is well known, the relative role of individual factors is less clear. "In many cases it is difficult to pinpoint the exact causes of coral reef declines now occurring around the world" (Bryant et al. 1998, 15). And as scientific understanding of the processes of coral reef degradation evolves, multilateral reports give somewhat conflicting information on particular causes of the problem. There is a general shift of attention from local causes such as eutrophication[13] to larger-scale causes such as global warming (Knowlton, personal communication). A report of the Global Task Team on the Implications of Climate Change on Coral Reefs, established in 1992 by UNEP, IOC, and IUCN, stated that the main threats to reefs are directly anthropogenic, while climate change poses only remote long-term risks (Wilkinson and Buddemeier 1996). *Reefs at Risk* did not consider at all natural threats and maintains that the main human threats to reefs are coastal development and overexploitation.[14] Another report, released in 1998, confirmed that the primary threats to reefs are local and regional anthropogenic stresses but submitted that the effects of global climate change are not negligible as previously thought (IGBP/NOAA 1998).[15] GCRMN's *Status 1998* downplayed the role of climate change and coral bleaching, but only two years later, *Status 2000* recognized the sharp turn in knowledge about causes of coral decline, and explicitly stated that climate change should be of primary concern. "Assessments to late 2000 are that 27 percent of the world's reefs have been effectively lost, with the largest single cause being the massive climate-related coral bleaching event of 1998." In subsequent reports from multilateral assessments, climate change as a cause of degradation is given a prominent place (GCRMN 2002; 2004).

In sum, knowledge on the causes of the problem is evolving rapidly and the information vacillates significantly. Judging from official reports, scientists seem to change their minds frequently. In the late 1990s, the prevalent views shifted to coral bleaching and climate change as the main concerns. It is necessary to point out that coral bleaching can occur for various reasons, including some that are not related to climate change. Bleaching occurs when the algae that provide coral polyps with nutrients are expelled from coral tissues. This breakdown of the symbiosis between corals and algae can be a result of very different types of stress: pollution, changes in water temperature, salinity, and possibly ultraviolet light (Bryant et al. 1998, 14). Hence, even though the scientific attention appears to be narrowing on coral bleaching as the main threat, a considerable multiplicity of causes remain. Nevertheless, there is no evidence of scientific controversy over the overall set of factors that are believed to cause coral degradation.

Sector III: Consequences of Coral Reef Decline

An astounding characteristic of coral reef research is the virtually complete absence of information on the consequences of coral reef degradation. The multilateral scientific assessments conducted by GCRMN are mute on the socioeconomic and ecological impact of the problem. Not only is such information missing from these reports, but there is no apparent research effort to study this aspect of the problem. The composition of the GCRMN is indicative in this respect: it involves many natural scientists but not social scientists to provide economic analysis of various scenarios for coral reef use. As its coordinator readily acknowledges, GCRMN focuses *exclusively* on the extent and causes of coral decline and never sought to provide information about the consequences of these problems for human communities (Wilkinson, personal communication, November 2, 2000).

There is only one study on the socioeconomic values of reefs. It estimated the value of Indonesian reefs at $121,000 per square kilometer and suggested that when fishery, tourism, and protection values of reefs are considered, the cost of destroying one square kilometer of coral reefs in Indonesia range from $137,000 to $1.2 million over a twenty-five-year period (Cesar 1996, 10). According to the coordinator of the GCRMN, this is the only existing study of benefits from reefs that implicitly addresses consequences of coral reef degradation (Wilkinson, personal communication, Nov. 2, 2000). This study is on a single country and is not incorporated into a multilateral assessment of coral reefs. Moreover, its author pointed out elsewhere that: "Some of the most important values of coral reefs, such as those to future generations and intrinsic values, cannot be quantified" (Cesar 1998, 164).

This is not to say that coral reef degradation is not a problem. Articles in popular magazines and political statements regularly make references to the important roles of coral reefs, implying grave consequences of coral decline. Scientists and activists habitually remark that coral reefs are the most diverse ecosystem in terms of gene pool, that they protect coasts from wave erosion, and that they support profitable tourism and sustain livelihoods of local communities who derive much of their protein intake from reef fish. According to one estimate, global coral reefs provide $375 billion worth of resources and services each year (Costanza et al. 1997, 256). They provide a barrier against waves and protect agricultural land, coastal dwellings, tourist beaches, and infrastructure from beach erosion. Some hotels pay as much as $100,000 per year to fight beach erosion (Cesar 1998, 166). In addition, frequent remarks are made on the potential to develop pharmaceutical products from coral or coral-related species.

But the point here is that there is very little scientific information about the consequences of coral reef decline and it is not included in multilateral assessments. There are two problems with this type of knowledge. First and foremost, GCRMN assessments are entirely void of any specific estimates of the ecological and socioeconomic values of reefs and of the corresponding impact of their decline. Only one global report attempts to address the effects of coral reef degradation, only to explicitly acknowledge the paucity of such data. With regard to biodiversity, *Reefs at Risk* only submits that information is missing: "Experts have barely begun to catalog the total number of species found within [reef] habitats" and even the roughest of estimates vary (Bryant et al. 1998, 8). No inventories of biodiversity have been made and the value, risk of loss, and even the amount of coral reef biodiversity have received little attention by scientists (Reakla-Kudla 1997, 84). "We don't know what risk of extinction is associated with reduction of reef area—we have no idea" (Knowlton, personal communication). "The broader ecological consequences of reducing biodiversity remain essentially uninvestigated for coral reefs" (Knowlton 2001, 5419).

Second, existing scientifically derived information does not seem to support popular claims about the consequences of reef decline. In particular, the destruction of coral reefs may not have the implications for biodiversity that are often assumed. Many species that dwell in reefs are not restricted to coral reefs and can occupy other habitats since "there is enormous ecological redundancy of species in reefs, i.e., many species can occupy a broadly similar niche" (Wood 1999, 10). Most reef-dwelling fish species, for instance, have ranges that extend outside the boundaries of reefs. "Should this be a general pattern, which seems likely, then even elimination of most coral reef habitats would probably not result in the extinction of a comparable proportion of coral reef builders and dwellers" (Knowlton 2001, 5423). Hence, even if we concede that the loss of marine species would have considerable negative impact, we still do not know how much biodiversity will be lost with the degradation of coral reefs.

Proponents of coral reef conservation often point out that reefs provide habitats to a large number of species, some of which could be of potential value for the production of pharmaceutical products. The medicinal value of coral species, however, remains in the realm of conjecture. There are two problems here. First, "the [pharmaceutical] potential has only barely been explored" and is presented in tentative terms: "Many families of organisms in [coral reefs] are *likely* to have species with chemical compounds of *potential* pharmaceutical value" (Adey 1998, 74; emphasis added). Second, even if future research shows that certain species that reside in reefs can be used to develop important drugs, the exact role of corals is unclear. If reefs are destroyed, the resident species may not disappear since they could survive in other habitats. Thus, based on the available information, the value of coral reefs to human health is unclear and does not provide compelling reasons for protecting them.

Similarly, the contribution of coral reefs to tourism is often lauded but rarely quantified. To take one example, the tourism industry in the Caribbean is valued at $8.9 billion in 1990 (Jameson et al. 1995, 24); yet, it is not clear what portion of this is attributable to coral reefs and how their degradation would subtract from tourist attraction. It is worth noting, however, that tourist companies and developers have not been active political lobbyists in coral reef politics (Colwell, personal communication).

Evaluating Scientific Knowledge on Coral Reefs

Despite the impressive array of research activities in which thousands of scientists are involved, existing knowledge on all three aspects of coral reef degradation is characterized with considerable uncertainty. Executive summaries of the most comprehensive multilateral scientific assessments explicitly state that the resulting global reports "contain much anecdotal information and assessments from experts, rather than sound monitoring data" (GCRMN 2002, 17). Although researchers and activists have a clear feeling that coral reefs are facing decline that is at least in part driven by human activities and that will have undesirable consequences, the science of corals has not progressed enough to provide either details or reliable data about coral responses to stress, their prospects of adaptation, or the ecological and social impact of reef degradation. While some of these gaps are due to shortage of funding and could be filled with more monitoring, other gaps exist due to fundamental limits to scientific understanding that could not be resolved in the short term. As the IGBP/NOAA report (1998) concluded:

> Long-standing lack of knowledge about the mechanisms of calcification, the nature of symbioses, the physiology of acclimatization, reproductive biology, . . . the nature and extent of biodiversity, and the long-term ecological structures and dynamics of coral reef communities hinder our ability to make decisions and useful predictions that address the issues raised by our rapidly developing understanding of large-scale processes.[16]

The transboundary effects of coral reef degradation are what we know least about. The collective research effort is seriously truncated in this important respect: it does not probe into the consequences of reef decline. By far, most research concentrates on monitoring and identifying reef conditions.

> Most available data collection is focused on the biological and physical dimensions of reefs: species found within these ecosystems, the location of these habitats, degree of degradation, etc. Socioeconomic and political information . . . that can be used to quantify the direct and indirect values derived from coral reef

ecosystems is important input for weighing development and management options. Collection of such policy-relevant data should be priority in future monitoring and assessment efforts. (Bryant et al. 1998, 39)

No one disputes the utter absence of socioeconomic information on the consequences of the problem. There are lingering debates among scientists about the existing state of knowledge but they concern only data on the extent and causes of coral decline. Some argue that there are major gaps in basic knowledge about coral reef ecosystems. Nancy Knowlton of the Smithsonian Tropical Research Institute argues that "many crucial pieces of information are missing," because biologists cannot reliably tell one coral species from another or calculate the densities needed for successful reproduction (Knowlton 1998, 183, 186). Even people on the opposite side of the fence, who maintain that knowledge from the natural sciences is sufficient, acknowledge that socioeconomic information is missing. "Calls that not enough is known about the biology and geology of coral reefs to manage them are false. . . . We lack economic, political and legal advice and expertise on the ground and where decisions are made to integrate knowledge and experience from the other disciplines" (Wilkinson and Salvat 1998, 19).

Explaining International Coral Reef Politics

Explanations of political processes and outcomes commonly used in the study of international relations cannot adequately capture the story of coral reef politics. Neo-Marxist perspectives that focus on the role of corporate actors would be amiss here because no business group has opposed policies for protection of coral reefs. The case could be made that companies that are against policies to combat climate change also account indirectly for the failure to protect corals from bleaching. Yet, climate-related bleaching is only one of the many causes of coral decline, and much could be done to address these other causes. In this respect, no group from any economic sector has gone up against proposals to manage coral reefs in a sustainable fashion. Therefore, we cannot account for the absence of international policy by referring to corporate interests.

Realist approaches that emphasize the role of powerful states would not fare well either. The absence of a binding international agreement on reefs cannot be explained with either resistance by a powerful state or by lack of political support from key states. On the contrary, the United States took the political and entrepreneurial leadership on coral reef initiatives, established ICRI, and has engaged in ambitious national policies to preserve the coral reefs under its own jurisdiction. Other wealthy states such as Australia, France, and Sweden are actively involved in ICRI and have helped sustain the initiative through financial and institutional support. However, no state has even suggested a preference for a legal treaty; rich and poor, strong and weak states alike want the initiative to remain informal.

And the knowledge-based school of thought that focuses on the activism of epistemic communities (Haas 1990, 1992; Jasanoff 1990) would encounter its Waterloo when trying to tackle the case. Scientific communities have been neither passive nor marginalized in coral reef politics. Quite the opposite: large networks of coral experts have actively engaged in research and exchange of information and have been perhaps the most active proponents of policies of preservation. Moreover, coral reef research is institutionalized in the political process: the GCRMN is the main operational unit of ICRI. One could argue that this does not necessarily undermine the epistemic communities theory, since Peter Haas and his followers explain *success* in environmental policymaking and do not claim to explain *failure* with the absence of epistemic communities. Arguably, if this school of thought focuses on identifying necessary but not sufficient conditions for regime formation, it may not be fair to expect it to explain failure in regime formation that could be due to other factors. But in this particular case, it is very difficult to find such other factors that explain the failure to introduce international policy on coral reefs. Again, no one disputes that coral reefs are in serious trouble; there are no political actors who oppose environmental policy; and the case is described as a win-win situation since the proposed policies would be beneficial for other realms such as infrastructure.

Knowledge and (In)Action: The Impact of Information

For any analyst who attempts to offer a knowledge-based explanation of the outcome, the puzzle in the coral reef story is: why is there so little action when there is so much research? Given the spate of institutionalized research activities and official scientific reports, and the fact that no one denies that coral reefs are in serious trouble, why is so little being done at the international level to protect coral reefs? One possible answer is that science does not count in politics. Since scientists have provided copious input through official reports of multilateral assessments, the conspicuous absence of even the desire to introduce an international legal regime may logically lead one to conclude that objective scientific information does not make much difference in politics.

An alternative and more plausible answer would be that, in the case of coral reefs, research has not provided the right *kind* of information. One of

GCRMN's reports notes that, "There often remains a gulf between what research scientists offer and what management really want" (GCRMN 1998). In particular, reports from multilateral assessments provide virtually no information on the consequences of the problem that would create a sense of urgency. Typically, calls for action do not state reasons for action. "We can no longer afford to only observe, define the problems facing coral reefs, and prescribe their solutions. We must act. We must issue a call to arms, to alert the world to the monstrous condition of the world's reefs" (Serageldin 1998b, 191). The plight of coral reefs is assumed to provide such a reason. But if reefs are degrading, what are the implications of this development for humans? More importantly, what are the cross-border negative consequences that would justify concerted international action? The important "so what" question is not addressed in multilateral assessments of coral problems. An ICRI report to the UN's Commission on Sustainable Development recognizes that "coral reef research has not always provided information useful to managers or policymakers as they endeavor to take timely action."[17]

Consequently, no socioeconomic group other than scientists and environmentalists push for action. Because the destruction of reefs undermines the recreational tourist and pharmaceutical businesses that are gradually losing their resource base, logically, these stockholders should have a strong interest in reef preservation. In reality, however, none of these interests groups have mobilized their political power to oppose destructive practices (Barber and Platt 1998, 41). Neither tourist companies nor coastal developers nor pharmaceutical companies have been visible political forces in international coral reef forums. In addition, activists involved in the network feel the absence of political lobbyists to push and make the case for sustainable management of coral reefs (Wilkinson and Salvat 1998, 18).

A Global Agenda on a Local Issue?

The argument advanced here, on basis of the empirical evidence, is that the missing knowledge about the cross-border consequences of reef decline conditions the unwillingness of states to even consider a legally binding international treaty. Existing information on coral reefs does not portray their degradation as a global issue that involves interdependence. Scientists and environmental activists alike perceive the problem as primarily local in character. "The problems [with coral reefs] are not specifically *global*, but a coincidence of related problems, occurring simultaneously at many locations" (Wilkinson and Salvat, 1998, 16; emphasis in the original). The initiatives launched in mid-1990s are trying to promote the notion that reefs are a global heritage but this discursive strategy has not been persuasive and reefs continue to be perceived as a local issue (Wilkinson and Salvat, 1998, 16). As one NGO activist points out, "Because they are fragmented and local, coral reefs do not tend to have global support. They are seen as a local issue, generally" (Colwell, personal communication).

We cannot dismiss the national benefits of coral reefs. Up to 25 percent of fisheries harvested in the developing countries are based on reef ecosystems (Serageldin 1998a). Those are said to contribute about one-quarter of the total fish catch and to provide food for one billion people in Asia alone (Jameson et al. 1995, 24).[18] But even if we leave aside the fact that there is very little information about such benefits, most of the consequences that could be expected from coral decline are exclusively local. It is not known if the decline of one country's reefs will affect another country. This makes it difficult to mobilize truly international policy efforts, since a state does not have clear pragmatic interests in protecting other countries' reefs. The importance of reefs for local communities and individual countries does not justify the need for international policy.

Because no cross-border impacts of reef decline are scientifically validated, the problem does not have clear elements of interdependence. Hence, existing information does not offer clear reasons for collective action through a system of state-to-state obligations. Even activists committed to coral reef preservation do not view international treaties as either necessary or adequate. One involved scientist, for instance, questioned the need for a formal international agreement: "I am not sure what a treaty would constitute, what its content would be since it is about local use of reefs." Another activist views a treaty as superfluous: "There is a variety of causes of degradation that are not amenable to any kind of interstate agreement" (Colwell, personal communication).

Indeed, when we turn to observe international coral reef politics, we see that the evolution and goals of the international political process match the local character of the issue, as defined by present knowledge about it. From the very beginning, participants defined a deliberate objective to turn the ICRI into a bottom-up process driven by local communities. According to the Strategic Plan, the GCRMN is intended to gradually devolve to lower levels, with support for it shifting to regions, countries and local organizations (Strategic Plan). In 1996, the management of ICRI changed from an executive committee to a coordinating and planning committee with a strong emphasis on regional capacity building, "with the aspiration that sooner or later the international coordinating role can be phased down" (Kenchington 1998, 14).

Similarly, proposed policies are targeted exclusively at local and national levels. Analysts of the problematic prescribe not international policy but local community action. The set of recommendations emerging from an international conference on reef problems include only national and local measures, and there is not even a mention of global or regional policy measures (Hatzi-olos 1998). Another policy framework put forward to combat cyanide fishing as a cause of reef decline in the Philippines also consists of a set of national policies (Barber and Platt 1998). Notably, the author of the only study on the consequences of coral decline does not deem necessary a global strategy and instead recommends local threat-based policy responses to coral mining, blast fishing, and overfishing; national responses to cyanide fishing and coastal for-est logging; and integrated coastal management to address sedimentation as a cause of reef decline (Cesar 1998, 168–170).

Given such characteristics, it becomes less surprising that no international treaty is in the making. It is the absence of reliable information about the so-cioeconomic consequence of the problem that conditions the absence of a for-mal binding agreement among states. As one scientist notes, "Hard decisions require hard science" (Knowlton 1998). And because researchers and analysts have not submitted specific estimates of either the socioeconomic or ecologi-cal impact of reef degradation, policy makers have not had strong reasons to undertake stringent remedial policies. And even if such information becomes available and justifies a need for action, such action is not likely to be codified in an international regime because the problem is perceived as local in char-acter.

The discovered match between information about the cross-border effects of a problem and the perceived common interests should not come as a sur-prise. A basic premise of regime theory is that international policy regimes are collective responses to transnational problems that cannot be managed effec-tively in a unilateral manner. The notion of "transnational" cannot be sepa-rated from available information about the problem: what makes a problem transnational is defined by its cross-border consequences. Hence, the forma-tion of common interests that stem from perceived interdependence is de-pendant on reliable information about the transboundary impact of an al-leged problem.

Conclusion

We cannot explain the absence of an international policy regime on coral reefs management if we focus on the scientific involvement in policymaking circles. Coral reef scientists have mobilized as political actors quite successfully, but this has not led to international policy coordination. The only way to under-stand the case in terms of science is to focus on the *content* of available scien-tific knowledge. One important reason for the absence of even efforts to form an international legal regime can be found in the virtual absence of information on the cross-border consequences of coral reef decline. There is a corresponding perception shared widely among scientists, activists, and policy makers alike that the problem is essentially local in character. Gaps of information exist in each of the three sectors of knowledge, but information about the extent and causes of degradation is accumulating while no research effort is made to study the effects of degradation. Multilateral scientific assessments of coral reefs supply information on the extent and causes of coral reef degradation, but submit virtually no data on the transboundary consequences of the problem. This deprives the issue of elements of interdependence, hampers the formation of common state interests, and helps explain why states do not consider it necessary to introduce an international treaty for comprehensive coral reef management.

The lack of intergovernmental policy should not be equated with absence of governance. Efforts at promoting sustainable coral reef management are made through other channels, including unilateral national policies, bilateral partnerships and nonstate initiatives. In December 2000, the U.S. Coral Reef Conservation Act established a reserve in the Hawaii Islands that contained nearly 70 percent of coral reefs under U.S. jurisdiction (Onion 2000). On the other side of the world, 33 percent of the Great Barrier Reef and associated ecosystems are declared protected areas or no-take zones (GCRMN 2004). And some individual countries help protect coral reefs outside their jurisdiction. Sweden, in partnership with the World Bank and Finland, launched the CORDIO project to help investigate the impacts of coral bleaching in the Indian Ocean and seek ways to improve local management of affected reefs.

In addition to national and bilateral governmental activities, a large number of NGOs such as the Coral Reef Alliance and REEF are active in the field of coral reef preservation. Three of them (Conservation International, The Nature Conservancy and the World Wildlife Fund) combined their expertise to develop training materials for developing and implementing marine protected areas in Southeast Asia and the Western Pacific. The International Marinelife Alliance developed and implemented a fishing reform program in the Philippines, consisting of community-based policies to enhance awareness, train fishermen in cyanide-free techniques, and facilitate law-making and enforcement efforts (Barber and Platt 1998). Another NGO, Coral Cay Conservation, helped establish seven marine protected areas along the 250 kilometers of reefs in Belize that were designated a World Heritage Site by the United Nations in 1996 (McWilliam 1997, 18). Hence, some action is being taken to sustainably manage coral reefs. These policy initiatives are undertaken exclusively on national and local levels, and the already loose and informal international initiative that exists is bound to devolve to local levels.

Notes

An earlier version of the chapter appeared as a journal article: Rado S. Dimitrov, "Confronting Non-Regimes: Science and International Coral Reef Policy," *Journal of Environment and Development*, vol. 11, no. 1 (March 2002), pp. 53–78.

1. Private communications with Richard Kenchington, head of the Secretariat of the International Coral Reef Initiative (1996–98), Stephen Colwell, executive director of Coral Reef Alliance, and a U.S. Department of State official who wished to remain anonymous.

2. Degradation is defined as major changes in species composition, species abundance, and productivity of coral reefs communities (Bryant et al. 1998, 17).

3. ICRI report to the UN Commission on Sustainable Development, available in electronic form at http://www.nos.noaa.gov/icri/csd/report.html (December 30, 2000).

4. Richard Kenchington, head of the ICRI's Secretariat, 1996–1998. Private communication, February 18, 2001.

5. Private communications with anonymous U.S. State Department official, January 9, 2001; Jamie Reaser, former U.S. State Department official and now assistant director, U.S. National Invasive Species Council, January 31, 2001; and Richard Kenchington, February 18, 2001.

6. Clive Wilkinson is the coordinator of the Global Coral Reef Monitoring Network.

7. ICRI report to UNCSD, available in electronic form at http://www.nos.noaa.gov/icri/csd/report.html (December 30, 2000).

8. Information about ICRI and its Secretariat can be found at the official Internet site at http://www.icriforum.org (February 11, 2005).

9. Later, this guesswork was presented as an established fact in GCRMN's first report, *Status 1998* (see below).

10. Middle East, Western Indian Ocean and Eastern Africa, South Asia, East Asian Seas, Pacific, and Caribbean and the tropical Americas.

11. Apart from GCRMN, there are several smaller regional programs for monitoring which are not covered in this study: the Caribbean Coastal Marine Productivity Program (CARICOMP), the Atlantic and Gulf Reef Assessment (AGRA) based at the University of Miami, Florida, and AQUANAUT run by ICLARM for training divers in assessment techniques (Wilkinson and Salvat 1998).

12. Incorporated in the report was a section with input from Reef Check, the volunteer and less scientific part of the monitoring program, that somewhat contradicted the main report and was more alarmist about coral bleaching.

13. Eutrophication is the process of oversaturation with nitrogen and phosphorus that leads to excessive plant growth and disrupts the functioning of an ecosystem.

14. Thirty-six percent of reefs were classified as threatened by overexploitation, and 30 percent by coastal development (Bryant et al. 1998, 20).

15. This report was a product of a large and highly interdisciplinary project that lasted for four years and studied the responses of coral organisms to global climate

change. It estimated that a doubling of carbon dioxide levels in the atmosphere would decrease by 10 to 20 percent the calcification of corals on which they depend for growth.

16. Available online at http://www.aims.gov.au/pages/research/coral-bleaching/global-change/global-change-02.html (February 11, 2005).

17. Available in electronic form at http://www.nos.noaa.gov/icri/csd/report.html (December 30, 2000).

18. According to one estimate, reefs provide 90 percent of all animal protein consumed in the South Pacific (Serageldin 1998a).

7

Knowledge, Power, and Interests
in Environmental Cooperation

Is knowledge possible, and if not, how do we *know* that?

—Woody Allen

THE RELATIONSHIP BETWEEN IDEAS AND HUMAN BEHAVIOR has been a lasting subject of intellectual endeavor. In a variety of thematic contexts, thinkers over the centuries have explored the connection between knowledge and action, between the ideational and the observable social world. How does what we know affect what we do? Is human behavior purposeful and rational? Do policy makers make decisions on the basis of expert information? This set of questions relates to a cluster of theoretical interests in the academic study of international relations where scholars have sought to identify when and why states cooperate, and what conditions affect collective action. How do states decide whether to address a problem collectively through international agreements? Why do societies respond to some environmental risks and not to others? The role of shared scientific knowledge in international environmental policy is a topic that straddles both sets of questions. Hence, investigating how scientific research information affects international environmental cooperation is a particularly worthwhile exercise.

Three features of this book make it uniquely positioned to advance our understanding of the role of shared knowledge in regime formation.

First, the broad comparative research design involving variance in the outcome of interest enables more widely generalizable conclusions. Regime theorists typically focus on "happy-end" stories of successfully concluded legal agreements and ignore instances where states forsake institutions for policy coordination. In the real world, however, there are important ecological problems that generate intense social discourse without leading to binding international agreements. We have much to learn from these negative cases where things do not happen. By exploring collective decisions *not* to cooperate we can understand better the conditions under which cooperation occurs. Previous chapters explored both positive and negative cases of institution building. Examining the deforestation and coral reef nonregimes and comparing them with existing regimes helps reveal a more complete picture of international regime formation and the circumstances that facilitate it.

Second, unlike other cognitivist interpretations, the account presented here focuses on the substantive content of information. As chapter 2 elaborated, there are no previous knowledge-based explanations of interstate governance. This assertion is certain to raise eyebrows, but consider this. Previous accounts that are dubbed cognitive in fact underscore the role of *actors* (epistemic communities) or *practices* (discourse) and not substantive research results and scientific claims. The epistemic communities' literature emphasizes the role of experts who infiltrate the policy process and facilitate policy formation. Other treatments of the science-policy connection highlight discursive practices and how existing information is presented and misrepresented (Litfin 1994). Still others emphasize the impact of "collective, deliberative *processes* of . . . reviewing and evaluating the state of knowledge" while explicitly arguing that the actual results of scientific research rarely exercise influence on policy outcomes (Parson 2003, 263–264). Everyone seems to have abandoned the original hypothesis that *information* affects policy, while IR scholars continue to speak of knowledge-based theories of regime formation. This book returns to the original supposition and places the impact of substantive scientific information back under the lens.

The third and most important analytical innovation that gives us better leverage over the research question is the distinction between different types of information. Instead of lumping together "scientific knowledge," the analysis here differentiates between three types of knowledge (about the extent, causes, and consequences of a problem), and examines their roles separately. The three sectors of knowledge vary independently from each other—in terms of quality of information and the degree to which it is accepted as reliable. For instance, information about the extent of an ecological development may be reliable but knowledge about its causes or consequences may be incomplete. The sectors of knowledge are therefore distinct variables that should be treated as such. This new analytical lens reveals uneven and differential roles that distinct types of information play in collective decision-making. The end result is a nuanced and more detailed picture of the interplay between knowledge, interests, and power.

Is good scientific information crucial for environmental policymaking? Some types are and other types are not. Treating scientific knowledge as a single variable prevents us from adequately assessing its role in decision-making or fully understanding the science-policy connection. Accurate identification of the role of science in international policymaking requires that we distinguish between different types of scientific information. Instead of asking "Does science matter?" it is more constructive to ask what kind of scientific information matters, and to provide a series of more precise suggestions about the influence of expert information. The results throw light on what constitutes usable knowledge and when natural scientific input is likely to affect environmental policy processes.

What Kind of Knowledge Matters?

The central finding is that *information about transboundary consequences of a problem is a key factor in international policymaking.* Reliable information about cross-border effects of a problem appears to be an important requirement in policy deliberations and increases the likelihood of international agreements. Within this universe of cases, there is a clear correspondence between this type of knowledge and the overall dynamics of regime making processes. Reliable and widely accepted knowledge about shared impacts of ozone depletion and acid rain served as a focal point in policy discussions on these ecological problems. It provided a constant background to negotiations and created zones of agreement. Conversely, gaps of information about negative cross-border effects severely hamper the process and may preclude the formation of international agreements. Because negative transboundary impacts of deforestation and coral reefs degradation are not scientifically ascertained, a country's benefits from remedial action in other countries remain unclear. This type of uncertainty reduces incentives to enter international agreements and diminishes countries' willingness to compromise with each other during political discussions.

Equally important, other types of information that are seemingly highly relevant are not actually essential prerequisites for decision-making. In particular, *conclusive information about the precise extent of a problem does not appear to be a critical requirement for international policy coordination.* Decision makers tolerate high degrees of uncertainty regarding the exact magnitude of an ecological development and can take costly policy action even in the absence of such knowledge. To use the language of causality, this particular type of information is not sufficient and not even necessary for regime formation. On the one hand, states created a strong policy regime to address ozone depletion despite the lack of conclusive evidence on the extent of ozone depletion. On the other hand, states have not constructed regimes on forests and coral reef management despite solid data about the high rates of deforestation and the extent of coral reef decline. The logical conclusion is that knowledge about the extent of the problem does not have a decisive influence on the policymaking processes.

The importance of a third type of information, on the causes of a problem, is more nuanced and ambiguous. *Good principal knowledge about particular human-related causes is needed before policy action can be undertaken.* This type of information is relevant to policy design since awareness of causes allows actors to identify possible solutions. How otherwise would actors know which human activities to regulate or what emissions to control? Uncertainty about the human causes dilutes incentives to undertake action in the first place. Knowledge about transboundary cause-effect relationships is particularly salient in international policymaking. The awareness that activities in one country contribute to a problem affecting territories and populations in other countries is a requirement for accepting the need for international cooperation under a multilateral treaty.

At the same time, however, *complete* information about the causes of a problem does not appear to be an essential requirement for international cooperation. *States occasionally take action without having precise estimates about the relative contributions of different causal factors.* Ozone depletion, for instance, is driven by various natural processes as well as human-made substances. At the time states committed themselves to collective action toward eliminating human-made ozone-depleting substances, scientists were unable to determine the relative contribution of these substances, compared to natural causes. This uncertainty did not prevent the emergence of strong international institutions for policy coordination.

These conclusions are based on comparative analysis of four cases. Previous chapters delved into four ecological problems and made extensive inventories of the state of knowledge on the three dimensions of each problem. The empirical findings are summarized in table 7.1.

Common to both cases of successful regime formation (ozone and acid rain) was the high degree of scientific consensus about the transboundary consequences of the problem. This involved reliable information about the negative effects of the ecological developments, as well as certainty that these effects could occur in countries other than the country of origin. There was scientific consensus on the negative impact of acidification on aquatic ecosystems, water supplies, and human health. Similarly, the consequences of ozone depletion were a matter of scientific consensus. The principal mechanisms through which increased UV radiation damages human health, terrestrial

TABLE 7.1
Summary of empirical findings

	Scientific Knowledge Base		
Cases	Transboundary Consequences	Extent of Problem	Causes of Problem
Ozone regime	strong	weak	medium
Acid rain regime	strong-medium	strong	strong-medium
Forests nonregime	weak	strong	strong
Coral reef nonregime	weak	medium	medium

plants, and aquatic life were well understood and never disputed by either scientists or negotiators. The transboundary dimension of the cause-effect relationship was well established in both cases: activities in one country could lead to negative impact in other countries.

In contrast, what characterizes both nonregimes (forests and coral reefs) was the poor knowledge about the transboundary consequences of the problems. Multilateral assessments produced solid information about the extent and causes of forest degradation and coral reef decline, but there was severe paucity of data on their cross-border effects. Most of the scientifically verified impacts are confined to the local and national levels. Furthermore, the perception of policy makers is consistent with research-derived information: they are dubious about the transboundary consequences of deforestation and coral reef degradation, or deny outright that there are any. As the next section elaborates, such statements are not motivated merely by political biases.

Regarding the second type of knowledge—the extent of the problem—the pattern indicates that such information does not play an important role in the political processes of regime formation. Across the cases, there is wide variance on this variable, without any corresponding variance on the political outcome (regime formation versus nonregime). The formation of the ozone regime was accompanied by significant scientific uncertainty about the precise extent of ozone depletion. The regime on acid rain was characterized by solid information on the magnitude of the problem—but so was the forest nonregime as well as, to a lesser degree, the corals nonregime. Given the absence of empirical patterns, we cannot conclude that knowledge about the exact extent of a problem makes a critical difference in international policy making.

Regarding the third type of shared knowledge—the causes of a problem—the patterns are less than clear because variance of this variable is insignificant. All four cases are characterized with relatively high scientific certainty about causes, and there is no obvious correspondence between this factor and political outcomes. Hence the conclusion that reliable information of this type is not particularly important in international efforts at regime formation. Scientific knowledge about causes of the problem was generally strong in all four cases, including cases where there was a failure to cooperate. Most notably, the ozone regime was created despite some gaps of information and unanswered scientific questions regarding the causes of ozone depletion.

Knowledge and Power

What is a plausible theoretical explanation of the observed pattern of correspondence between international regime processes and information about transboundary consequences? One possible interpretation would focus on the relationship between power and knowledge and the idea that the exercise of power shapes information according to preexistent interests. Intellectual descendants of Michel Foucault are inclined to regard knowledge as a dependent variable shaped by power. A number of important works examine the production of knowledge as a sociological phenomenon and are united in viewing knowledge as socially constructed (Mulkay 1978; Latour and Woolgar 1979; Jasanoff 1990; Miller and Edwards 2001a; Munton 2001). Cognitivist students of global environmental politics tend to focus on the extent to which political actors control processes of generating, ordering, and using information (Jasanoff 1986, 1990; Litfin 1994; Miller and Edwards 2001a; SLG 2001; Lidskog and Sundqvist 2002). Scientific research relies on funding whose allocation is political, and the political biases of the sponsors possibly compromise the neutrality of researchers. Power also affects how information is transmitted from the scientific to the political realm and interpreted.[1]

A significant windfall of disaggregating types of knowledge is that it gives us additional purchase on the interplay between power and knowledge and allows us to see things that would otherwise remain hidden. Basic facts in all four cases do not allow us to interpret existing shared knowledge as a function of power or as a contrivance in its exercise. Certainly, we cannot completely dismiss the political manipulation of science: powerful political actors can and do affect which scientific projects are funded, who conducts them, and how the results are used. At the very least, however, the empirical evidence presented here serves as a reminder about the limits to which information is malleable and knowledge volatile.

According to the "power-knowledge" line of argument, knowledge is epiphenomenal: it is constructed by powerful political actors who generate and mold information to buttress their negotiating positions and support their interests. This string of logic could turn the research question on its head by treating knowledge as a dependent rather than a causal variable: why was consensual knowledge about consequences available in the two regime cases but not in the forestry and coral reef cases? This question redirects the analytical scrutiny toward the impact of interests and power on agenda-setting in scientific research, what information is sought and produced, and what knowledge becomes a broadly accepted basis for decision-making. Hence, the argument would proceed, what really helps interpret the two cases is not the available information but the exercise of power that shaped the legitimization of some scientific claims over others.

The problem with this theory is that facts and logic get in the way. When the theory is operationalized and its logical derivatives are tested, they do not find strong support in the empirical cases. How would we know whether power shapes knowledge? If knowledge was clay in the hands of political actors, one would logically expect such actors to "produce" information that suits their interests and, conversely, to contest information that undermines their negotiating positions. This did not happen in either of the cases examined here. Even powerful political actors did not always manage to generate scientifically validated information that suits their interests. Furthermore, they were not able to suppress information that runs counter to their preferences. Often they do not even *attempt* to contest such information.

In the ozone case, the United States sought an international treaty and took the political and entrepreneurial leadership in the negotiating process. U.S. research institutions were the prime producers of ozone science, and that should have provided government actors with an opportunity to massage information. Yet, the United States was not able to produce evidence about the extent of ozone depletion: very significant uncertainties persisted and were not resolved until after the Montreal Protocol was signed. Moreover, American negotiators and policy makers never disputed the information gaps in that particular sector of knowledge. If power shaped knowledge, why was the United States unable to "produce" reliable information on this important aspect of the problem?

Similarly, even ardent proponents of a forest treaty, such as Canada, the Scandinavian countries, and Switzerland, readily acknowledge the considerable scientific uncertainty about the consequences of deforestation. These political actors do not even attempt to manipulate existing knowledge about the problem to strengthen their negotiating positions and further their interests. In the case of coral reef degradation, key information about consequences is lacking, even though the leaders of the political initiative are Western countries. These powerful actors have strong scientific research capabilities and a political will to engage in coral reef management—but obviously these do not translate into an unlimited capacity for knowledge fabrication.

The power-over-knowledge thesis encounters its most formidable Waterloo in the acid rain case. Political efforts to suppress information and misrepresent scientific knowledge were made but did not succeed. Reluctant to embark on costly policies, government actors in the United States and the United Kingdom denied evidence and emphasized existing scientific uncertainties. Despite these political efforts at manipulation, research findings consistently refuted their claims and scientific conclusions went against the governments' preferences. Such research came not only from other countries but also from American and British researchers at the National Academy of Sciences and the Royal Society. Even studies sponsored by the governments and the corporate actors in these countries "got out of hand" and revealed that enough was known about the problem to justify policy action. Thus, concerted efforts by powerful political actors to obstruct research and to perpetuate myths of scientific uncertainty eventually failed. "Although one government might lose interest in [scientific] studies, and even seek to obstruct them, the integrity of participating scientists could, in the end, preserve the credibility of the exercise" (Wetstone 1987, 175).

Knowledge and Interests

The state of existing scientific knowledge about ecological problems cannot be explained as an epiphenomenal function of political power, but it does have independent influence on the formation of state interests and eventually collective policy decisions. Neoliberal institutionalism is a theoretical perspective through which we can make better sense of the empirical pattern between shared knowledge and collective decisions. This school of thought, whose origins are associated with the work of Robert Keohane and Kenneth Oye, has a long tradition and incorporates a variety of perspectives. The kernel of neoliberal institutionalist thought shared by all its varieties is emphasis on the role of common interests in world politics. According to this argument, actors take collective action when they perceive common interests under conditions of interdependence.

The role of scientific information and shared knowledge in environmental cooperation could adequately be understood in terms of interest formation. Interests are future-oriented ideas: they are preferences for a particular future. The consideration of alternative futures is therefore intrinsic in the process through which actors calculate their interests. As the analyses of the individual cases already showed, knowledge about a problem's consequences exerts influence on the formation of interests along three main pathways: by making utility calculations possible, by portraying the degree of interdependence involved in the issue, and by offering fuel for rhetorical arguments.

Information and Utility Calculations

According to even the most basic notion of rationality, the expectation of utility is an integral part of the rationale for action.[2] Even critics of rational choice theory agree that actors seek to benefit from their own actions. There are various types of perceived utility, some of which have little to do with the transboundary problem at hand: obtaining information about other countries, scoring domestic or international political points by joining a regime, shielding oneself from domestic criticism, or strengthening political alliances can be reasons for entering international institutions. Assuming that a policy regime is at least partly a response to perceived problems, its utility is in preventing or ameliorating the problem's negative effects. Indeed, the cognitive act of defining something as a problem presupposes and is based on undesirable impact. A particular event, trend, or development is perceived as a "problem" only by virtue of its unpalatable consequences. To assess the stakes regarding an ecological development, actors seek to know what ramifications this development may have. Reliable information about the impact of a problem plays an integral role in this process, by allowing actors to make utility calculations. It does not determine the final decision but enables the policy maker to make such considerations and to weigh the costs against the benefits of policy action.

Scientific knowledge does not exercise its role in a deterministic way. Expert information cannot dictate the particular choice of policy and therefore cannot explain the particular design of a regime. Available scientific data only set the parameters within which political discussions take place and demarcate the *range* of policy options that are considered by political actors. Nor does the availability of reliable scientific information about negative consequences guarantee that policy action will be taken at all. Regime formation may fail for various other reasons since many political, economic, and personal considerations as well as the dynamics of interaction among actors affect collective decisions. Even if policy makers know with certainty that an ecological problem will have negative transboundary impact, states may not reach an agreement to coordinate policy because the political or economic costs of action would be too high. The socioeconomic costs of forest protection, for instance, would be considerable since forest utilization involves a number of economic and broader social interests. It is therefore dubious whether the policy outcome would have been different even if there had been solid information about the impact of deforestation.

Yet, reliable knowledge about the consequences of a problem is an important enabling condition because it allows a meaningful discussion of the problem, of actors' interests in addressing it, and of the general policy options. Indeed, when states have taken action, the scientific information about negative impacts was solid and the knowledge was accepted and shared. In short, knowledge about transboundary effects of a problem does not determine the outcomes of decision-making and negotiations; rather, it facilitates utility calculations and the formation of international regimes.

Knowledge and Perceived Interdependence

The second pathway through which this type of knowledge affects interests is by supplying elements of interdependence involved in the issue. A premise of regime theory is that international policy regimes are collective responses to transnational problems that cannot be managed effectively in a unilateral manner. Yet, the notion of transnational hinges on information about the problem: what makes a problem transnational is defined by its cross-border dimensions. Hence, the formation of common interests that stem from perceived interdependence is dependent on reliable information about the transboundary impact of an alleged problem. How this connection plays out in the cases was elaborated in previous chapters, but some additional observations would be useful.

In the case of ozone depletion and acid rain, multilateral research produced evidence and scientific consensus that the shared consequences of the problem would be grave. Correspondingly, the benefits from precluding ozone depletion and ameliorating acidification were compelling and were seen as such by all actors—even by those for whom the costs of action were greatest. In the forestry and coral reef cases, on the other hand, policy makers do not have solid information about the cross-border consequences of these problems and are therefore unconvinced about the benefits of international policy coordination under a treaty. Even forest convention advocates admit that the problems can be effectively addressed through unilateral policies. Few see a clear reason to commit their countries to international obligations, particularly given the high socioeconomic costs involved in sustainable forest management.

Elements of interdependence implied by cross-border impact strongly affect collective decision-making, and their relevance is clearly reflected in perceptions of policymakers. In comparing deforestation to ozone depletion, Great Britain's senior forestry official for international policy commented, "Ozone depletion was a case where national actions create an international problem. Deforestation is seen as an international problem but in fact the links are not so easy to establish" (Dudley, interview). And an Indian negotiator noted, "Transboundary issues are easier to be addressed by a treaty than localized problems. For example, climate change is a transboundary issue but forests are not. What happens to one's forests will not affect other countries" (Oberai, interview). Remarkably, even the most eager supporters of a treaty recognize that "for an issue to trigger an international (policy) response, there have to be global dimensions, there has to be a problem that is shared . . . common impacts. . . . Forests don't affect everyone in the same sense" (Fullerton, interview).[3]

Some readers may object that what explains the cases is not the stock of available information but the "character of the problems." Yet, we cannot regard the two in isolation from each other. Social scientists have rightfully rejected objectivist notions of issue characters that exist independently from social cognition. What matters is how actors see a problem, and that perception is based to a large extent, if not entirely, on the information that these actors possess. Quite simply, what helps define the nature of the issue is shared knowledge about it. One could speak of the local character of coral reef degradation only because there is no scientific evidence of transboundary effects. It is reasonable to refer to the character of the problem *as defined by existing information about it.*

Information and Argumentation

Finally, information affects negotiations when it is used by actors who make arguments to support their positions. When data about the negative impact of a problem are reliable, those who want a treaty could point to the consequences of the problem and use them to argue that we need action. And when such impacts cross borders, treaty proponents could more easily make an argument that we need multilateral action. On the other hand, when information about effects is not reliable or when it is certain that such effects are not transboundary, this weapon for argumentation is snatched from the hands of treaty proponents. In forestry deliberations, for instance, no country has been able to offer convincing reasons why there should be an international legally binding agreement, and the countries that want one (for other reasons) have not been able to make a convincing case for a treaty. At the same time, the gaps of information are used as effective weapons in the hands of treaty opponents who argue that forest protection could be handled effectively in a unilateral manner without making international commitments under a treaty.

Implications for IR Theory and Practice

The findings presented here support neoliberal institutionalist claims about the importance of common interests for the establishment of international institutions, as well as studies showing that high externalities are likely to lead to convergence in state behavior (Sprinz and Vaahtoranta 1994; Botcheva and

Martin 2001). States enter agreements when they expect benefits from collective action and when these benefits cannot accrue from unilateral policies. In environment management, governments enter mutual obligations under a treaty in order to collectively address a shared ecological problem that involves interdependence. What defines interdependence is the existence of perceived and reciprocal cross-border impacts. Actors are likely to perceive interdependence when two conditions are present: when a problem has consequences for all parties involved and when activities in one country could contribute to the problem and affect other countries. These two elements (shared consequences and shared origin of the problem) create interdependence and may provide reasons for policy cooperation among states. Indeed, within the small universe of cases examined here, legal regimes are created when there is reliable evidence of negative consequences of a transboundary problem.

On Multicausality

Social scientists rarely make universally valid propositions that hold across all times and places; we typically formulate conditional hypotheses that apply to specific contexts. Every theory comes with scope conditions that delineate the parameters within which it is valid (Walker and Cohen 1985). The scope condition of my theoretical argument pertains to concern about ecological problems: as long as states are concerned about a potential transboundary problem, the availability of reliable information about cross-border impacts is critically important for the emergence of collective policy.

Nothing in the present analysis should be taken to imply that states create policy agreements *only* to ameliorate transboundary ecological problems. Governments can form policy regimes for a variety of reasons. Sometimes the main concern is indeed transboundary impacts. Other times the rationale is based on political, economic, and normative considerations barely related to ecological problems. Concerns about economic competitiveness are often acute, and some countries see international agreements as instrumental in creating level playing fields, by securing reciprocal commitments among treaty participants. Treaties can also be tools for securing mutual benefits at the expense of nonparticipating countries. The cooperative arrangement between Norway and Russia regarding fisheries in the Barents Sea, for instance, helped these two countries exclude third parties from utilization of living resources.[4]

The decision to uphold an international treaty could also be motivated by social norms, as appears to be the case with the International Whaling Commission. Scientists report that certain whale species are no longer threatened with extinction and testify that renewed whaling on a limited basis could be sustained without jeopardizing the survival of the species. Yet, many governments prefer to maintain the current moratorium on whaling, against the will of countries such as Japan, Norway, and Iceland. This decision is clearly not based on science and is likely motivated by environmental norms and/or the opportunity to score domestic political points for being "green." The creation of another institution, the North Atlantic Marine Mammal Commission, in turn, can be explained partly by a desire to escape the restrictions of the International Whaling Commission. In any of these cases, the political will to reach and uphold policy agreements outstripped the scientific documentation of aspects of the problem.

The present analysis is premised on a belief in multicausality, the view that multiple factors work to shape social reality, and that any particular causal influence takes place in conjunction with other factors. The availability of reliable information about transboundary impacts of a problem does not guarantee that governments will engage in international cooperation since obstacles of a completely different nature may preclude collective action. Furthermore, ascertaining the important role of information does not imply that there are no other important factors. The cases under consideration here do indeed display variance on research-derived information that could possibly be treated as a causal variable. But they also differ along a number of other axes, including levels of externalities, opportunity costs, the distribution of power across coalitions, the type of product, and the distribution of costs and benefits among domestic actors. One might argue, for instance, that the four cases display variance on the nature of the problem—the two regimes address pollution and the two nonregimes involve natural resources—and that such typology of issues holds explanatory power. Given such multidimensionality, it would be unwise to expect (or to attempt to provide) an exhaustive single-variable explanation. Each of the above factors could be used as a basis for alternative explanations, and the account offered here is not intended to refute those. It advances not a competing but a complementary explanation and illuminates the impact of a particular type of information that, in conjunction with other factors, has made regime formation easier in some cases and overwhelmingly difficult in others.

It is also worth considering that shared knowledge about consequences may be an integral and indispensable part of other "alternative" explanations as well. One such explanation may focus on the environmental externalities of economic activities. In the ozone and acid rain cases, we have a relatively certain global externality that accrues to present generations. In the forestry and coral reef cases, on the other hand, externalities are far from clear and may accrue disproportionately to future generations. Such differences could help explain the lower level of cooperation on forestry and coral reefs as well as the more limited role of scientific assessments. We cannot, however, discuss externalities without reference to negative impacts, and those are matters of scientific knowledge. Is not the level of externality defined by the socioeconomic consequences of a problem? Therefore, an explanation focusing on externalities cannot be divorced from a discussion of scientifically derived information. Similarly, we cannot explain international cooperation exclusively with the position of the United States. Why did the United States want an ozone treaty, and how did knowledge about negative consequences help shape its national position? Information about the disastrous impact of ozone depletion on human health was an important reason why the United States wanted regulation at both national and international levels. This factor helps shape other factors that come to characterize a case and therefore provides the basis not for a competing explanation but a complementary one. The state of knowledge on cross-border consequences is one element of a broader picture, albeit a very important element.

Alternative Explanations of Regime Formation

While it is not the purpose of this book to refute competing theoretical explanations of regime formation, it is worth noting that some of the factors that are often said to shape world politics exerted very little influence in the cases investigated here. For instance, realist expectations about the role of a world hegemony find only partial support. The U.S. skepticism and occasional opposition to the acid rain accords did little to sway other countries and failed to prevent the emergence of a strong international policy regime.

At first glance, the preferences of the United States could explain other individual cases. It is tempting to entertain the idea that the ozone talks succeeded and the forest talks failed to produce agreements because the United States supported the former and opposed the latter. But the position of the United States on forests changed 180 degrees in the mid-1990s, with no corresponding change in either the other actors' positions or the general political outcomes. Negotiating a global forest convention was an American cause, and the United States was one of the strongest treaty proponents at the early stages. Yet, developing countries blocked negotiations and managed to keep them out of the agenda of the 1992 Earth Summit. Because this state of affairs remained unaffected by the subsequent sharp turn of the United States, we cannot reasonably explain the outcome with preferences of the hegemony.

Similarly, the American position regarding ozone depletion vacillated considerably and the Reagan administration came close to refusing to sign both the Vienna Convention and the Montreal Protocol. This fluctuation did not affect the formation of the regime: the political movement by other states toward a binding agreement was powerful and did not falter despite uncertainty about what the United States would do.

Likewise, corporate influences made very small dents in multilateral policy-making processes. Their powerlessness in the acid rain case is obvious and quite striking: governments embarked on costly policies that were highly detrimental to large numbers of powerful businesses. On the surface, the interests of large industries could explain the ozone regime since DuPont came to support international regulations, but the U.S. government pushed for a regime even earlier, when DuPont was strongly against it. The limited usefulness of neo-Marxist ideas becomes even more apparent when we look at the cases in conjunction with each other and focus on the variance between them. Corporate preferences differ ostensibly within each pair of same-outcome cases, which suggests that they did not make a critical difference. Negotiations on both ozone depletion and acid rain led to successful regime formation even though the policy costs and economic implications were very different: relatively minor economic importance of ozone-depleting substances versus far-reaching ramifications of reducing acidifying air pollutants (regulation would affect transportation, power production, coal mining, and various manufacturing industries). Corporate interests regarding the two nonregimes are also very different. Forest protection would hurt enormously profitable industries, while coral reef protection could actually benefit tourism and pharmaceutical companies. This is why industries provide strong opposition on forests and no opposition whatsoever on corals and yet the outcomes of the two cases are essentially the same: nonregimes.

International norms do not appear capable of generating collective policy in environmental management either.[5] From a broader historical perspective, the evolution of environmental norms could perhaps offer a satisfactory interpretation of the overall proliferation of environmental agreements and the overall rise of global environmental politics (Meyer et al. 1997). Within a single time frame, however, and against the same normative background, some negotiations fail and others succeed in leading to an agreement.

Norms cannot easily explain such variance. On the contrary, it appears that regimes form where environmental norms are weak and fail where norms are strong. The acid rain and ozone regimes addressed ecological problems that were novel, esoteric, and poorly understood by the general public. These problems had not existed in the public awareness long enough to generate norms but nevertheless compelled governments to seek to ameliorate them through international coordinated policies. On the other hand, the forest problematic has been in the focus of long traditions of environmental movements, and forest protection enjoys considerable public support. Despite the centrality of trees as symbols for environmental protection and the recognition that coral reefs are the richest ecosystems, both forests and coral reefs remain unaddressed by international agreements. The four cases thus offer little evidence that norms make significant difference in global environmental politics. Norms may add fuel to policy processes but they are certainly not primary driving forces behind regime formation.

The role of NGOs and transnational networks of activists in these particular cases also appears to be less significant than some IR literature leads us to believe. In both of the nonregime cases, NGOs were very active politically: they lobbied their governments, engaged in campaigns to raise awareness about ecological problems, participated in international governmental conferences, and contributed to negotiation processes. In the coral reef case, in particular, NGOs and scientists are prominent participants in deliberations and perhaps the main engine behind the ICRI. These efforts failed to make much difference in the end, as far as international policy coordination is concerned: no government has advocated a coral reef treaty, and efforts to create a global forest convention have failed consistently.

Ironically, NGOs were not the main driving force in the cases of successful regime creation (governments were), and even when they tried to influence governments, they did not sway the policy process. They were active in negotiations on the nitrous protocol to the LRTAP convention on acid rain but eventually governments decided to *reduce* their own initial ambitions and adopted weaker policy targets than originally envisioned. In sum, neither civil society pressures, nor international environmental norms, nor hegemonic power, nor corporate influences can account for either the achievement of environmental cooperation or the failures to create international policy regimes.

Rationality and Veils of Uncertainty

The findings suggest that international policymaking processes display a significant degree of large-scale rationality, at least over the long term. They portray international policy coordination as a purposeful problem-solving activity. States act to prevent or ameliorate negative consequences of problems and do so collectively through coordinated policy when they perceive added value in multilateral (versus unilateral) actions. Governments enter international agreements when the consequences of the problem are transnational and when the activities in any country can lead to negative impacts on other countries (as in the cases of ozone depletion and acid rain). Conversely, they are reluctant to make commitments under treaties when the transboundary character of an issue is dubious (in the cases of deforestation and coral reefs). In this context, information about the cross-border consequences of a problem is central to deliberations regarding the desirability of collective action.

By themselves, local impacts of a problem are not sufficient to generate incentives for collective action. Both acid rain and deforestation have negative local effects caused by activities within national borders. However, concerns with these local cause-effect links carried uneven weight in considering the utility of international cooperation. In the case of acid rain, controlling emissions would bring both local and transnational benefits from reducing acidification, and the local benefits of reducing one's own industrial emissions served to reinforce incentives to enter international agreements with other states. In contrast, the purely local effects of deforestation proved insufficient for an international treaty by themselves because they were not supplemented with cross-border effects that would translate into corresponding benefits from forest protection in other countries.

Local environmental externalities may warrant national policies but offer little reason for international policy. What makes a problem transnational is not that it occurs in every country but the cross-border cause-effect relationship. For instance, noise pollution and street litter are global problems in the sense that they can be found in every major city around the world. But they are not transnational problems because their causes are purely local and only local populations suffer their consequences. City authorities and national governments may consider addressing them through local and national policies, but there is no reason why they should negotiate global treaties to deal with them. In this respect, the distinction between global and transnational is important.

The empirical findings as well as their interpretation offered here fit with rationalist approaches to the study of international relations. Rationalist theorizing has come under heavy criticism, for its problematic assumptions that available strategies and the outcome from each strategy are fully known to the parties and that their interests and the ordering of their preferences are fixed and known. Constructivists argue that interests are not exogenously given but derive from values that vary across space and time and show how interests are affected by sociocultural context, issues of identity, the role of norms, and processes of ideational change (Haas 1982; Kratochwil 1989; Wendt 1992; Lumsdaine 1993; Price 1997). Indeed, rationalistic approaches are not well equipped to address the role of values in interest formation and cannot adequately explain why different actors choose to pursue very dissimilar ends.

The limitations of rational-choice assumptions need not detract from its achievements. Nor do they *necessarily* imply that perceived interests and rational calculations of costs and benefits are not central to decision-making. "It is essential to take account of the underlying constellation of interests, even if the assumptions of the rational choice approach are overly rigid and should be avoided" (Zürn 1998, 629). The cases examined here suggest that there is overall rationality behind collective decisions on policy coordination. The cases offer no evidence of strict rationality on the part of policy makers in deciding what exactly to do, when to do it, and how to do it. Shared scientifically derived knowledge clearly cannot explain the precise policy choices or their timing, but it can help explain when countries are likely to engage in collective action and when they are not.

Disaggregating knowledge enables findings that have theoretical implications even beyond the cases under examination here. The ideas expressed here modify propositions made in game theory, namely that complexity and uncertainty may be positive factors in negotiations because they may produce a "shadow of the future" (Oye 1986) or a "veil of uncertainty" that prevents actors from seeing the implications of different outcomes for their interests (Young 1994).[6] In such conditions, they may be more willing to cooperate in the creation of insurance regimes (Keohane 1984).

Considering different types of information, some veils of uncertainty may be indeed beneficial in negotiations but other veils may be detrimental to the chances of collective action. States could decide to follow the precautionary principle and take costly policy action despite uncertainty and/or incomplete information. It is crucial to emphasize, however, that such uncertainty pertains to particular aspects of the ecological problems: the precise extent of the problem and the relative contributions of its causes. Complete information on such matters is indeed not necessary for cooperative action. One may even argue that the veil of uncertainty created by gaps of this type of information facilitates regime formation. Whether states take action *despite* such uncertainty or *because* of it should be further explored and theorized.

Other types of uncertainty, however, have the opposite effect and hamper policymaking. In particular, gaps of information about the ecological and socioeconomic consequences of a problem are clearly detrimental to efforts at international regime formation. In light of the findings, the proposition may have to be qualified as follows: a veil of uncertainty about the *magnitude* of the problem facilitates or at least does not prevent regime formation, while a veil of uncertainty about *the consequences* of an environmental problem has a highly negative impact on negotiations and reduces incentives to engage in collective action.

Implications for Policymaking and International Law

Some readers are less interested in theories of international politics or international legal doctrines and more concerned with environmental degradation and the need for prompt environmental policy at national and international levels. Apart from its theoretical import, this book offers suggestions to policy makers and natural scientists interested in ways to strengthen the science-politics interface and optimize the use of scientific research in policy-making.

How should societies respond to complex environmental risks when they have incomplete information about them? Traditional scientific standards require high levels of statistical correlation and establishing strict causal links between cause and effect. Yet, absence of evidence is no evidence of absence (of harm). Ecological impacts cannot always be quantified and their timing and magnitude cannot be predicted with certainty. Because of restrictive paradigms, science has frequently failed to predict serious negative impacts of anthropogenic substances and activities on human health and the environment. This is why advocates of the "precautionary principle" in international law argue that irreducible uncertainty should be integrated into management decisions and that incomplete information should not prevent environmental regulations (Tickner 2003). The principle postulates that when environmental threat is possible, preventive action ought to be taken even in the face of scientific uncertainty.[7]

The precautionary principle is gaining wider acceptance in international environmental law (Trouwborst 2002). Legal historians trace its origins back to German national environmental legislation and identify the 1976 air pollution act of the Federal Republic of Germany as the first policy instrument incorporating precaution. Germany also gets credit for introducing and promoting the concept at the international level, during negotiations regarding protection of the North Sea. The principle gradually permeated regional and global environmental politics, spreading through environmental law sector by sector (Trouwborst 2002). Today, more than fifty multilateral agreements are said to contain references to precaution, in one version or another. These include the International Convention on Oil Pollution, the Bamako Convention on Hazardous Waste, the Framework Convention on Climate Change, the Convention on Biological Diversity, the Convention on Persistent Organic Pollutants, and the Protocol on Biosafety. Observers note that by the mid-1990s, the precautionary principle was being incorporated into virtually every international policy document related to environmental management (Cameron 2001).

The contentious implication of the precautionary principle is that policy decisions should be made without the full support of expert information. This controversial point has generated heated debates among various social actors who have a stake in environmental policymaking: philosophers, biologists, economists, policy makers, and corporate and environmental activists.[8] Proponents point out the merits of precaution in protecting human and environmental health, and argue that the precautionary principle should be embraced as a guide in policymaking (O'Riordan et al. 2001; Gollier and Treich 2003; Tickner 2003). Opponents stress the importance of scientifically established facts and insist on policy based on traditional cost-benefit analysis and risk assessment using available information (Hammitt 2000; Morris 2000).

Bypassing the normative question of whether the precautionary principle should be applied, we can illuminate the empirical question of what governments actually do in the face of scientific uncertainty about ecological issues. Evidence supports the view that governments opt for precaution when they are uncertain about the extent of an ecological problem. Contrary to widespread academic notions, however, governments do not apply the precautionary principle under uncertainty about the transboundary consequences of a problem.

The advice for policy makers that draws on the lessons from this study is to appraise carefully the state of expert knowledge about the consequences of a problem before they embark on expensive political initiatives. The forest case, in particular, provides a dramatic example of how futile political efforts can be when the information base for decision-making is weak. In the end, the many global and regional conferences on international forest management wasted precious financial and political resources since they led neither to a policy agreement nor to commitments of additional funding for national forest policies.

Considerable financial and political resources go into organizing and holding conferences that occasionally last for weeks. Additional preparatory meetings, including regional expert meetings, precede each conference. The costs involved, including prices of transcontinental round-trip tickets, hotel accommodations, and gourmet meals, are staggering. The expenditure for simultaneous translation at a single UN conference exceeds $5,000 per day. In trying to generate support for a forest convention, Canada invested in lobbying other governments and in sponsoring the many meetings of the Costa Rica–Canada initiative. These resources and efforts made little difference in changing other governments' positions and no difference at all in affecting the outcome of the regime-making efforts. Policy makers could have saved resources if they had conducted a more careful analysis of the existing scientific information on deforestation. Such an analysis would have revealed that the probability of multilateral accord is meager, given the uncertainty about cross-border consequences of deforestation.

Recommendations can also be made on where to focus scientific research on ecological problems in ways that strengthen efforts to introduce responsible environmental policy. Biologists, chemists, atmospheric scientists, and other natural scientists worldwide try to help in policymaking and are often frustrated when policy makers do not heed their input. Of course, knowledge has inherent value in itself, and research furthers the progress of science in ways that are not always predictable. However, as far as "mandated research" is concerned—whose explicit purpose is to provide input for policy makers and help them make decisions—the design and goals of scientific assessments become important. In particular, assessments should focus on research on the consequences of ecological problems. As the coral case illustrates vividly, even ambitious scientific assessments are not likely to facilitate environmental policy if their design omits research on the consequences of the problem. When there is no conclusive information about the transboundary impact of a problem, then perhaps no effort should be wasted in discussing international treaties.

Achievements and Research Horizons

The study of global governance has much to gain from broad comparative research that covers both positive and negative cases. Explorations of multilateralism are incomplete without probing instances where social actors abstain from collective action, to clarify not only why states cooperate but also why and when they do not cooperate. Widening the scope of comparison to include both regimes and nonregimes strengthens the conclusions about the role of scientific knowledge in regime formation. It allows us to see not only the conducive influence of research-derived information in cases of successful regime formation but also the impeding force of scientific uncertainty in nonregimes. The duality of analyzing both sides of the coin increases our confidence in the strength of the conclusions.

The results of the investigation help us understand some of the reasons why some environmental problems trigger international policy responses while others do not. They reveal to what extent the willingness of states to engage in multilateral action relates to the nature of the issue at hand as defined by shared knowledge about it. The findings clarify which type of shared information is most critical in joint decision-making and warrant the conclusion that reliable knowledge on transboundary externalities facilitates collective action. At the same time, policy makers are willing to tolerate uncertainty regarding other important aspects of a problem. States often follow the precautionary principle and act even in the absence of information about the precise extent of an ecological development. These observations lead to specific policy recommendations that could enhance decision-making in the environmental realm and offer ideas on how to design scientific assessments for more effective and influential input in policymaking.

Discovering the important role of information regarding cross-border consequences is compatible with basic premises of rationalism and neoliberal institutionalism, intellectual traditions that regard states as purposeful actors that create international institutions to pursue common interests more effectively (Koremenos et al. 2001). This is why the apparent match between perceived interests and transboundary ecological impacts should not be particularly surprising. Yet, none of the findings should be regarded as self-evident since they are made possible only by distinguishing between types of information. This analytical step makes possible a breakthrough in revealing clear empirical patterns between collective action and shared knowledge.

Disaggregating the concept of knowledge in analyzing its influence on international policymaking proves to be a valuable tool in exploring the connection between ideas and behavior. The new analytical framework creates broader opportunities to study the interaction between knowledge and interests as well as the relationship between power and knowledge. It enables us to arrive at findings that are more consistent with theoretical expectations about the importance of information and shared knowledge. Eventually, it helps reduce tensions that have haunted previous academic work on the connection between expert knowledge and politics at the international level.

Previous knowledge-based explanations cannot help us understand outcomes because they use an undifferentiated concept of knowledge. From the perspective of the epistemic communities tradition, the failure of regime formation in the forest case would be puzzling given the impressive array of research efforts that are highly institutionalized in the policymaking structures and the steady stream of reports that provide solid information about the extent of deforestation. The puzzle dissolves only when we differentiate between types of information, which enables us to see gaps in data about the consequences of deforestation. In the ozone case, previous accounts overemphasize the uncertainty about the extent of depletion that existed when international agreements were made, and overlook the reliable and undisputed scientific knowledge about the detrimental shared *impact* of potential ozone depletion—information that facilitated reaching these agreements. Thus, it is not possible to provide an adequate knowledge-based explanation of the cases unless we distinguish between different sectors of knowledge.

The centrality of these cases in global environmental politics warrants that these propositions are taken seriously and further tested. At most, they help explain why some environmental problems trigger international policy responses and others do not. At the very least, they demonstrate that proper identification of the role of science in international policymaking requires that we distinguish between different types of scientific information. The analytical framework advanced here is hence a valuable addition to the research agenda of knowledge-based approaches to the study of international cooperation. What we need are further comparative studies that examine the differential role of types of shared knowledge in international environmental politics.

The research agenda can be extended in a number of directions. It would be interesting to explore the role of other types of knowledge that were not investigated here, such as knowledge about policy options. Is science able to tell with certainty whether a particular policy will indeed reduce the problem? What would be the effectiveness of alternative policy options in addressing the problem and reducing its impacts? And how does such information affect decision-making? Examining the influence of information about available policy options, technical solutions, their costs, and effectiveness is a particularly promising avenue for further research, and there are already some productive analyses of this topic (Parson 2003).

It would also be useful to change the dependent variable and study the impact of shared knowledge not on regime formation but on regime design or policy implementation. It does appear, for example, that better understanding of the extent of ozone depletion and its causes contributed to strengthening the already existing policy regime later on. Similarly, improved knowledge about causes of acid rain drove the expansion of the regime into new binding protocols to the convention on transboundary air pollution. Thus, although complete information about the extent and causes of a problem does not appear necessary for overall regime formation, the state of such knowledge may relate to other aspects of regime development such as regime scope and strength. These and other questions merit further research.

Notes

1. One academic debate pertains to the desirability of insulating science from politics. Some argue that attempts at strict separation may hurt advisory processes (Jasanoff 1990), while others observe that separation is beneficial at early stages of knowledge production and engagement between scientists and policymakers is better for later stages of policy formulation (Andresen et al. 2000).

2. On the widely used concept of utility, consult Bruce Bueno de Mesquita's expected utility theory of conflict as well as the work of James Fearon, Duncan Snidal, Kenneth Oye, and James Morrow, among others.

3. Also confirmed by Richard Ballhorn, chief negotiator for Canada at IFF-4. Interviewed December 1999.

4. I am grateful to Oran Young for drawing my attention to this case.

5. Gregory Raymond (1997) and Martha Finnemore and Kathryn Sikkink (1998) have made comprehensive reviews of scholarly work on norms in the social sciences.

6. This idea was first developed by Geoffrey Brennan and James M. Buchanan (1985) and later applied to the analysis of environmental regimes by Oran Young (1994).

7. The principle does not have a definition that is universally accepted. Conceptual inventories have uncovered as many as nineteen different formulations (Sandin 1999). Nevertheless, the common kernel of meaning involves linkage between scientific uncertainty and policy action: when the possibility of environmental threat arises, preventive action ought to be taken even when the relevant scientific information is incomplete or unreliable. The postulate has a reactive and a proactive version. First, scientific uncertainty about a potential problem should not stop governments from taking regulatory policy action to protect the environment and human health. The Organization for Economic Cooperation and Development declared: "the absence of complete information should not preclude precautionary action to mitigate the risk of significant harm to the environment" (cited in Trouwborst 2002, 27–28). Reversely, governments should not allow new substances or activities such as genetically engineered foods if their potential impacts are not fully understood. The 1982 World Charter for Nature stipulates that "where potential adverse effects [of socioeconomic activities] are not fully understood, the activities should not proceed." Thus, the precautionary principle implies that scientific uncertainty should be treated as either a green light for regulatory action or as a red light at the crossroads of policy choices.

8. See, for instance, special issues of *Foundations of Science* 2 (1997), *Human and Ecological Risk Assessment* vol. 6, no. 3 (2000), and *Journal of Risk Research* vol. 5, no. 4 (2002).

References

Abrahamsen, G. 1984. "Effects of acidic deposition on forest soil and vegetation." In *Ecological Effects of Deposited Sulphur and Nitrogen Compounds.* Edited by J. Beament, A. D. Bradshaw, P. F. Chester, M. W. Holdgate, M. Sugden, and B. A Thrush. London: The Royal Society.

Adey, W. H. 1998. "Coral reefs: Conservation by valuation and the utilization of pharmaceutical potential." In *Coral Reefs: Challenges and Opportunities for Sustainable Management.* Edited by M. E. Hatziolos, A. J. Hooten, and M. Fodor. Washington, D.C.: World Bank.

Adger, W. N., K. Brown, R. Cervigni, and D. Moran. 1995. Total Economic Value of Forests in Mexico. *Ambio* 24(5):286–96.

Alcamo, Joseph, Roderick Shaw, and Leen Hordijk (eds.). 1991. *The RAINS Model of Acidification.* IIASA Executive Report 18. Laxenburg, Austria: IIASA.

Anderson, J. G., W. H. Brune, and M. J. Proffitt. 1989. Ozone Destruction by Chlorine Radicals within the Antarctic Vortex: The Spatial and Temporal Evolution of $ClO-O_s$ Anticorrelation Based on In Situ ER-2 Data. *Journal of Geophysical Research* 94:11465–79.

Andresen, Steinar, and Willy Østreng (eds.). 1989. *International Resource Management: The Role of Science and Politics.* New York: Belhaven Press.

Andresen, Steinar, Tora Skodvin, Arild Underdal, and Jørgen Wettestäd. 2000. *Science and Politics in International Environmental Regimes: Between Integrity and Involvement.* New York: Manchester University Press.

Bakken, Per M. 1989. "Science and politics in the protection of the ozone layer." In *International Resource Management: The Role of Science and Politics.* Edited by Steinar Andresen and Willy Østreng. New York: Belhaven Press.

Barber, C. V., and V. R. Platt. 1998. "Policy reform and community-based programs to combat cyanide fishing in the Asia-Pacific region." In *Coral Reefs: Challenges and*

Opportunities for Sustainable Management. Edited by M. E. Hatziolos, A. J. Hooten, and M. Fodor. Washington, D.C.: World Bank.

Baumgartner, F. R., and B. D. Jones. 1993. *Agendas and Instability in American Politics.* Chicago: University of Chicago Press.

Beament, James, A. D. Bradshaw, P. F. Chester, M. W. Holdgate, M. Sugden, and B. A. Thrush (eds.). 1984. *Ecological Effects of Deposited Sulphur and Nitrogen Compounds.* London: The Royal Society.

Beck, Ulrich. 1992. *Risk Society: Toward a New Modernity.* London: Sage.

Benedick, Richard Elliot. 1998. *Ozone Diplomacy: New Directions in Safeguarding the Planet,* 2nd edition. Cambridge, Mass.: Harvard University Press.

Bernstein, Steven, and Benjamin Cashore. 2004. "Non-state global governance: Is forest certification a legitimate alternative to a global forest convention?" In *Hard Choices, Soft Law: Combining Trade, Environment, and Social Cohesion in Global Governance.* Edited by John Kirton and Michael Trebilcock. Aldershot, England: Ashgate Press.

Biggs, R. H., and S. V. Kossuth. 1978. "Effects of ultraviolet-B radiation enhancement under field conditions on potatoes, tomatoes, corn, rice, southern peas, peanuts, squash, mustard and radish." UV-B Biological and Climatic Effects Research (BACER), Final Report. Washington, D.C.: EPA.

Binns, W. O., and D. B. Redfern. 1982. *Acid Rain and Forest Decline in West Germany.* Forestry Commission Research and Development Paper 131. Farnham, Hants, UK: Forestry Commission.

Blyth, M. M. 1997. Ideas and Institutions. *Comparative Politics* 29(2):229–50.

Boehmer-Christiansen, Sonja. 1989. "The role of science in the international regulation of pollution." In *International Resource Management: The Role of Science and Politics.* Edited by Steinar Andresen and Willy Østreng. London: Belhaven Press.

Boehmer-Christiansen, Sonja, and Jim Skea. 1991. *Acid Politics: Environmental and Energy Politics in Britain and Germany.* London: Belhaven Press.

Botcheva, Liliana, and Lisa Martin. 2001. Institutional Effects on State Behavior: Convergence and Divergence. *International Studies Quarterly* 45:1–27.

Brennan, Geoffrey, and James M. Buchanan. 1985. *The Reason of Rules: Constitutional Political Economy.* Cambridge, UK: Cambridge University Press.

Brewer, Gary D., and Peter DeLeon. 1983. *The Foundations of Policy Analysis.* Homewood, Ill.: Dorsey Press.

Brickman, Ronald, Sheila Jasanoff, and Thomas Ilgen. 1985. *Controlling Chemicals: The Politics of Regulation in Europe and the United States.* Ithaca, N.Y.: Cornell University Press.

Bryant, D., L. Burke, J. McManus, and M. Spalding (eds.). 1998. *Reefs at Risk. A Map-Based Indicator of Threats to the World's Coral Reefs.* Washington, D.C.: World Resources Institute, International Center for Living Aquatic Resources Management, World Conservation Monitoring Centre, and the United Nations Environmental Programme.

Cagin, Seth, and Philip Dray. 1993. *Between Earth and Sky.* New York: Pantheon Books.

Caldwell, Lynton Keith. 1996. *International Environmental Policy.* Durham, N.C.: Duke University Press.

Cameron, James. 2001. "The precautionary principle in international law." In *Reinterpreting the Precautionary Principle*. Edited by Tim O'Riordan, James Cameron, and Andrew Jordan. London: Cameron May.

Cashore, Benjamin, Graeme Auld, and Deanna Newsom. 2004. *Governing through Markets: Forest Certification and the Emergence of Non-state Authority*. New Haven, Conn.: Yale University Press.

Cesar, Herman. 1996. *Economic Analysis of Indonesian Coral Reefs*. Washington, D.C.: World Bank.

———. 1998. "Indonesian coral reefs: A precious but threatened resource." In *Coral Reefs: Challenges and Opportunities for Sustainable Management*. Edited by M. E. Hatziolos, A. J. Hooten, and M. Fodor. Washington, D.C.: World Bank.

Clark, William, Ronald Mitchell, David Cash, and Frank Alcock. 2002. "Information as influence: How institutions mediate the impact of scientific assessments on global environmental affairs." Faculty Research Working Paper RWP02-044. John F. Kennedy School of Government, Harvard University.

Collingridge, David, and Collin Reeve. 1986. *Science Speaks to Power: The Role of Experts in Policymaking*. New York: St. Martin's Press.

Costanza, Robert, Ralph d'Arge, Rudolf de Groot, Stephen Farber, Monica Grasso, Bruce Hannon, Karin Limburg, Shahid Naeem, Robert V. O'Neill, Jose Paruelo, Robert G. Raskin, Paul Sutton, and Marjan van den Belt. 1997. The Value of the World's Ecosystem Services and Natural Capital. *Nature* 387:253–60.

Crutzen, Paul. 1974. A Review of Upper Atmospheric Chemistry. *Canadian Journal of Chemistry* 52:1569–81.

Dauvergne, Peter. 2001. *Loggers and Degradation in the Asia-Pacific: Corporations and Environmental Management*. Cambridge: Cambridge University Press.

Davenport, Deborah S. 2005. An Alternative Explanation for the Failure of the UNCED Forest Negotiations. *Global Environmental Politics* 5(1):105–30.

DeLeon, Peter. 1999. "The stages approach to the policy process: What has it done? Where is it going?" In *Theories of the Policy Process*. Edited by Paul Sabatier. Boulder, Colo.: Westview.

DeSombre, Elizabeth R., and Joanne Kauffman. 1996. "The Montreal Protocol multilateral fund: Partial success story." In *Institutions for Environmental Aid*. Edited by Robert O. Keohane and Marc A. Levy. Cambridge, Mass.: MIT Press.

Dimitrov, Radoslav S. 2002. Confronting Non-Regimes: Science and International Coral Reef Policy. *Journal of Environment and Development* 11(1):53–78.

———. 2004. "Lost in the woods: International forest policy." In *Science and Politics in the International Environment*. Edited by Neil E. Harrison and Gary C. Bryner. Lanham, Md.: Rowman & Littlefield.

———. 2005. Hostage to Norms: States, Institutions and Global Forest Politics. *Global Environmental Politics* 5(4):1–24.

Dixon, R. K., S. Brown, R. A. Houghton, A. M. Solomon, M. C. Trexler, and J. Wisniewski. 1994. Carbon Pools and Flux of ·Global Forest Ecosystems. *Science* 263:185–90.

Douglas, Mary, and Aaron Wildavsky. 1982. *Risk and Culture: An Essay on the Selection of Technical and Environmental Dangers*. Berkeley: University of California Press.

Drabløs, D., and A. Tollan (eds.). 1980. *Ecological Impact of Acid Precipitation.* Proceedings of an international conference, Sandefjord, Norway, May 11–14. Oslo: SNSF.

Dürch, H. U. 1974. The Ozone Distribution in the Atmosphere. *Canadian Journal of Chemistry* 52:1491–504.

E/CN.17/1997/12. *Report of the Intergovernmental Panel on Forests to the UN Commission on Sustainable Development.* United Nations.

E/CN.17/IFF/1998/L.1. *Report on the first session of the Intergovernmental Forum on Forests.* United Nations.

E/CN.17/IFF/2000. *Final Report of IFF to the UN Commission on Sustainable Development.* United Nations.

ECE/LRTAP. 1995. *Strategies and Policies for Air Pollution Abatement: 1994 Major Review.* Geneva: Economic Commission for Europe.

Emmett, Edward. 1986. "Health effects of ultraviolet radiation." In *Effects of Changes in Stratospheric Ozone and Climate Change,* vol. 2. Edited by James Titus. Washington, D.C.: UNEP/EPA.

EPA (Environmental Protection Agency). 1979. *Acid Rain Research Summary.* Washington, D.C.: EPA 600/8-79-028.

———. 1986. *Regulatory Impact Analysis: Protection of Stratospheric Ozone.* Washington D.C.: EPA.

———. 1987. *Assessing the Risks of Trace Gases that Can Modify the Stratosphere.* Washington, D.C.: EPA.

ERL (Environmental Resources Limited). 1983. *Acid Rain: A Review of the Phenomenon in the EEC and Europe.* London: Graham and Trotman.

FAO (Food and Agriculture Organization). 1976. *Forest Resources in the Asia and Far East.* Rome: FAO.

———. 1982. *Tropical Forest Resources.* Rome: FAO.

———. 1987. *Small-Scale Forest-Based Processing Enterprises.* Rome: FAO.

———. 1993. *Forest Resources Assessment: Tropical Countries.* Rome: FAO.

———. 1995a. *Forest Resources Assessment 1990: Global Synthesis.* FAO Forestry Paper 124. Rome: FAO.

———. 1995b. *State of the World's Forests.* Rome: FAO.

———. 1995c. *Non-Wood Forest Products,* Report of the International Expert Consultation on Non-Wood Forest Products. Rome: FAO.

———. 1996. *Survey of Tropical Forest Cover.* Rome: FAO.

———. 1997. *State of the World's Forests.* Rome: FAO.

———. 2001. *Forest Resources Assessment 2000: Main Report.* Rome: FAO.

Farman, Joseph C., B. G. Gariner and J. D. Shanklin. 1985. Large Losses of Total Ozone in Antarctica Reveal Seasonal ClO_x/NO_x Interaction. *Nature* 315:207–10.

Finnemore, Martha, and Kathryn Sikkink. 1998. International Norms Dynamics and Political Change. *International Organization* 52(4):887–917.

Gale, Fred P. 1998. *The Tropical Timber Trade Regime.* New York: St. Martin's Press.

GCRMN (Global Coral Reef Monitoring Network). 1998. *Status of Coral Reefs of the World: 1998.* Townsville, Queensland: Australian Institute of Marine Science. Available at: http://www.aims.gov.au/pages/research/coral-bleaching/scr1998/scr-00.html.

———. 2000. *Status of Coral Reefs of the World: 2000*. Townsville, Queensland: Australian Institute of Marine Science.

———. 2002. *Status of Coral Reefs of the World: 2002*. Townsville, Queensland: Australian Institute of Marine Science.

———. 2004. *Status of Coral Reefs of the World: 2004*. Townsville, Queensland: Australian Institute of Marine Science.

GEA (Global Environmental Assessments Project). 1997. *A Critical Evaluation of Global Environmental Assessments: The Climate Experience*. Calverton, Md.: CARE.

Gehring, Thomas. 1994. *Dynamic International Regimes: Institutions for International Environmental Governance*. Frankfurt: Peter Lang.

Goldstein, Judith, and Robert O. Keohane (eds.). 1993. *Ideas and Foreign Policy: Beliefs, Institutions, and Political Change*. Ithaca, N.Y.: Cornell University Press.

Gollier, Christian, and Nicolas Treich. 2003. Decisionmaking under Scientific Uncertainty: The Economics of the Precautionary Principle. *The Journal of Risk and Uncertainty* 27(1):77–103.

Gorham, Eville. 1958. Atmospheric Pollution by Hydrochloric Acid. *Quarterly Journal of the Royal Meteorological Society* 84:274–76.

Grayson, A. J., and W. B. Maynard. 1997. *The World's Forests—Rio + 5: International Initiatives towards Sustainable Management*. Oxford: Commonwealth Forestry Association.

Haas, Ernst B. 1975. Is There a Hole in the Whole? Knowledge, Technology, Interdependence, and the Construction of International Regimes. *International Organization* 29:827–76.

———. 1982. Words Can Hurt You; Or, Who Said What to Whom about Regimes. *International Organization* 36(2):207–43.

Haas, Peter M. 1990. *Saving the Mediterranean: The Politics of International Environmental Cooperation*. New York: Columbia University Press.

———. (ed.). 1992a. *Knowledge, Power and International Policy Coordination*. Special Issue of *International Organization* 46(1).

———. 1992b. Banning Chlorofluorocarbons: Epistemic Community Efforts to Protect Stratospheric Ozone. *International Organization* 46(1):187–224.

———. 1993. "Stratospheric ozone: Regime formation in stages." In *Polar Politics: Creating International Environmental Regimes*. Edited by Oran Young and Gail Osherenko. Ithaca, N.Y.: Cornell University Press.

———. (ed.). 1997. *Knowledge, Power, and International Policy Coordination*. Columbia: University of South Carolina Press.

Haas, Peter M., Robert O. Keohane, and Marc A. Levy. 1993. *Institutions for the Earth: Sources of Effective International Environmental Protection*. Cambridge, Mass.: MIT Press.

Haggard, Stephan, and Beth A. Simmons. 1987. Theories of International Regimes. *International Organization* 41(3):491–517.

Haigh, N. 1989. New Tools for European Air Pollution Control. *International Environmental Affairs* 1:26–38.

Hajer, Maarten A. 1995. *The Politics of Environmental Discourse, Ecological Modernization, and the Policy Process*. Oxford: Claredon Press.

Hall, Peter, (ed.). 1989. *The Political Power of Economic Ideas: Keynesianism across Nations*. Princeton, N.J.: Princeton University Press.

Hammitt, James K. 2000. Global Climate Change: Benefit-Cost Analysis vs. the Precautionary Principle. *Human and Ecological Risk Assessment* 6(3):387–98.

Harrison, Neil E., and Gary C. Bryner (eds.). 2004a. *Science and Politics in the International Environment*. Lanham Md.: Rowman & Littlefield.

———. 2004b. "Thinking about science and politics." In *Science and Politics in the International Environment*. Edited by Neil E. Harrison and Gary C. Bryner. Lanham Md.: Rowman & Littlefield.

Hasenclever, Andreas, Peter Mayer, and Volker Rittberger. 1997. *Theories of International Regimes*. Cambridge, UK: Cambridge University Press.

Hatziolos, M. E. 1998. "Summary and recommendations." In *Coral Reefs: Challenges and Opportunities for Sustainable Management*. Edited by M. E. Hatziolos, A. J. Hooten, and M. Fodor. Washington, D.C.: World Bank.

Hatziolos, M. E., A. J. Hooten, and M. Fodor (eds.). 1998. *Coral Reefs: Challenges and Opportunities for Sustainable Management*. Proceedings of an associated event of the Fifth Annual World Bank Conference on Environmentally and Socially Sustainable Development, October 9–11, 1997. Washington, D.C.: World Bank.

Hempel, L. C., and S. Morozova. 1999. "Science into policy: Designing coral reef management from the benthos up." Paper presented at the International Conference on Scientific Aspects of Coral Reef Assessment, Monitoring, and Restoration, Ft. Lauderdale, Florida.

Hettelingh, Jean-Paul, Robert J. Downing, and Peter A. M. de Smet (eds.). 1991. *Mapping Critical Loads for Europe: CCE Technical Report No. 1*, RIVM Report no. 259101001. Bilthoven, the Netherlands: LRTAP Coordinating Center for Effects, Netherlands National Institute for Public Health and Environmental Protection.

Hiller, R., L. Giacometti, and K. Yuan. 1977. Sunlight and Cataract: An Epidemiological Investigation. *American Journal of Epidemiology* 105:450–59.

Hoskins, Marilyn. 1990. The Contribution of Forestry to Food Security. *Unasylva* 41(1).

House of Commons Environment Committee. 1984. *Fourth Report: Acid Rain*. London: HMSO.

Humphreys, David. 1996. *Forest Politics: The Evolution of International Cooperation*. London: Earthscan Publications.

———. 2003. Life Protective or Carcinogenic Challenge? Global Forests Governance under Advanced Capitalism. *Global Environmental Politics* 3(2):40–55.

———. 2004. Redefining the Issues: NGO Influence on International Forest Negotiations. *Global Environmental Politics* 4(2):51–74.

Hunter, David. 1989. CFC Prices Soar as Capacity Is Cut. *Chemical Week*, April 26, p. 14.

Hutchinson, Thomas. C., and Magda Havas (eds.). 1980. *Effects of Acid Precipitation on Terrestrial Ecosystems*. NATO Conference on Effects of Acid Precipitation on Vegetation and Soils; Toronto, May 1978. New York: Plenum Press.

IGBP/NOAA. 1998. *Coral Reefs and Global Change: Adaptation, Acclimation or Extinction*. Report of working group 104 of the Scientific Committee on Oceanic Research.

[On-line.] Available at: http://www.aims.gov.au/pages/research/coral-bleaching/global-change/global-change-02.html

IPCC (Intergovernmental Panel on Climate Change). 1996. *Climate Change 1995.* Cambridge, UK: Cambridge University Press.

ITTO (International Tropical Timber Organization). 1996. *ITTO: Ten Years of Progress.* Yokohama: ITTO.

Jameson, S. C., J. W. McManus, and M. D. Spalding. 1995. *State of the Reefs: Regional and Global Perspectives.* Washington, D.C.: U.S. Department of State.

Jasanoff, Sheila. 1986. *Risk Management and Political Culture: A Comparative Study of Science in the Policy Context.* New York: Russell Sage Foundation.

———. 1990. *The Fifth Branch: Science Advisers as Policymakers.* Cambridge, Mass.: Harvard University Press.

Johnston, H. 1971. Reduction of Stratospheric Ozone by Nitrogen Oxide Catalysts from Supersonic Transport Exhaust. *Science* 173:517–22.

Jones, Charles O. 1984. *An Introduction to the Study of Public Policy,* 2nd edition. North Scituate, Mass.: Duxbury Press.

Keck, Margaret E., and Kathryn Sikkink. 1998. *Activists beyond Borders: Advocacy Networks in International Politics.* Ithaca, N.Y.: Cornell University Press.

Keith, L. D. 2000. "Coral reefs overwhelmed." *ABC News.* [On-line.] Available at: http://abcnews.go.com/sections/science/DailyNews/coralreef000516.html.

Kelly, John. 1986. "How might enhanced levels of solar UV-B radiation affect marine ecosystems?" In *Effects of Changes in Stratospheric Ozone and Climate Change,* vol. 2. Edited by James Titus. Washington, D.C.: UNEP/EPA.

Kenchington, Richard. 1998. "Status of the international coral reef initiative." In *Coral Reefs: Challenges and Opportunities for Sustainable Management.* Edited by M. E. Hatziolos, A. J. Hooten, and M. Fodor. Washington, D.C.: World Bank.

Keohane, Robert O. 1984. *After Hegemony: Cooperation and Discord in the World Political Economy.* Princeton, N.J.: Princeton University Press.

———. 1988. International Institutions: Two Approaches. *International Studies Quarterly* 32: 379–96.

———. 1989. *International Institutions and State Power: Essays in International Relations.* Boulder, Colo.: Westview.

Keohane, Robert O., and Elinor Ostrom (eds.). 1995. *Local Commons and Global Interdependence.* London: Sage.

King, Gary, Robert O. Keohane, and Sidney Verba. 1994. *Designing Social Inquiry: Scientific Inference in Qualitative Research.* Princeton, N.J.: Princeton University Press.

Kingdon, John W. 1984. *Agendas, Alternatives, and Public Policies.* Boston: Little, Brown.

Kitcher, Philip. 1989. "Explanatory unification and the causal structure of the world." In *Scientific Explanation.* Edited by Philip Kitcher and Wesley C. Salmon. Minneapolis: University of Minnesota Press.

Knowlton, Nancy. 1998. "Hard decisions and hard science: Research needs for coral reef management." In *Coral Reefs: Challenges and Opportunities for Sustainable Management.* Edited by M. E. Hatziolos, A. J. Hooten, and M. Fodor. Washington, D.C.: World Bank.

———. 2001. *The Future of Coral Reefs.* Proceedings of the National Academy of Sciences 98(10):5419–25.

Koch, N. E., and M. Linddal. 1993. "Commentary on the results of the assessment." In *The Forest Resources of the Temperate Zones: The UN-ECE/FAO 1990 Forest Resources Assessment,* Vol. II: *Benefit and Functions of the Forest.* New York: United Nations.

Kolk, Ans. 1996. *Forests in International Environmental Politics: International Organizations, NGOs and the Brazilian Amazon.* Utrecht, Netherlands: International Books.

Koremenos, Barbara, Charles Lipson, and Duncan Snidal. 2001. *The Rational Design of International Institutions.* Cambridge, Mass.: Cambridge University Press.

Krasner, Stephen (ed.). 1983. *International Regimes.* Ithaca, N.Y.: Cornell University Press.

Kratochwil, Friedrich V. 1989. *Rules, Norms, and Decisions: On the Conditions of Practical and Legal Reasoning in International Relations and Domestic Affairs.* Cambridge, Mass.: Cambridge University Press.

Krugg, Edward C., and Charles R. Frink. 1983. Acid Rain on Acid Soil: A New Perspective. *Science* 221:520–25.

Kuhn, Thomas. 1970. *The Structure of Scientific Revolutions.* Chicago: University of Chicago Press.

Latour, Bruno, and S. Woolgar. 1979. *Laboratory Life: The Social Construction of Scientific Facts.* Princeton, N.J.: Princeton University Press.

Levy, Marc A. 1993. "European acid rain: The power of tote-board diplomacy." In *Institutions for the Earth: Sources of Effective International Environmental Protection.* Edited by Peter M. Haas, Robert O. Keohane, and Marc A. Levy. Cambridge, Mass.: MIT Press.

Lidskog, Rolf, and Göran Sundqvist. 2002. The Role of Science in Environmental Regimes: The Case of LRTAP. *European Journal of International Relations* 8(1):77–101.

Lipschutz, Ronnie D. 2001. Why Is There No International Forestry Law? An Examination of International Forestry Regulation, Both Private and Public. *UCLA Journal of Environmental Law and Policy* 19(1):153–79.

Litfin, Karen T. 1994. *Ozone Discourses: Science and Politics in Global Environmental Cooperation.* New York: Columbia University Press.

———. 1995. Framing Science: Precautionary Discourse and the Ozone Treaties. *Millennium: Journal of International Studies* 24(2):251–77.

Lowrance, William W. 1976. *Of Acceptable Risk: Science and the Determination of Safety.* Los Altos, Calif.: W. Kaufmann.

Lumsdaine, David Halloran. 1993. *Moral Vision in International Politics: The Foreign Aid Regime, 1949–1989.* Princeton, N.J.: Princeton University Press.

Lundvist, Lennart J. 1980. *The Hare and the Tortoise: Clean Air Policies in the United States and Sweden.* Ann Arbor: University of Michigan Press.

Magnuson, J. J., J. P. Baker, and E. J. Rahel. 1984. "A critical assessment of effects of acidification on fisheries in North America." In *Ecological Effects of Deposited Sulphur and Nitrogen Compounds.* Edited by James Beament, A. D. Bradshaw, P. F. Chester, M. W. Holdgate, M. Sugden, and B. A. Thrush. London: The Royal Society.

Mahoney, James, and Gary Goertz. 2004. The Possibility Principle: Choosing Negative Cases in Comparative Research. *American Political Science Review* 98(4):653–69.

Maugh, Thomas H. 1984. Acid Rain's Effects on People Assessed. *Science* 4681:1408–10.

McConnell, J. C. 1974. Uncertainties in Stratospheric-Mesospheric Modeling. *Canadian Journal of Chemistry* 52(8):1625–33.

McCormick, John. 1985. *Acid Earth: The Global Threat of Acid Pollution*. London: Earthscan.

McInnis, Daniel F. 1992. "Ozone layers and oligopoly profits." In *Environmental Politics: Public Costs, Private Rewards*. Edited by Michael S. Greve and Fred L. Smith, Jr. New York: Praeger.

McWilliam, F. 1997. Turning the Tide. *Geographical Magazine* 69(3):18–19.

Merton, Robert K. 1973. *The Sociology of Science: Theoretical and Empirical Investigations*. Chicago: University of Chicago Press.

Meyer, John W., David John Frank, Ann Hironaka, Evan Schofer, and Nancy Brandon Tuma. 1997. The Structuring of a World Environmental Regime, 1870–1990. *International Organization* 51(4):623–51.

Miles, Edward L. Arild Underdal, Steinar Andresen, Jørgen Wettestäd, Jon Birger Skærseth, and Elaine M. Carlin. 2002. *Environmental Regime Effectiveness: Confronting Theory with Evidence*. Cambridge, Mass.: MIT Press.

Miller, Clark A. and Paul N. Edwards (eds.). 2001a. *Changing the Atmosphere: Expert Knowledge and Environmental Governance*. Cambridge, Mass.: MIT Press.

———. 2001b. "Introduction: The globalization of climate science and climate politics." In *Changing the Atmosphere: Expert Knowledge and Environmental Governance*. Edited by Clark A. Miller and Paul N. Edwards. Cambridge, Mass.: MIT Press.

Ministry of Food, Agriculture and Forestry. 1982. *Forest Damage Due to Air Pollution: The Situation in the Federal Republic of Germany*. Bonn: The Ministry of Food, Agriculture and Forestry.

Molina, Mario J., and F. Sherwood Rowland. 1974. Stratospheric Sink for Chlorfluoromethanes: Chlorine Atom Catalyzed Destruction of Ozone. *Nature* 249:810–12.

Morris, Julian (ed.). 2000. *Rethinking Risk and the Precautionary Principle*. Oxford: Butterworth Heinemann.

Mulkay, M. 1978. Consensus in Science. *Sociology of Science* 17:107–22.

Muniz, I. P. 1984. "The effects of acidification on Scandinavian freshwater fish fauna." In *Ecological Effects of Deposited Sulphur and Nitrogen Compounds*. Edited by James Beament, A. D. Bradshaw, P. F. Chester, M. W. Holdgate, M. Sugden, and B. A. Thrush. London: The Royal Society.

Munton, Don. 2001. "Constructing International and Domestic Environmental Interests: Acidification in Ontario, 1917–1991." Paper presented at the annual meeting of the International Studies Association, Chicago.

Munton, Don, Marvin Soroos, Elena Nikitina, and Marc A. Levy. 1999. "Acid rain in Europe and North America." In *The Effectiveness of International Environmental Regimes: Causal Connections and Behavioral Mechanisms*. Edited by Oran R. Young. Cambridge, Mass.: MIT Press.

Myers, Norman. 1980. *Conversion of Tropical Moist Forests*. Washington, D.C.: National Academy of Science.

———. 1989. *Deforestation in Tropical Forests and Their Climatic Implications*. London: Friends of the Earth.

Myers, Norman, and Jennifer Kent. 2001. "Forestry." In *Perverse Subsidies: How Tax Dollars Can Undercut the Environment and the Economy*. Edited by Norman Myers and Jennifer Kent. Washington, D.C.: Island Press.

NAS (National Academy of Sciences). 1981. *Atmosphere-Biosphere Interactions: Toward a Better Understanding of the Ecological Consequences of Fossil Fuel Combustion*. Washington, D.C.: National Academy Press.

NASA (National Aeronautics and Space Administration) 1986. *Present State of Knowledge of the Upper Atmosphere: An Assessment Report*. Washington, D.C.: NASA.

Nelson, Barbara. 1984. *Making an Issue of Child Abuse: Political Agenda Setting for Social Problems*. Chicago: University of Chicago Press.

Nilsson, J. (ed.). 1986. *Critical Loads for Nitrogen and Sulphur*. Stockholm: Nordisk Ministerrad.

Nilsson, Sten. 1996. *Do We Have Enough Forests?* IUFRO Occasional Paper No. 5. Vienna: International Union of Forest Research Organizations.

NRC (National Research Council). 1975. *Environmental Impact of Stratospheric Flight. Biological and Climatic Effects of Aircraft Emissions in the Stratosphere*. Washington, D.C.: National Academy of Sciences.

———. 1976. *Halocarbons: Effects on Stratospheric Ozone*. Washington, D.C.: National Academy Press.

———. 1979a. *Stratospheric Ozone Depletion by Halocarbons: Chemistry and Transport*. Washington, D.C.: National Academy of Sciences.

———. 1979b. *Protection Against Depletion of Stratospheric Ozone by Chlorofluorocarbons*. Washington, D.C.: National Academy of Sciences.

———. 1982. *Causes and Effects of Stratospheric Ozone Reduction: An Update*. Washington, D.C: National Academy of Sciences.

———. 1983. *Acid Deposition: Atmospheric Processes in Eastern North America: A Review of Current Scientific Understanding*. Washington, D.C.: National Academy Press.

———. 1984. *Causes and Effects of Changes in Stratospheric Ozone: Update 1983*. Washington, D.C.: National Academy of Sciences.

———. 1996. *Understanding Risk: Informing Decisions in a Democratic Society*. Washington, D.C.: National Academy Press.

Nriagu, J. O. (ed.). 1978. *Sulfur in the Environment*. New York: John Wiley.

Nyyssönen, A., and A. Ahti (eds.). 1997. *Proceedings of FAO Expert Consultation on Global Forest Resources Assessment 2000*. Research Paper 620. Helsinki: Finnish Forest Research Institute.

Oden, Svante 1968. The Acidification of Air and Precipitation and Its Consequences in the Natural Environment. *Ecology Committee Bulletin*, No. 1. Stockholm: Swedish National Research Council.

OECD. 1972. *Cooperative Technical Programme to Measure the Long-Range Transport of Air Pollutants*. Paris: OECD Environment Directorate.

———. 1977. *The OECD Programme on Long Range Transport of Air Pollutants: Summary Report*. Paris: OECD Environment Directorate.

Onion, Amanda. 2000. "New protection: Commerce secretary announces new measures." *ABC News*, December 1. [On-line.] Available at: http://www.abcnews.go.com/sections/science/DailyNews/corals001211.html

O'Riordan, Tim, James Cameron and Andrew Jordan (eds.), 2001. *Reinterpreting the Precautionary Principle*. London: Cameron May.

Oye, Kenneth A. (ed.). 1986. *Cooperation under Anarchy*. Princeton, N.J.: Princeton University Press.

Päivinen, R., and A.J.R. Gillespie. 2000. *Estimating Global Forest Change 1980–1990–2000*. Rome: FAO.

Park, Chris. 1987. *Acid Rain—Rhetoric and Reality*. London: Methuen.

Parson, Edward, A. 1993. "Protecting the ozone layer." In *Institutions for the Earth: Sources of Effective International Environmental Protection*. Edited by Peter M. Haas, Robert O. Keohane, and Marc A. Levy. London: MIT Press.

———. 2003. *Protecting the Ozone Layer: Science and Strategy*. Oxford: Oxford University Press.

Parson, Edward A., and William C. Clark. 1995. "Sustainable development as social learning: Theoretical perspectives and practical challenges for the design of a research program." In *Barriers and Bridges to the Renewal of Ecosystems and Institutions*. Edited by Lance H. Gunderson, C. S. Holling, and Stephen S. Light. New York: Columbia University Press.

Paterson, Matthew. 1996. *Global Warming and Global Politics*. New York: Routledge.

Patrick, Ruth, Victoria P. Binetti, and Steven G. Halterman. 1981. Acid Lakes from Natural and Anthropogenic Causes. *Science* 4481:446–48.

Persson, R. 1975. *Forest Resources of Africa*. Stockholm: Department of Forest Survey.

Pimentel, David, Michael McNair, Louise Buck, Marcia Pimentel, and Jeremy Kamil. 1997. The Value of Forests to World Food Security. *Human Ecology* 25(1):91–120.

Pitelka, Louis F., and Dudley J. Raynal. 1989. Forest Decline and Acidic Deposition. *Ecology* 70(1):2–10.

Porter, Gareth, Janet Welsh Brown, and Pamela Chasek. 2000. *Global Environmental Politics*. Boulder, Colo.: Westview, 3rd edition.

Price, Richard M. 1997. *The Chemical Weapons Taboo*. Ithaca, N.Y.: Cornell University Press.

Przeworski, Adam, and Henry Teune. 1970. *The Logic of Comparative Social Inquiry*. New York: John Wiley.

Rahn, R. O. 1979. Non-dimer Damage in Deoxyribonucleic Acid Caused by Ultraviolet Radiation. *Photochemical and Photobiological Reviews* 4:267–330.

Railton, Peter. 1989. "Explanation and metaphysical controversy." In *Scientific Explanation*. Edited by Philip Kitcher and Wesley C. Salmon. Minneapolis: University of Minnesota Press.

Raymond, Gregory A. 1997. Problems and Prospects in the Study of International Norms. *Mershon International Studies Review* 41:205–45.

Reakla-Kudla, M. L. 1997. "The global biodiversity of coral reefs: A comparison with rain forests." In *Biodiversity II: Understanding and Protecting Our Natural Resources*. Edited by M. L. Reakla-Kudla, D. E. Wilson, and E. O. Wilson. Washington, D.C.: Joseph Henry Press.

Repetto, Robert. 1988. "Overview." In *Public Policies and the Misuse of Forest Resources.* Edited by Robert Repetto and Malcolm Gillis. Cambridge, Mass.: Cambridge University Press.

Rittberger, Volker, and Peter Meyer (eds.). 1993. *Regime Theory and International Relations.* New York: Oxford University Press.

Roan, Sharon. 1989. *Ozone Crisis: The 15-Year Evolution of a Sudden Global Emergency.* New York: John Wiley and Sons.

Rochefort, D. A., and Roger W. Cobb (eds.). 1994. *The Politics of Problem Definition: Shaping the Policy Agenda.* Lawrence: University Press of Kansas.

Rowe, R., N. P. Sharma, and J. Browder. 1992. "Deforestation: Problems, causes, and concerns." In *Managing the World's Forests: Looking for Balance between Conservation and Development.* Edited by N. P. Sharma. Dubuque, Iowa: Kendall/Hunt.

Rowland, F. S. 1986. A Threat to Earth's Protective Shield. *EPA Journal* 12(10).

Rowlands, Ian H. 1995. *The Politics of Global Atmospheric Change.* Manchester, UK: Manchester University Press.

Sabatier, Paul, and H. C. Jenkins-Smith (eds.). 1993. *Policy Change and Learning: An Advocacy Coalition Approach.* Boulder, Colo.: Westview.

Saito, I., H. Sugiyama, and T. Matsura. 1983. Photochemical Reactions of Nucleic Acids and Their Constituents of Photobiological Relevance. *Photochemistry and Photobiology* 38:735–43.

Sand, Peter H. 1992. *Effectiveness of International Environmental Agreements: A Survey of Existing Legal Instruments.* Cambridge, UK: Grotius Publications.

Sandin, Per. 1999. Dimensions of the Precautionary Principle. *Human and Ecological Risk Assessment* 5(5):889–907.

Schindler, D. W. 1988. Effects of Acid Rain on Freshwater Ecosystems. *Science* 4836:149–57.

Schon, Donald A., and Martin Rein. 1994. *Frame Reflection: Toward the Resolution of Intractable Policy Controversies.* New York: Basic Books.

Schreiber, R. Kent, and James R. Newman. 1988. Acid Precipitation Effects on Forest Habitats: Implications for Wildlife. *Conservation Biology* 2(3):249–59.

Sebenius, James K. 1992. Challenging Conventional Explanations of International Cooperation: Negotiation Analysis and the Case of Epistemic Communities. *International Organization* 46(1):323–65.

Serageldin, I. 1998a. "Coral reef conservation: Science, economics, and law." In *Coral Reefs: Challenges and Opportunities for Sustainable Management.* Edited by M. E. Hatziolos, A. J. Hooten, and M. Fodor. Washington, D.C.: World Bank.

———. 1998b. "Epilogue." In *Coral Reefs: Challenges and Opportunities for Sustainable Management.* Edited by M. E. Hatziolos, A. J. Hooten, and M. Fodor. Washington, D.C.: World Bank.

Shackley, Simon and Brian Wynne. 1995. Global Climate Change: The Mutual Construction of an Emergent Science-Policy Domain. *Science and Public Policy* 22(4):218–30.

Skocpol, Theda. 1984. "Emerging agendas and recurrent strategies in historical sociology." In *Vision and Method in Historical Sociology.* Edited by Theda Skocpol. Cambridge, UK: Cambridge University Press.

Skolnikoff, Eugene. 1997. *Same Science, Differing Policies: The Saga of Global Climate Change*. Report No. 22 of the MIT Joint Program on the Science and Policy of Global Change. Cambridge, Mass.: MIT Press.

SLG (The Social Learning Group). 2001. *Learning to Manage Global Environmental Risks*. Cambridge, Mass.: MIT Press.

Smith, Robert A. 1872. *Air and Rain: The Beginnings of a Chemical Climatology*. London: Longmans, Green.

Solomon, Susan. 1988. The Mystery of the Antarctic Ozone "Hole." *Reviews of Geophysics* 26(1):131–48.

Sommer, Adrian. 1976. Attempt at an Assessment of the World's Tropical Forests. *Unasylva* 28:112–13.

Spalding, M., C. Ravilious, and E. P. Green. 2001. *World Atlas of Coral Reefs*. Berkeley: University of California Press.

Sprinz, Detlef F. 1999. "Research on the Effectiveness of International Environmental Regimes: A Review of the State of the Art." Paper presented at the 40th Annual Convention of the International Studies Association, Washington, D.C., February 16–20.

Sprinz, Detlef F., and Tapani Vaahtoranta. 1994. The Interest-Based Explanation of International Environmental Policy. *International Organization* 48(1):77–105.

Stein, Janice Gross (ed.). 1989. *Getting to the Table: The Processes of International Prenegotiation*. Baltimore: The John Hopkins University Press.

Stoel, Thomas B. 1983. "Fluorocarbons: Mobilizing concern and action." In *Environmental Protection: The International Dimension*. Edited by David A. Kay and Harold K. Jacobson. Montclair, N.J.: Allanheld, Osmun.

Stolarski, Richard. 1988. The Antarctic Ozone Hole. *Scientific American* 258:30–36.

Stolarski, Richard, and Ralph J. Cicerone. 1974. Stratospheric Chlorine: A Possible Sink for Stratospheric Ozone. *Canadian Journal of Chemistry* 52:1610–15.

Strategic Plan of the IOC/UNEP/IUC Global Coral Reef Monitoring Network. [Online.] Available at: http://coral.aoml.noaa.govgcrmn/gcrmn-strat.html.

Swedish Ministry of Agriculture. 1982. *The 1982 Stockholm Conference on the Acidification of the Environment, June 28–30*. Stockholm: Departementens Reprocentral.

Swedish Ministry of Foreign Affairs and Swedish Ministry of Agriculture. 1972. *Pollution Across National Boundaries: The Impact on the Environment of Sulfur in Air and Precipitation Sweden's Case Study for the United Nations Conference on the Human Environment*. Stockholm: Royal Ministry of Foreign Affairs and Royal Ministry of Agriculture.

Tarasofsky, Richard G. 1995. *The International Forests Regime. Legal and Policy Issues*. Gland, Switzerland: International Union for the Conservation of Nature and World Wildlife Fund.

———. 1999. Assessing the International Forest Regime. Gland, Switzerland: International Union for the Conservation of Nature and World Wildlife Fund.

Teramura, Alan H. 1986a. "Overview of our current state of knowledge of UV effects on plants." In *Effects of Changes in Stratospheric Ozone and Climate Change*, vol. 1. Edited by James Titus. Washington, D.C.: UNEP/EPA.

————. 1986b. "The potential consequences of ozone depletion upon global agriculture." In *Effects of Changes in Stratospheric Ozone and Climate Change*, vol. 2. Edited by James Titus. Washington, D.C.: UNEP/EPA.

Thompson, Bruce E. 1986. "Is the impact of UV-B radiation on marine zooplankton of any significance?" In *Effects of Changes in Stratospheric Ozone and Climate Change*, vol. 2. Edited by James Titus. Washington, D.C.: UNEP/EPA.

Tickner, Joel A. (ed.). 2003. *Precaution, Environmental Science and Preventive Public Policy*. Washington, D.C.: Island Press.

Titus, James (ed.). 1986. *Effects of Changes in Stratospheric Ozone and Global Climate*. Washington, D.C.: U.S. Environmental Protection Agency and United Nations Environmental Programme.

Tolba, Mostafa, and Iwona Rummel-Bulska. 1998. "The story of the ozone layer." In *Global Environmental Diplomacy: Negotiating Environmental Agreements for the World, 1973–1992*. Edited by Mostafa Tolba and Iwona Rummel-Bulska. Cambridge, Mass.: MIT Press.

Trouwborst, Arie. 2002. *Evolution and Status of the Precautionary Principle in International Law*. The Hague, Netherlands: Kluwer Law International.

Ulrich, Bernhard, R. Mayer, and P. K. Khanna. 1979. *Deposition of Air Pollutants and Their Effects on the Wooded Ecosystems in Solling*. Report to the Deutsche Forschungsgemeinschaft, vol. 58. Göttingen, Germany: University of Göttingen.

Ulrich, Bernhard, and J. Pankrath (eds.). 1983. *Effects of the Accumulation of Air Pollutants in Forest Ecosystems*. Proceedings of an international workshop at the University of Göttingen. Dordrecht, The Netherlands: D. Reidel Publishing Company.

UNECE/FAO. 2000. *Forest Resources of Europe, CIS, North America, Australia, Japan and New Zealand—Main Report*. Geneva: Food and Agriculture Organization.

VanderZwaag, D., and D. MacKinlay. 1996. "Towards a global forests convention: Getting out of the woods and barking up the right tree." In *Global Forests and International Environmental Law*, Canadian Council of International Law. London: Kluwer.

Veron, J.E.N. 1995. *Corals in Space and Time: The Biogeography and Evolution of the Scleractinia*. Sydney: University of New South Wales Press.

Victor, David G., Kal Raustiala, and Eugene B. Skolnikoff (eds.). 1998. *The Implementation and Effectiveness of International Environmental Commitments: Theory and Practice*. Cambridge, Mass.: MIT Press.

Vogel, David. 1986. *National Styles of Regulation: Environmental Policy in Great Britain and the United States*. Ithaca, N.Y.: Cornell University Press.

Walker, Henry A., and Bernard P. Cohen. 1985. Scope Statements: Imperatives for Evaluating Theories. *American Sociological Review* 50:288–301.

Watson, Robert T., F. Sherwood Rowland, and John Gille. 1988. *Ozone Trends Panel: Executive Summary*. Washington, D.C.: NASA.

Waxler, Morris. 1986. "Ozone depletion and ocular risks from ultraviolet radiation." In *Effects of Changes in Stratospheric Ozone and Climate Change*, vol. 1. Edited by James Titus. Washington, D.C.: UNEP/EPA.

Weale, Albert, and Andrea Williams. 1998. "National science and international policy." In *The Politics of International Environmental Management*. Edited by Arild Underdal. Boston: Kluwer.

Wendt, Alexander. 1992. Anarchy Is What States Make of It. *International Organization* 41:335–70.

Westoby, Jack. 1989. *Introduction to World Forestry: People and Their Trees.* Oxford: Basil Blackwell.

Wetstone, Gregory. 1987. "A history of the acid rain issue." In *Science for Public Policy.* Edited by Harvey Brooks and Chester L. Cooper. Oxford: Pergamon.

Wetstone, Gregory, and A. Rosencrantz. 1983. *Acid Rain in Europe and North America.* Washington, D.C.: Environmental Law Institute.

Wettestäd, Jørgen. 1998. "Participation in NO_x policymaking and implementation in the Netherlands, UK, and Norway: Different approaches but similar results?" In *The Implementation and Effectiveness of International Environmental Commitments: Theory and Practice.* Edited by David Victor, Kal Raustiala, and Eugene B. Skolnikoff. Cambridge, Mass.: MIT Press.

———. 1999. *Designing Effective Environmental Regimes: the Key Conditions.* Cheltenham, UK: Edward Elgar.

———. 2000. "The ECE convention on long-range transboundary air pollution: From common cuts to critical loads." In *Science and Politics in International Environmental Regimes. Between Integrity and Involvement.* Edited by Steinar Andresen, Tora Skodvin, Arild Underdal, and Jørgen Wettestäd. Manchester, UK: Manchester University Press.

Wettestäd, Jørgen, and Steinar Andresen. 1991. *The Effectiveness of International Resource Cooperation: Some Preliminary Findings.* Lysaker, Norway: Fridtjof Nansen Institute.

———. 1994. The Effectiveness of International Resource and Environmental Regimes. *International Studies Notes* 19(3):49–52.

Wilkinson, Clive. 1993. "Coral reefs are facing widespread devastation." In *Proceedings of the 7th International Coral Reef Symposium, Guam, Micronesia, June 22–27, 1992.* Mangilao: University of Guam Marine Laboratory.

Wilkinson, Clive, and R. Buddemeier (eds.). 1996. *Global Climate Change and Coral Reefs: Implications for People and Reefs.* Gland, Switzerland: IUCN.

Wilkinson, Clive, and Bernard Salvat. 1998. "Global coral reef monitoring network: Reversing the decline of the world's reefs." In *Coral Reefs: Challenges and Opportunities for Sustainable Management.* Edited by M. E. Hatziolos, A. J. Hooten, and M. Fodor. Washington, D.C.: World Bank.

WMO (World Meteorological Organization). 1982. *Report of the Meeting of Experts on Potential Climate Effects of Ozone and Other Minor Trace Gases.* WMO Global Ozone Research and Monitoring Project Report No. 14. Geneva: WMO.

———. 1986. *Atmospheric Ozone 1985. Assessment of Our Understanding of the Processes Controlling Its Present Distribution and Change.* Report no. 16 of the Global Ozone Research and Monitoring Project. Geneva: WMO.

———. 1990 *Scientific Assessment of Stratospheric Ozone: 1989.* Report no. 20, WMO Global Ozone Research and Monitoring Project. Geneva: WMO.

Wood, R. 1999. *Reef Evolution.* Oxford: Oxford University Press.

Woodin, S. J. 1989. Environmental Effects of Air Pollution in Britain. *Journal of Applied Ecology* 26(3):749–61.

World Bank. 1991. *The Forest Sector.* Washington, D.C.: World Bank.

WRI (World Resources Institute). 1999. *Critical Consumption Trends and Implications: Degrading the Earth's Ecosystems.* Washington, D.C.: WRI.

Wright, R. F. 1977. "Historical changes in the pH of 128 lakes in southern Norway and 130 lakes in southern Sweden over the period 1923–1976." SNSF project report TN 34/77.

Wynne, Brian. 1995. "Public understanding of science." In *Handbook of Science and Technology Studies.* Edited by S. Jasanoff, G. E. Markle, J. C. Petersen, and T. Pinch. London: Sage.

Yandle, Bruce. 1989. *The Political Limits of Environmental Protection. Tracking the Unicorn.* Westport, Conn.: Quorum Books.

Young, Oran R. 1989. *International Cooperation: Building Regimes for Natural Resources and the Environment.* Ithaca, N.Y.: Cornell University Press.

———. 1991. Political Leadership and Regime Formation: On the Development of Institutions in International Society. *International Organization* 45(3):281–308.

———. 1994. *International Governance. Protecting the Environment in a Stateless Society.* Ithaca, N.Y.: Cornell University Press.

———. (ed.). 1997. *Global Governance: Drawing Insights from the Environmental Experience.* Cambridge, Mass.: MIT Press.

———. 1998. *Creating Regimes: Arctic Accords and International Governance.* Ithaca, N.Y.: Cornell University Press.

———. 1999. *The Effectiveness of International Environmental Regimes: Causal Connections and Behavioral Mechanisms.* Cambridge, Mass.: MIT Press.

Young, Oran R., and Gail Osherenko (eds.). 1993. *Polar Politics: Creating International Environmental Regimes.* Ithaca, N.Y.: Cornell University Press.

Zürn, Michael. 1998. The Rise of International Environmental Politics: A Review of Current Research. *World Politics* 50:617–49.

Interviews

Tasso Rezende de Azevedo, deputy director of Brazil's Secretariat of Biodiversity and Forests, Ministry of Environment. June 2003, May 2004, Geneva.

Richard Ballhorn, head of the Canadian delegation at the fourth session of the Intergovernmental Forum on Forests. February 2000, New York.

Astrid Bergquist, deputy director, Division for Energy and Primary Industries, Ministry of Industry, Employment and Communications, Sweden. December 1999 (Ottawa), February 2000 (New York), June 2003, and May 2004 (Geneva).

Jacques Carette, head of the Canadian delegation at the third session of the UN Forum on Forests. June 2003, Geneva.

Bernard Chevalier, head of the International Affairs Division, Ministry of Agriculture of France. December 1999, Ottawa.

Stephen Colwell, executive director of Coral Reef Alliance. November 16, 2000 (telephone).

Mike Dudley, head of International Division, U.K. Forestry Commission. Interviewed December 10, 1999, Ottawa.

Concenção Ferreira. Portuguese Directoriat-General of the Forests and speaker on behalf of the EU at the fourth session of IFF. February 2000, New York.

Manuel Sobral Filho, executive director, International Tropical Timber Organization. November 10, 2002, Yokohama.

Mike Fullerton, Canadian delegation, Forest Service, Division for International Affairs. December 1999 (Ottawa), February 2000 (New York), and May 2004 (Geneva).

Robert Hendricks, U.S. Forest Service, delegate at UNFF sessions. May 2004, Geneva.

Peter Holmgren, coordinator of FAO's Forest Resources Assessments. March 19, 2003, Viterbo, Italy.

Jorge Illueca, assistant executive director, Division of Environmental Conventions, United Nations Environment Programme. November 2001 (Montreal) and May 2004 (Geneva).

Olav Bakken Jensen, advisor, Norwegian delegation, Ministry of the Environment. June 2003, Geneva.

Richard Kenchington, head of the Secretariat of the International Coral Reef Initiative (1996–98). February 18, 2001 (telephone).

Nancy Knowlton, Smithsonian Tropical Research Institute. December 20, 2000 (telephone interview).

Evgeny Kuzmichev, deputy chief, Federal Forest Service of Russia, delegate at the fourth session of the Intergovernmental Forum on Forests. February 10, 2000, New York.

Jan MacAlpine, U.S. delegation, senior forest officer, U.S. State Department, Office of Ecology and Terrestrial Conservation. December 1999 (Ottawa), February 2000 (New York), November 2002 (Yokohama), and May 2004 (Geneva).

Jag Maini, head of the Secretariat of the Intergovernmental Forum on Forests. December 1999, Ottawa.

William Mankin, director of Global Forestry Action Project, a collaborative initiative of Sierra Club, Friends of the Earth, and the Natural Wildlife Federation. December 1999 (Ottawa), February 2000 (New York) and May 2004 (Geneva).

Mike McNamara, Australian delegation at the third and fourth sessions of UNFF, general manager, Forest Industries, Department of Agriculture, Fisheries and Forestry. June 2003 and May 2004, Geneva.

Christian Mersmann, director of United Nations Development Programme's Programme on Forests (PROFOR). December 1999, Ottawa.

C. P. Oberai, inspector-general of forests, Ministry of Environment and Forests, India. December 1999, Ottawa.

Knut Øistad, deputy director general of Norway's Ministry of Agriculture and delegate at IFF and UNFF sessions. December 1999 (Ottawa), February 2000 (New York), and June 2001 (New York).

Pekka Patosaari, coordinator and head of the United Nations Forum on Forests. June 2003 and May 2004, Geneva.

Franz X. Perrez, chief negotiator for Switzerland and head of Global Affairs Section, Swiss Agency for the Environment, Forests and Landscape. May 2004 (Geneva) and May 2005 (New York).

Jose Antonio Prado, officer for International Relations, Forests and the Environment, Ministerio de Agricultura, Chile. December 10, 1999, Ottawa.

Rob Rawson, co-chair of the International Tropical Forest Council and assistant-secretary of Agriculture, Fisheries and Forestry, Australia. December 5, 1999, Ottawa.

Jamie Reaser, assistant director, U.S. National Invasive Species Council, and former U.S. State Department official. January 31, 2001 (telephone).

Milena Roudna, Global Relations Department, Ministry of Environment, the Czech Republic. December 9, 1999 (Ottawa).

Denise Rousseau, Deputy Director of Environment and Sustainable Development Division, Canadian Department of Foreign Affairs. May 2004 (Geneva).

Carole Saint-Laurent, representative of the International Union for Conservation of Nature at international forest meetings. November 2002 (Yokohama), June 2003, and May 2004 (Geneva).

Alastair Sarre, Secretariat of the International Tropical Timber Organization. November 2003, Yokohama.

Peter Schültz, senior staff-officer (Forests), Department of Nature Management, the Netherlands. December 9, 1999, Ottawa.

José M. Solano, head of International Forest Policy Service, Ministerio de Medio Ambiente, Spain. December 7, 1999, Ottawa.

Birgitta Stenius-Mladenov, director of Political Department, Finland's Ministry of Foreign Affairs. December 6, 1999, Ottawa.

Bai-Mass M. Taal, senior programme officer for Biodiversity/Forests, United Nations Environmental Programme. December 10, 1999.

Barbara Tavora, Brazilian delegation, later policy advisor at the United Nations Forum on Forests Secretariat. December 1999 (Ottawa) and June 2003 (Geneva).

Evelyn Trines, Science and Technology Program, Secretariat of the Framework Convention on Climate Change. December 10, 1999, Ottawa.

U.S. Department of State official. Anonymous. January 9, 2001 (telephone).

Everton Vargas, Minister of External Relations and head of Brazil's delegation at IFF-4. February 5, 2000, New York.

Genevieve Verbrugge, International Coral Reef Initiative Secretariat, France. February 2000, New York.

Don Wijewardana, New Zealand's director of International Forest Policy, Ministry of Agriculture and Forestry. June 6, 2003, Geneva.

Clive Wilkinson, coordinator of the Global Coral Reef Monitoring Network. November 2, 2000 (telephone).

Stuart Wilson, Forests Monitor. Interviewed February 2000 (New York) and May 2004 (Geneva).

Index

About the Author

Radoslav S. Dimitrov is assistant professor in the Department of Political Science at the University of Western Ontario, where he teaches international relations. He works for the Earth Negotiations Bulletin as an analyst at global environmental negotiations at the United Nations and other international institutions. His research on environmental norms, policy regimes, environmental security, coral reefs management, and global forest politics appears in *International Studies Quarterly*, *Global Environmental Politics*, *The Journal of Environment and Development*, *The International Journal of Global Environmental Issues*, and *Society and Natural Resources*.